EDUCATION FOR DEMOCRATIC CITIZENSHIP: A CHALLENGE FOR MULTI-ETHNIC SOCIETIES

edited by

Roberta S. Sigel
Rutgers University

Marilyn Hoskin
Buffalo State College

LEA LAWRENCE ERLBAUM ASSOCIATES, PUBLISHERS
1991   Hillsdale, New Jersey   Hove and London

Lawrence Erlbaum Associates, Inc., Publishers
365 Broadway
Hillsdale, New Jersey 07642

Library of Congress Cataloging in Publication Data

Education for democratic citizenship : a challenge for multi-ethnic
    societies / edited by Roberta S. Sigel and Marilyn Hoskin.
        p.. cm.
    Papers originally presented at a conference sponsored by the
Spencer Foundation.
    Includes bibliographical references and index.
    ISBN 0-8058-0725-X.
    1. Civics--Study and teaching--Congresses. 2. Democracy--
Congresses. 3. Intercultural education--Congresses.
4. Immigrants--Education--Congresses. 5. Education and state--
Congresses. I. Sigel, Roberta S. II. Hoskin, Marilyn B.
III. Spencer Foundation.
LC1091.E44 1991
307.11'5--dc20   90-49721
                                                          CIP

Printed in the United States of America
10 9 8 7 6 5 4 3 2 1

ACKNOWLEDGMENTS

The collection presented here stems from a conference funded by the Spencer Foundation of Chicago. Special thanks in preparing this volume are due to the Foundation without whose support and encouragement the enterprise could not have been undertaken. Thanks are also due to Rutgers University which provided the facilities, and to its late President Edward Bloustein who opened the conference. A special thanks is reserved for Lauren Burnbauer of the political science department who helped with, and supervised, many of the organizational tasks, and did so with flair and great tact.

Contents

INTRODUCTION

1 Democracy in the Multi-Ethnic Society

Roberta S. Sigel

Temptation is strong to label the winter of 1989–1990 as the winter when democracy spread with astonishing rapidity to nations hitherto seemingly immune to it. Not unexpectedly, this unanticipated event has been greeted with much hope and enthusiasm, especially in the modern, post-industrialist democracies. In our euphoria, however, we must not lose sight of the fact that these countries, although desiring democracy, often find themselves at a loss how to define it, let alone implement it. The practice of democracy does not, ipso facto, follow the desire for it; it has to be learned.

This observation, however, applies with equal force to the well-established democracies of the West. Democratic citizens are not born; they are made. Citizenship education is meant to accomplish this learning task. It is a task that has become increasingly urgent over the past few decades, because the post-World War II period has seen massive population changes in these countries, mostly due to large-scale in-migration from Asia, Africa, and Latin America (as Hoskin details in Chapter 2). Today, many post-industrial nations have to be characterized as multi-ethnic ones, and the probability is great that they will remain so. There is, of course, nothing intrinsically incompatible between democratic practices and multi-ethnic living. But, as the events of the post-war period have shown, host populations have not always accepted this simple truism. Some nations, over the past decades, have witnessed public expressions of hostility to newcomers, and, at times, even acts of violence against them. It is becoming increasingly clear that hosts and newcomers alike have to *learn* what it means to live democratically in a multi-ethnic world and, to accept diversity without fear or rancor.

This book will illustrate how six post-industrial nations (Canada, The Federal Republic of Germany, Israel, The Netherlands, The United Kingdom, and The United States) have met, or failed to meet, this challenge, what they have done, or need to do, in the near future in order to promote the practice of democratic living and citizenship for the people in their midst—newcomers and hosts alike. Each of the six countries—as Hoskin's next chapter relates—is experiencing a large influx of new populations, some permanent immigrants, others guest workers, refugees, or nationals of former colonial holdings.

This volume is based on the contributions made by scholars from the above countries to a conference funded by the Spencer Foundation, and held in the fall of 1988 on the campus of Rutgers University. The conferees were given the charge to ask themselves, and to ask each other: What can we as educational researchers or practioners do to prepare our youth for cooperative, constructive living in a democracy? How can we meet that challenge?

To answer that question, we asked the contributors to keep in mind that:

> Immigration represents a meeting of two worlds: the world of the immigrant and the world of the host society. In this meeting both worlds are at risk. Unless somehow transformed the immigrant may subtly alter the host society; naturally enough, therefore, the host society attempts to transform the immigrant. (Merelman, 1989 p. 5)

The immigrant, on the other hand, may resist being transformed, may even resent the effort, and/or may find the transformation impossible to achieve unless assisted and guided by the schools and other support structures offered in the host country. But, even under the most propitious of circumstances, "the immigrant cannot avoid 'placing in question' the culture of the approached group. . . . The transformation process, therefore, can never be automatic. Immigration, in short, becomes a gigantic exercise in socialization . . ." (Merelman, 1989 pp. 5–6).

To socialize its youth for democratic adult citizenship is, of course, one of the educative tasks the state's schools are supposed to perform for all the pupils. That is, schools are expected to instruct them (overtly or not) in the principles on which democratic governance rests, and in the norms and behaviors these entail, and which should guide its citizens. All too often the educational systems have tended to ignore or deemphasize this obligation—feeling indifferent about it or assuming that it would occur unaided.

In the case of the "native" population, this assumption might have been given some credence by the fact that a certain value consensus seems to exist, so that the acceptance of some fundamental beliefs and congruent behaviors can be taken for granted. To offer an example from the American scene, American school children, much like adults, usually subscribe to the notion of majority rule (although they may vary among themselves as to what that implies). Consequently, they tend to respect electoral outcomes, no matter how distasteful they might find them. And, because values taught in school tend to be reinforced by the family, the mass media, and other institutions, major energies need not be devoted to explain why the majority—rather than the elders, the religious leaders, or the well-born—should rule.

No such value consensus can be automatically assumed among the newcomers. Immigrants:

> sit on the periphery of culture. Immigrants function as naive anthropologists struggling to understand the meanings embedded in cultural displays. As Alfred Schutz puts it, the immigrant "becomes essentially the man who has to place in question nearly everything *that seems to be unquestionable to the members of the approached group. To him the cultural pattern of the approached group does not have the authority of a tested system of recipes"* . . . (Schutz, 1944 p. 502; italics mine). . . . being an immigrant dictates that one carried the culture of a foreign land, and is therefore automatically excluded from the shared, implicit meanings that members of the host society take for granted. . . . (Merelman, 1989 pp. 6–7)

Consequently, citizenship education for immigrants may have to involve socialization to new socio-political values, some of which not only may seem strange, but even undesirable to the recent arrival. More than that, the new values may conflict fundamentally with those of the family. To cite but one example, schools in western democracies seek to convey the notion that all citizens are created equal, and that men and women are entitled to the same rights and privileges. This notion, however, conflicts in serious ways with what is taught in the families of many recent immigrants who adhere to more patriarchical family patterns. How should the policy maker and the educator resolve such conflict without undermining, on the one hand, the young person's bond to the family, and without, on the other hand, incapacitating him or her from functioning in a way consistent with the demands and norms of the dominant society? In short, how much should we expect him or her to become transformed, and how much will the host society have to transform itself in order to accommodate the newcomer constructively and harmoniously?

Putting the question this way is not meant to imply that only the minority student should be the target of resocialization. As we said earlier, to live effectively in a democratic society, nonminority youths are equally in need of socialization. They must learn to accept the realities of multi-ethnic living, to become acquainted with, and respectful of, the value and living patterns of other ethnic groups, without blindly assuming that their own culture is superior, and therefore immune to change or improvement.

Helping students to reach that understanding presents educators with a daunting challenge. They, after all, are also part of the mainstream culture. Many of them had been trained to become teachers at a time when it was not customary to question the cultural superiority of one's country, and the rectitude of its course. This message they tended to convey to students via history courses—courses that usually extolled the nation's glorious past. Nothing more seemed to be required. To wit, not so long ago, several of the nations represented in this volume featured no such thing as citizenship education, taking for granted that all students, whatever their backgrounds, would subscribe to the dominant culture's value system, because so "clearly" it was superior to their own (see Adler and Rubinstein, also Lister in this volume).

Of all the nations, the United States was perhaps the least confident that socialization attempts were superfluous. It felt the need to offer citizenship training to all its youth and made especially determined efforts to "Americanize" newcomers as soon as possible, to encourage them to shed the ways of "the old country" quickly. Much was made of the metaphor of the "melting pot," portraying it as one of the United States' great, conscious achievements. It was only recently that people began to show much awareness that the metaphor also implies that the indigenous characteristics of parts (in this case people), by being "melted down" or otherwise being transformed, are essentially deprived of their identity.

Until recently, the model from which the above six nations operated was essentially an assimilationist one. It is based on the assumption that it is in the best interest of society, and of the newcomer (in fact it is the latter's duty), to adopt and conform to the common culture as fast as possible, and to abandon those earlier acquired beliefs and traditions which conflict with it. In this model, great cultural diversity and strong ethnic attachments are seen as being dysfunctional for the welfare of the modern nation. It is what some people have called a "deficiency model," in that it argues that those groups which have "characteristics that cause their members to function unsuccessfully in the common culture are deficient . . ." (Banks, 1977 p. 230).

Among scholars—even if not always among practioners—this model has lost a good deal of credibility (for an exception, see Jensen, 1980), and has been rejected in favor of the so-called pluralist model. Although the term "cultural pluralism" conveys different meanings to different scholars, and although distinctions are made between different forms of cultural pluralism, a fair amount of agreement exists that it rests on the recognition of the legitimacy and validity of different cultural experiences and heritages, and argues that these experiences are entitled to articulation in the common culture, enriching rather than diminishing said culture. Cultural pluralists envision an organic relationship in which the individual freely partakes of his or her own distinctive heritage, but also becomes an integral part of the history and experience of the common culture.

Not surprisingly, social scientists, especially those doing educational research, prefer this model to the assimilationist model, because they hold the latter to be fallacious. Where assimilationists tend to consider ethnic bonds as primitive or primordial, cultural pluralists—such as Apter (1977) and Levine (1973)—argue that these bonds meet significant needs which modern living cannot satisfy completely. Cultural pluralists advocate this model, not only for philosophical reasons, but also for practical ones. Commenting on surveys conducted in many different multi-ethnic countries, Torney and Tesconi (1977) write: "Unless students in this very pluralistic situation are provided with extensive educational experience to equip them to cope with this diversity, they will be overwhelmed by it and low intercultural tolerance will result" (p. 120). It goes without saying that democratic citizenship is incompatible with intercultural intolerance.

Clearly, as the Torney and Tesconi citation suggests, it is to the schools that we tend to look in this context. This volume is no exception. The major emphasis in the chapters which follow is on the way in which the schools offer, or should offer, students the "extensive educational experience to equip them to cope with this diversity." Moreover, the chapters also make clear that educating for democratic citizenship cannot be restricted to, let alone be equated with, a course or two on civics or citizenship, or studies in democracy. Such courses may be useful to enrich pupils' understanding of their society, and its political processes, but that is but one part of the educational equation. The school is also a microcosm of society—hence how it comports itself in the classroom, how it deals with controversies and authority relationships, the treatment it accords students, etc., makes an equally important and perhaps more lasting contribution to the student's democratic orientations. It is for that reason, as Felsenthal and Rubinstein write in this volume, we cannot: "afford the luxury of letting the schools be . . ." (Chapter 6).

This volume's emphasis on the schools, however, is not meant to imply that the schools should, or even are, in a position to shoulder the full responsibility for the task. Obviously, many other societal institutions also have to do their part. Four chapters in this volume do focus on these (Rubinstein and Adler—Chapter 5, Black—Chapter 10, Ungerleider—Chapter 9, and Hoskin—Chapter 11). These four chapters highlight different ways in which countries affect the ease or difficulty with which newcomers can become integrated. They single out immigration policies, and public and private agencies for the purpose of helping the newcomer find his or her way in a strange new country, and the resources spent on multi-ethnic and multilingual education, to name a few. Such auxiliary efforts are vital if the schools are to perform the task of democratic citizenship education in multi-ethnic societies. Nonetheless, in this volume we choose to emphasize the role of the schools precisely because they alone are in contact with almost all of the country's youth, and this contact takes place at a time when the young people are at the most impressionable, reachable age in their lives. If the thoughts and suggestions of the contributors to this volume will prove helpful to educators as they prepare young people for democratic living in a multi-ethnic society, it will have accomplished its goal.

REFERENCES

Apter, D. E. (1977). Political Life and Pluralism. In M. M. Tumin & W. Plotch (Eds.), *Pluralism in a democratic society* (pp. 58–91). New York: Praeger.

Banks, J. A. (1977). Cultural Pluralism: Implications for Curriculum Reform. In M. M. Tumin & W. Plotch (Eds.), *Pluralism in a democratic society* (pp. 226–248). New York: Praeger.

Jensen, A. R. (1980). *Bias in mental testing*. New York: The Free Press.

Levine, R. A. (1973). *Culture, behavior, and personality*. Philadelphia: University of Pennsylvania Press.

Merelman, R. M. (1989). *Cultural Displays: An Illustration from American Immigration*. Mimeograph.

Torney, J. V. & Tesconi, C. A. (1977). Political Socialization Research and Respect for Ethnic Diversity. In M. M. Tumin & W. Plotch (Eds.), *Pluralism in a democratic society* (pp. 95–132). New York: Praeger.

Schutz, A. (1944). A Stranger: An Essay in Social Psychology. *American Journal of Sociology*, 499–508.

2 The Challenge of the Multiethnic Society

Marilyn Hoskin

Among the most dramatic features of the post-World War II period has been that of population movement and resettlement. Such migration is notable first for its sheer magnitude, involving major relocation of upwards of 100 million people since 1944. It is all the more significant because it shows no signs of abating. Indeed, the pressures from groups wanting to relocate have increased dramatically, both from predictable sources (primarily third world nations), and unanticipated quarters (Eastern Europe), leaving virtually no region unaffected. Faced with fairly rigid and narrow legal channels for movement, potential immigrants have turned to other means—illegal entry, political asylum, international refuge—and tested their limits severely. Given the strains which such movements have created, it is not surprising that immigration issues have assumed an unprecedented urgency across sending as well as receiving nations.

Major population shifts are inherently disruptive. Even where migration is relatively carefully planned and controlled, the shifts create imbalances in the labor market, skew national or regional demographics, and raise questions about absorptive capacity. When they involve major differences in background or economic status, the shifts are likely to be socio-culturally disruptive as well. In the last two decades large numbers of Asians, Blacks, and Hispanics have brought unfamiliar and often unwelcome traditions to their new homes. They have also brought needs—educational, social, and economic—which leaders in host societies have had difficulty in meeting. With increasing demands on their resources, even traditionally liberal nations have found themselves strained by the demands of the contemporary multiethnic society.

Given the fact that migrations are as old as time itself, it is somewhat surprising that processes of integration and assimilation continue to be so troublesome for host societies. Virtually all nations engage in endless and frequently acrimonious debate over how to balance benefits and costs in their admission policies. Paradoxically, however, few have displayed much of an ongoing official interest in immigrants after they have cleared customs. Instead, most governments have assumed that whereas immigration policy is their preserve, social, economic, and political integration is the responsibility of other institutions—schools, community organizations, ethnic networks, local governments, and society in general. As a general rule, that process has usually allowed gradual movement of immigrants into the mainstream of their respective host societies without long-term threat to their established systems.

Despite a reasonably successful past, however, immigration inspires tremendous conflict whenever new pressures appear, and most scholars, educators, and political leaders agree that the quiescence of the past is unlikely to continue. The problem of educating both majority and minority segments of the democratic multiethnic society looms as a major challenge in the decades ahead. At stake is not just the ability of schools to provide training in basic skills, or even the inculcation of rudimentary democratic values. It is, rather, the ability of the systems to bring their minority populations into the political life of the nation in the face of circumstances which are likely to be both formidable and unprecedented. In the following sections we elaborate on these circumstances as they define problems and processes of democratic education, introduce the challenges which face governments and schools, and suggest how several nations discussed in this volume are working to facilitate political integration within their multiethnic societies.

THE PROBLEM OF NUMBERS

However the count is done, the scale of population movement in the past three decades has been enormous. To the surprise of many, the massive deportations and flows of voluntary migrants that followed World War II did not correct the imbalances created by its casualties and territorial changes. Nor did they meet the unanticipated labor needs created by economic growth in the 1950s and 1960s. Most important, they also did not curb the desires of millions of others to migrate to lands of greater opportunity and freedom.

Although precise migration figures are difficult to obtain, national statistics illustrate the magnitude of movement. In West Germany the number of foreigners grew from under 300,000 in 1960 to 4.7 million in 1988, an all-time high. During the same interval, the minority population of Britain and Switzerland tripled; in the Netherlands it increased sixfold. Between 1959 and 1980, 10 percent of the population of Cuba emigrated. Even with a slowdown in the immigration rate in the last decade, the foreign-born in Canada have grown to represent 16 percent of the total population, and more than twice that proportion in large metropolitan areas. A backlog of over 2 million applicants exists—double the 1981 number—for the 270,000 places reserved through United States policy for immigrants who are not dependents of current residents. As Jonathan Power (1979) has noted, population increases are not just additive. At this time most Western democracies "have reached a stage where the numbers of immigrants are so large that the sheer dynamics have become self-sustaining" (p. 24).

As high as such figures are, they represent only legal immigrants or resident aliens—categories whose importance is being eclipsed by dramatic increases in nontraditional immigrants. Estimates of the annual number of new illegal aliens in the United States run as high as 3 million. The Canadian agency in charge of asylum requests has developed a backlog of over 20,000 cases, and the number of applicants for refugee status in Germany in 1988 increased 80 percent over 1987, to over 100,000. In addition, some 200,000 resettlers from former German territories entered the Federal Republic in 1988, and the number who will enter under the massive exodus from Eastern Europe will approach half a million. That number for 1988, entering a nation the size of Oregon, is close to the total number of regular immigrants admitted to the United States in the same year. In short, nontraditional channels are adding migrants in dramatic quantities, not just restructuring the manner in which they enter.

More important than actual numbers is the question of whether they are perceived as manageable or appropriate numbers. Surveys conducted in Britain since the late 1960s have consistently revealed that a large majority of citizens there (75–85%) thought that there were "too many" immigrants. Even in nations traditionally seen as open to immigration (Canada, Israel, and the United States), legislative debates are increasingly concerned with questions of capacity and possible damage to national identity. Official policy in Germany maintains that "the absorptive capacity of the Federal Republic has been exhausted at around 4.4 million foreigners; in some areas with a proportion over 20% it is exceeded." (Federal Ministry of the Interior, 1985; p. 5) Public opinion in these states has tended to mirror this apprehensiveness, inspiring calls to limit entry or restrict the rights of foreigners. To be sure, immigration has always generated fears and negative reactions, and perhaps the popular desire to close the door to an attractive site is inevitable. Resistance recurs despite decades of successful absorption of immigrants. Nonetheless, it would be shortsighted to ignore the fact that the numbers involved since 1945, and particularly since 1960, have created especially urgent concern about population control across nations.

THE CLASH OF CULTURES

At least as significant as the increasing size of minority populations is the change in countries of origin. Prior to 1965, immigrants to the United States and Canada came mostly from Europe, and immigrants to Europe came largely from other European nations. By the early 1980s, the large majority of new entrants were non-European, with large contingents from Latin America and Southeast Asia. Britain, whose history has been dominated by movement of its citizens to colonial territories, found that pattern reversed after 1945, when successive waves of Commonwealth immigrants from the Caribbean, South Asia, and Africa sought entry. The southern Europeans, North Africans, and Turks, whose labor had been eagerly recruited by Common Market nations in the early 1960s, have been joined by hundreds of thousands of asylum-seekers from the Middle East and Africa since 1980.

Although there has been considerable international pressure on in-migration nations not to discriminate in their policies, their reluctance to embrace the shift to third world immigrants has been almost universal. Opening the doors to those with dramatically different backgrounds, religions, and traditions has always generated fears that the new foreigners would be unwilling or unable to assimilate, and the magnitude of current movements has undoubtedly exacerbated those concerns. Oscar Handlin's (1951) conclusion that such problems were resolvable as long as the migrants and their host population were similar, suggests that the current prospects for easy integration are poor (p. 13).

It should be noted that the factors which work against acceptance of migrants tend to be cumulative. In the United States, for example, early groups of immigrants were poor but strictly regulated in their entry, and generally familiar in their Anglo-European background. They would start out in the lowest job categories, but move willingly into mainstream society. Newer groups, on the other hand, have been very poor, ineffectively regulated, and overwhelmingly unfamiliar in their non-European backgrounds. Thus, where earlier immigrants might have experienced temporary periods in the lowest jobs and social strata, newer arrivals are frequently referred to as a permanent, but angry underclass. The clear implication has been that they will not be able to better their lot, and that they will form distinctive and hostile subcultures. Whether or not such fears are a product of ignorance or conscious beliefs that mobility and integration have reached finite limits in host societies, citizens are clearly more apprehensive about the minorities who have arrived since 1960 than they have been about previous groups.

Interestingly, even governments with relatively liberal immigration policies actually emphasize the differences which minorities represent. Canada refers to "visible minorities in official policy statements and promotes "multiculturalism" as a situation in which distinctly foreign traditions coexist alongside the native culture. British policy distinguishes between "patrials," "new Commonwealth," and other immigrants; Israel reserves the term "Sabra" for native-born residents; and Germany still employs common usage of "guestworker" labels to designate foreigners who are not officially expected to become lifelong residents. Even governments that support diversity as beneficial to their societies, maintain official terminology whose connotations are not necessarily positive or even neutral. Thus, cultural or racial differences of new migrants, already dramatic by historical standards, are often accentuated by the very governments which facilitated their entry into the host societies.

ACCOMMODATING NEW MINORITIES

One apparently immutable characteristic of the postindustrial age has been the reduction or elimination of all manner of national barriers: trade, transportation, and technology. A corollary of this trend is the possibility that large-scale, ongoing population movements are inevitable. Anthony Richmond, for example, maintains that inherently postindustrial conditions—increasingly open communication and information, ease of transportation, and the spread of political and economic aspirations—create pressures for free movement which defy any expectation that borders could be effectively closed (Richmond, 1988).

Given these trends and the magnitude of population changes which have occurred in recent years, it is surprising that receiving nations have been so slow to adjust to the reality of multiethnic societies. For example, official policy continues to assume that Germany is not an immigration state, and that foreigners will not seek German citizenship. Having neither anticipated nor planned for the scale of immigration which took place between 1960 and 1980, British governments still leave critical matters of economic and social assistance to localities. Even where the influx of foreigners has been long-term and varied (as in Canada, Israel, and the United States), questions of language, preference hiring, and cultural identity are still controversial. Although basic rights of access to social benefits and education have been largely assured, the reluctance of host governments to promote or expand them has been widespread.

It is undoubtedly an understatement to note that ethnic minorities have emerged as significant subpopulations across the industrialized world. At one level, they represent a vast resource of untapped talent and ambition, lacking only the commitment and means to develop their potential. At another level, they represent an overwhelming socio-economic burden for their hosts, who must find creative ways in which to transform dependency into productivity and loyalty to their new state. And, at still a third level, they are dangerously vulnerable to "scapegoating," as well as neglect, as they wait for opportunity to enter the mainstream. What Hoffman-Nowotny (1979) refers to as "the transfer of tensions" (p. 231) encompasses all the fears and hostilities which surface in employment, housing, and social and political interaction in general. Host nation residents link minorities to neighborhood deterioration, unemployment, strains on the welfare system, and rising crime rates. In such a context, their contributions to society are unlikely to be fully appreciated, and their potential for being productive citizens is almost certainly limited.

DEMOCRATIC EDUCATION IN THE MULTIETHNIC SOCIETY

Can there be straightforward governmental or societal responses to the dilemmas presented by new ethnic minorities in democratic nations? All such nations desire social harmony, and at some level virtually all recognize the need for dedicated efforts to bring minorities into their nations' mainstreams. Not surprisingly, all have looked to their school systems to educate new minorities in the ways of democracy. Minority adults would have to understand and respect laws, but they would also need to appreciate norms and rights associated with places of work and residence. Their children would have to learn about the structure and rules of the society in which they were most likely to live. To function at all, they would have to learn skills. But to function in ways which would contribute to the long-term health of the system, they would have to have positive educational experiences that would make them internalize democratic values as well. However else they might differ, most receiving nations have agreed that they have a commitment to democratic education for those residing within their borders.

Beyond the global agreement to educate, however, consensus has been elusive. Disagreement or confusion on more specific questions has riddled the task with major problems. First, as noted above, there is at best an uneasy ambivalence associated with the fact that minorities are there to begin with. Where few would argue that their own citizens deserve the resources necessary for a quality education, many would, and do, question the extent of the state's obligation to provide the schooling which minorities may require. At issue are both the additional funds needed to accommodate large numbers of minority children, and the special needs which many of them have for language or remedial instruction.

Second, and perhaps more basic, is the fact that no universal understanding—much less definition—of "education for democratic citizenship" exists to guide those who are charged with providing it. Traditional educators stress the centrality of a basic civics curriculum, taught through a perspective of positive socialization to existing institutions and procedures. Others see its fundamental ingredient as the development of critical thinking skills, capable of application to all manner of social, political, or philosophical questions. Still others approach democratic education through the discussion of controversial and basic issues with no underlying pedagogy or commitment to existing political structures. Whatever the virtues of any of these or other approaches, the fact that they are both numerous and divergent indicates that students will not be exposed to a unified conception of democracy.

If division of opinion and teaching philosophy complicates the provision of "democratic education," so too does the division of responsibility for education more generally. In some western democracies, educational matters are the preserve of state and local governments whose approaches and policies vary widely. The idea of national involvement or control is frequently suspect. This is particularly so in the United States. In practice, that means that the concept of education for democratic citizenship is itself subject to literally hundreds of variations in meaning. It also means that the delivery of education to minorities may well differ tremendously—in the extent of commitment to special educational needs, the enthusiasm for minority children, the willingness to entertain requests from their parents, even in what they are taught. In short, the decentralization that these states consider fundamental to their democratic character almost certainly inhibits the possibility of anything approaching a national operationalization of democratic education.

Undoubtedly related to the close scrutiny that localites exercise over their schools in decentralized systems, is an almost universal tendency of schools to avoid controversy in their curricula. Subjects such as race relations, political ideology, or changing morals do generate intense community concern. But such concern usually manifests itself in objections to the inclusion of polemical subjects, rather than support for student exposure to them. As a result, social studies in the elementary and secondary schools have developed a well-deserved reputation for focusing on factual and non-controversial aspects of social and political life. Although such aspects represent real components of the democratic system, they do not embrace some of its most important elements—namely, those of political opposition, conflict, and competing interests. Needless to say, these latter elements are critical to understanding minority issues that multiethnic democracies face.

It is important to note that there has never been anything approaching agreement in contemporary democratic systems that the responsibility for "education for citizenship" lies primarily with the schools. Citizens have always been expected to learn about democracy by observing and participating in the system itself. Most organizations to which people belong incorporate democratic principles and processes, and they represent member interests in a broader orbit, which includes other organizations and government. In addition, people take many of their cues about how to treat others from events, from groups, from the implementation of official policy, and from public leaders. The time that the schools could devote to helping pupils to understand issues such as minority relations is clearly minuscule relative to the time and coverage provided by real world observation. There is thus some logic to the argument of many educators that their primary responsibility consists of training students in basic skills, which the latter may then apply to complicated social and political issues. The question that is as yet unresolved is how much those issues need to be included, or at least introduced, in the classroom in order to fulfill society's expectations that democratic education be provided to all citizens.

Even if schools are defined as the primary provider of citizenship education, other non-institutional sources may play this role as well. National and local traditions are certainly influential in determining how native citizens, as well as new minorities, view their respective places in the system. Official policies provide relatively clear statements of the values being promoted. Interpretations by subnational governments of their role in providing socioeconomic and political aid to minorities serve to define their expectations, as well as those of the society. More particularly, political leaders can and do play crucial roles in assessing whether policies toward minorities are appropriate, just, and adequate. In short, education dedicated to democratic citizenship is clearly a multi-faceted phenomenon in any society, and is all the more complicated when applied to multiethnic societies.

THE CHALLENGE OF DEMOCRATIC EDUCATION IN
MULTIETHNIC SOCIETIES

However unique many of the situations alluded to here may appear at first blush, there are a number of important similarities which characterize the experiences of multiethnic societies. For better or worse, the movement of migrants from less developed to more developed economies appears to be a permanent feature of the postindustrial world. The resulting multiethnic societies present new and potentially difficult situations for both host and minority populations.

Almost without exception, modern multiethnic societies have demonstrated a clear reluctance to deal comprehensively with such situations directly. Most have responded to problems with established minorities by restricting further immigration. Only when those steps failed to alleviate domestic pressures have they developed major efforts to address the myriad of issues presented by sociocultural diversity, and many of those efforts have been limited or tentative. And, although all systems facing such a challenge would have to make adjustments, democracies have a special responsibility to keep their opportunity structures open. Their consistent reluctance to embrace liberal policies must, in this light, be seen as pessimistic indication of how migration issues might be resolved.

For the issues addressed in this volume, the most relevant commonality which links multi-ethnic democracies is ambivalence about their educational obligations. All recognize the importance of basic education, but their enthusiasm and ability to provide the means to realize that goal has been limited. All realize that minorities have special needs, but many cannot decide whether such needs demand bilingual instruction, and study of the homeland, or a greater emphasis on mainstreaming into the host culture. Perhaps most important, all feel threatened, to varying degrees, by the mathematical reality that the increases in numbers of minority children will outpace those of the majority for the indefinite future. In such situations, schools feel the pressure to provide appropriate education, because of both the pressure of conflicting concepts of appropriate education, and the pressure of some of their constituents who resent the very presence of minorities with special educational needs.

It is not surprising that in this context the issues associated with education for democratic citizenship are still mired in confusion. Even if we assume that schools bear primary responsibility for democratic education, the next and more difficult question is who should be responsible for defining and implementing the appropriate curriculum or curricula. Although government is an easy response, it is evident that some governments are reluctant to intervene in matters of curriculum, and especially reluctant to appear to be establishing mandatory standards. But even if they were willing to take the initiative (and the heat) involved in setting such expectations, it is not clear that governments have any greater vision of their goals than others who have tried to define them.

On the other hand, if schools are expected to teach basic skills, as opposed to socializing students to democratic values and participatory norms, the question turns to whether government should assume an independent and primary commitment to help minorities become fully participating citizens. At issue are how strong legislation aiding minorities should be, how generously government should support local and private integration programs, and what the official position should be on promoting cultural diversity. Each of these concerns has the potential to be a major debate in its own right, as illustrated by conflict over naturalization in Germany, disagreement about multiculturalism in Canada, or dispute about levels of welfare support in Britain. The rather tepid governmental initiatives in each of these areas suggest, however, that governments have preferred not to take on the major responsibility for democratic education. For better or for worse, governments assume that schools' responsibilities are fundamental, at the same time that schools assume that extra-curricula experiences—largely out of their control or purview—are critical to the task of educating minorities.

However wide-ranging the debates over democratic education are, two points are central and clear. One is that there is little evidence to support the traditional expectation that all minorities will somehow gradually, weave their own way into the mainstream socio-economic and political world. The post-1960 populations are too large, and the obstacles too great, to assume that they would take that path naturally and without major disruption to the host system. Second, wavering government policies and unprepared school structures cannot be counted on to create the proper mix of formal and informal citizenship education. Although governments and schools have made some, even major, attempts to meet the challenges posed by new minorities, there is a wide-ranging consensus that those efforts have not been adequate to meet current and future needs.

In this context, it is fitting that we begin to reassess the issue of education for democratic citizenship by taking stock of current problems, and the attempts of educational institutions and governments to deal with them. The essays in this volume are written to address precisely these concerns, to compare experiences across nations, and to assess how successfully or unsuccessfully democratic education is operationalized in contemporary multiethnic societies.

We should note at the outset what this collection of studies will not attempt to do. It will not try to cover all, or even most nations which are experiencing the strains of new ethnic minorities. Nor will it provide a great deal of historical context to explain the current array of political and educational factors which are determining the quality of minority life in host societies. Finally, it will not attempt to review or analyze the myriad of programs with which different systems have experimented as they faced the challenges of new minorities. The conference which inspired the papers included here specifically avoided the omnibus emphasis in soliciting and discussing current research.

On the other hand, the range and variety of experiences examined here are extensive. They represent nations whose relationship to new minorities is rooted in colonial history (Britain), religious statehood (Israel), planned recruitment and settlement (Canada), and unplanned immigration (Germany and the Netherlands). Despite this difference in background, however, they all have found the new demands on their systems trying. They have all looked to schools as educators, and they have all faced the dissonance between policy and commitment and societal resistance. As a group they provide a wealth of experience and detail. As a result, this volume is dedicated to an examination of attempts to reconcile new citizens and old traditions, across a significant range of societies, through the limited yet broadly employed lens of "education"—which is to say education as both official institution and as a body of unofficial norms.

In presenting these cases, our intent is threefold. First, we explore important traditions and mores that have served to define the major parameters of ethnic minority education in receiving nations. Second, we examine the paramount role that major social groups, silent majorities, and vocal oppositions have played in constraining lawmakers as they define official policy, and set the tone for integration or isolation of minorities in these states. Finally, we analyze throughout the essays the critical role which educational commitment has played, or may play, in shaping or overcoming other social forces. In drawing the various experiences together, we may thus attempt to offer an assessment of the aids and obstacles which characterize the integration of minorities across the several democratic nations discussed here.

REFERENCES

Federal Ministry of the Interior. (1985). *Report of Policy and Laws Related to Foreigners in the Federal Republic of Germany*. Bonn: Government Printing Office.

Handlin, O. (1951). *The Uprooted: The Epic Story of the Great Migrations that Made the American People*. Boston: Little Brown.

Hoffman-Nowotny, J. J., & Killias, M. (1979). Switzerland. In D. Kubat (Ed.), *The Politics of Migration Policies* (pp. 226–241). New York: Center for Migration Studies.

Power, J. (1979). *Migrant Workers in Europe and the United States*. New York: Praeger.

Richmond, A. (1988). "Caribbean Immigrants in Britain and Canada: Socio-Economic Adjustment." *International Migration*, 26, pp. 356–385.

THE PROBLEM OF MINORITIES IN THE SOCIO-POLITICAL SYSTEM

As we noted in the introductory chapters, host nations vary tremendously in their commitment to the democratic education of ethnic minorities. Such variation is at least in large part a function of history, tradition, and the conception of society that principle groups in the host nation hold. In this section, we present some of the context in which democratic education has been addressed. As the literature on non-integration of ethnic groups is extensive at this general level, we offer perspectives from three nations whose multi-ethnic circumstances differ quite dramatically, in an attempt to alert readers to both major differences and similarities.

Israelit Rubenstein's and Chaim Adler essay presents the case of Israel, perhaps the only modern state with a genuinely aggressive commitment to immigration. They discuss the question of whether minority groups "automatically" adjust to each other, and to the system which has attracted them, by examining three minority groups whose origins lie in non-democratic nations. They find, not surprisingly, that first generation immigrants are quiescent and uninvolved citizens, but the mobility of the second and later generations translates into greater participation and demands for minority rights. Perhaps more interesting is the fact that even in a highly structured educational curriculum, the high school instruction

in democracy appears to have had little impact on actual attitudes or behavior. In this and a later chapter, the specific issue of whether a nationally
designed curriculum can ensure a common identification and loyalty is
raised. As the authors indicate, even a consciously tolerant yet integrative
state cannot assume that formal education and strong positive national
orientations will overcome the difficulties that minorities present.

Variations on the magnitude of the integration task are presented by
Clive Harber's research on political education in Britain and Hartmut
Esser's chapter on second generation foreigners in Germany. Both nations
represent reluctant hosts, with Britain accepting, but not welcoming arrivals
from former colonial territories, and Germany continuing to insist that
second generation foreigners were not going to settle in the country permanently. Harber elaborates on the stifling obstacles of a racist climate,
and how that translates into a reluctance to change in the schools, and in
turn, an alarming level of ignorance of the dimensions of multiethnic relations among children. His work supports the conclusion reached by others
in this volume that students learn not from formal courses, but from the
"hidden curriculum," which is authoritarian and hierarchical.

Interestingly, Britain is one of those relatively rare cases where a "national curriculum" has actually been discussed. Harber presents a shrewd
analysis of how genuine educational reform fares in a political context that
has few genuine supporters. The net result has been a stalemate in which
ambitious programs for political education wither, or gradually downscale
to routine civics courses. Not surprisingly, Harber's conclusion is that a
hostile context can fatally undermine efforts to create a real democratic
education program.

Esser takes the analysis of this type of situation one step further by
documenting that poor performance in school is directly related to characteristics that the immigrants bring with them into the school setting—
especially language skills, age at entry, and cultural distance—and for
which the schools obviously fail to make the necessary remedial conces-
sions. He investigates the validity of two popular but mutually contradictory
myths. One is that some groups (those most like the hosts) integrate well,
but others (notably those considered less "like" Germans) do not perform
very well, thereby creating doubts and fears among those in the host population. Another myth is the idea that sooner or later (with later usually
meaning the second or third generation), virtually all migrants assimilate,
with or without specific assistance. Either myth then permits the schools
not to extend themselves greatly on behalf of the immigrant child. Using
data from groups of Turkish and Yugoslav students, Esser is able to show
that differences between the two groups, in their ability to integrate into
the host society, are related mostly to socioeconomic background factors,
whereas purely national differences have only minor impact. On the brighter

side, generational time does reduce obstacles to integration. Those who came earlier, or who were born in the host society, have greater language and social skills that facilitate their move into the mainstream of German society.

Esser's research differs from most of the chapters in this book, in that it relies heavily on quantitative analyses to test some of his underlying assumptions. This approach is an important addition to the volume, in that it illustrates both a significant pattern (the absence of differences between second generation groups), and a flexible model which can be modified to study intergroup and intergenerational differences. As he notes, the model has immediate substantive statistical utility, as well as broader theoretical promise.

In all three cases, the presence of cultural differences is compounded by either insensitive socio-educational climates, or by official distinctions, not to say outright discrimination, from which minorities suffer as they attempt to fit into their new societies. All three cases define the persistence of a major identity issue, which confronts and perhaps derails superficial official commitment to provide democratic education for minority populations and host. The essays in this section thus alert us to some of the fundamental issues of social and political structure, which can make or break efforts to come to grips with the education of ethnic minorities in these states.

3 Anti-Racism and Political Education for Democracy in Britain

Clive Harber
University of Birmingham

INTRODUCTION

This paper examines the issue of political education for democracy in relation to Britain as a multiethnic society. It begins by arguing that Britain is not a fully democratic country. In particular, racism among white power holders, which is predominantly directed at "black" people of Asian or Afro-Caribbean origin, and that is essentially anti-democratic, still permeates most British social and political institutions. The social institution with which this paper is most concerned—the school—presently does little to enhance democracy, and is a factor in the reproduction of racism. Political education, it is argued, can make a significant contribution to the development of more democratic norms among all young people, but this is most important for young white people who, as the children of the politically dominant ethnic group, must learn genuinely to value equal rights for all citizens. However, the British government now seems implacably opposed to such education, and it is difficult to be optimistic about the future.

BRITISH DEMOCRACY

Britain's political system is anachronistic and fixed in time. As a result, it can perhaps best be described as a partial democracy, as there are key features of the system that do not fit easily with democratic ideals. The

25

head of state is an hereditary monarch who does not usually wield effective political power, but who can have political influence in certain circumstances, as in the event of an election not producing a clear result, she will be involved in the political bargaining that must take place. More importantly, the respect and authority afforded to the monarch (and her wider family) in British society helps to legitimate the idea of deference to hereditary political power.

The British House of Lords has the power to delay and refer back, and thus change and even defeat, much legislation stemming from the House of Commons. Indeed, since the early 1980s, with the demise of the Labor Party, and divisions among opposition parties, there has been much talk of the House of Lords being the only effective opposition to the government. However, this cannot be reconciled with any notion of democracy, as by far the majority of members of the House of Lords are there on hereditary grounds, and as a result there is a built-in Conservative Party bias.

Unfortunately, the elected chamber of Parliament, the House of Commons, is also unrepresentative of the views of the British people. Some 58 percent (i.e., nearly three-fifths) of those who voted in the 1987 general election did not vote for Mrs. Thatcher's Conservative Party, yet her party ironically obtained exactly this share (58%) of the seats in the House of Commons. Conversely, the minor opposition parties obtained 27 percent of the popular vote, but only 7 percent of the seats in Parliament. Such unrepresentative results are a consequence of the simple majority electoral system that is unique to Britain among the democracies of Western Europe. As a result, "Our government has less electoral support than any other government in power in a European democracy" (Ridley, 1987). The claim of the British government that it has a mandate from the people is therefore not based on the electoral facts.

Recent legislation in Britain permits tenants, in homes owned by local councils, to vote on whether they wish to opt out of council control, and come under the control of private landlords. In this important matter, the undemocratic principle has been adopted that all those that do not vote will be counted as voting for the change to a private landlord. Thus, in Torbay in Devon, 2,210 tenants voted to stay under local authority control, and only 787 voted to opt out. However, 3,209 tenants did not vote, and so this is regarded as a majority in favor of opting out (*Guardian*, August 11, 1988)!

A final example is that in British government a higher value is still placed on secrecy than openness. Rather than a Freedom of Information Act putting the onus on government to justify why something should be secret, the 1911 Official Secrets Act makes it an offense for anybody who has signed the Act to pass on information to "unauthorized persons." This gives the government of the day considerable power over the flow of information—technically even the number of teaspoons in the House of Commons is a secret. Not surprisingly the Act has come under considerable criticism because governments have seemed less concerned with using the Act to protect national security, than to avoid political embarrassment.

In describing Britain as a "civic culture," Almond and Verba (1963) were impressed with the large number of British voters who felt themselves capable of influencing government. However, in a reassessment of Britain as a civic culture, Kavanagh (1981) has noted the increase in more direct forms of political protest in Britain recent years. Kavanagh quotes one survey in which one-fifth were ready to engage in illegal acts for political ends, and 56 percent said "yes" when asked if it was **ever** justified to break the law to protest about something you feel is very unjust or harmful. Often these replies were made in relation to civil liberties and human rights (and it is interesting to note that Britain has a poor record in terms of the cases upheld against it at the European Court of Human Rights). Not surprisingly, given the unrepresentative and unresponsive nature of British political institutions, Kavanagh (1981) notes that such feelings were "related to dissatisfaction with perceived government performance and the state of democracy in Britain" (p. 79).

RACISM IN BRITAIN

Black people, in particular, may well not be satisfied with democracy in Britain. Some writers have argued that marginalization caused by racism has denied black people the normal channels for resolving their grievances, and that the resulting political alienation was a major factor in the urban riots that have occurred in a number of British cities in the 1980s (Young & Lea, 1982). What is the nature and extent of racism in Britain?

It must be borne in mind that even now Britain is a colonial power (e.g., Hong Kong, the Cayman Islands, and the Falklands), and that the majority of Britain's colonies only became independent relatively recently. Slavery and imperialism could only be justified by an ideology that accepted that there was a separate black "race" that was inferior to the white "race," and racism is therefore a major cultural legacy of this aspect of British history. Negative images of black people and culture along with parallel images of white superiority have permeated literature, films, language, school books, and general folk-lore. Not surprisingly, although various intellectual and political counter-currents do exist, all British institutions are affected by the attitudes and practices that result from this cultural legacy. One clear example is politics itself—the first black members of parliament since 1945 (four out of 650—all Labor Party) were not elected until 1987. A book on the sociology of race relations in Britain, by Richardson and Lambert (1985) gave two further examples:

. . . a recent report by the Policy Studies Institute (1983) discovered that racial prejudice and racial talk are pervasive in the Metropolitan Police Force. The researchers found that a rhetoric of racial abuse ("nigger," "coon," "wog,") was not only tolerated, but actually cultivated in the occupational cultures of the police, a group holding a powerful and publicly sensitive position. Likewise, the mass media have been identified as a particularly insidious source of racist sentiments (Hartmann & Husband, 1974). They have been accused of treating blacks in Britain as alien "outsiders" and therefore as a "problem" rather than an asset. Instead of vigorously condemning white racism they have exaggerated immigration figures; instead of investigating the underprivileged positions of blacks in this country, they have spotlighted black crime rates. (p. 46)

Another review of research literature on the role of the mass media in race relations in Britain (Pilkington, 1984, pp. 153–160) concluded that "All in all there do seem good grounds for believing that the news media do play a major part in defining for people what the major issues are in race relations," (p. 160), but unfortunately ". . . the media continue to present black people in a negative light" (p. 155).

In particular, Pilkington (1984) notes that the conclusions of the research on the media aimed primarily at children are "uniformly bleak." Speaking of comics he states that:

An image of the world is conveyed that derives from colonialism and visualizes both black people and the countries they come from as "primitive." Such assumptions are also apparent in children's popular fiction. Again if blacks do figure, they are allotted limited roles, tending to oscillate between "naughty, evil and menacing roles," such as the golliwogs in the Noddy series, on the one hand, and being "merry, simple, childlike people," such as Little Black Sambo, on the other. (pp. 153–154)

Smith (1977) sums up the position:

In most organizations, the proportion of people who are active and vociferous in their opposition to the minority groups is small, but the majority feels some sympathy for these attitudes, or at any rate is prepared to tolerate them. (quoted in Pilkington, 1984, p. 380)

Even while working on this paper three examples of this were reported. A government-funded research project found evidence of racial discrimination in the recruitment, deployment, and promotion of nurses in the National Health Service (*Guardian*, August 6, 1988). The Commission for Racial Equality noted an increase of race discrimination cases being brought against large, "respectable" employers such as the BBC, British Airways, and the Department of Employment itself (*Observer*, August 7, 1988). A Law Society survey uncovered just 70 solicitors of Afro-Caribbean back-

ground, and 22 of African background among the 48,000 practicing solicitors in England and Wales. The society is to launch a drive to tackle
the discrimination faced by recruits from racial minorities (*Guardian*, August 18, 1988).

The most recent Policy Studies Institute survey of race relations in
Britain (Brown, 1984) again provides clear evidence of continuing structural inequalities in terms of housing and employment opportunities. While
it also notes that such disadvantages stem from more than one source
(e.g., language problems and the position of migrants and their children
at the lower end of the existing and inflexible British class structure), ". . .
it is clear that racialism and direct racial discrimination continue to have
a powerful impact on the lives of black people" (p. 318). Indeed, they
argue that the collapse of demand for labor in Britain in the 1980s has not
only created higher rates of unemployment among blacks, it has also provided extra fuel for racism and racial discrimination among whites: "We
therefore find that many Asian and West Indian people feel that these
problems have worsened, while in the 1974 survey they were outnumbered
by those who felt that things were getting better" (p. 317).

Finally, the PSI study found that racial violence was a serious problem.
A Home Office report in 1981 had found that Asians were 50 times more
likely than whites to be victims of racially motivated crimes and West
Indians 36 times more likely. The PSI study stated that:

> The survey not only shows that violent racially-motivated attacks on black
> people are a common and frightening aspect of racialism in Britain, but also
> that only half of Asian men and women, and less than a third of West Indian
> men and women felt that their ethnic group could rely on the protection of
> the police against them. This was backed up by a surprisingly high level of
> support for the idea of organizing self-defense groups. Our analysis suggests
> that the 1981 Home Office report *Racial Attacks* did not overestimate the
> number of racial attacks that became known to the police and suggests that
> many more of these incidents go unreported. (pp. 321–322)

A survey of racial violence and harassment in housing published in 1987
(Commission for Racial Equality) found that racial attacks were increasing,
not only in areas where black ethnic minorities are well represented, but
also where their numbers are low. One example from this depressing publication illustrates the point. A study carried out in the Newham area of
London in 1986 found that one in four of Newham's black residents had
been victims of some form of racial harassment in the previous 12 months.
This included insulting behavior, attempted and actual damage to property, attempted theft, threats of damage, or violence and physical assault
(p. 9).

SCHOOLS AND DEMOCRACY

Schools in Britain have not played a major role in education for democracy, either through school and classroom organization, or through taught courses of political education. Pupils have learned political values at school via the hidden curriculum, but these have tended to be authoritarian, hierarchical, bureaucratic and, as the next section will discuss, ethnocentric and racist.

Like many other institutions in Britain, schools do not have an organizational style which is democratic. Students in state secondary schools are subjected to patterns of authority which correspond to the non-participatory role they are expected to play in society. Shipman (1971) argues that the majority are "treated as subordinate at school and prepared for menial status at work." The organizational style of school is essentially authoritarian and bureaucratic. "Punctuality, quiet, orderly work in large groups, response to orders, bells and timetables, respect for authority, even tolerance of monotony, boredom, punishment, lack of reward and regular attendance at place of work are habits to be learned at school. . . . Education not only prepares for new ways of living it also stresses attitudes to authority that can help to preserve the existing distribution of power" (pp. 47, 54–55). According to one management consultant, the organizational model that schools in Britain most closely resemble is that of a prison. "The inmates' work routine is disrupted every 40 minutes; they change their places of work and supervisors constantly; they have no place they can call their own; and they are often forbidden to communicate and cooperate with each other" (Charles Handy quoted in the *Sunday Times*, May 2, 1984).

Not only is it possible to count the case studies of democratic schools in the state sector in Britain on one hand, but those that have tried to operate in this way have been plagued with difficulties created by the press and local politicians (Fletcher, Caron, & Williams, 1985; Harber & Meighan, 1989).

The converse of this is the leadership training/elite socialization that takes place in British public schools (i.e., expensive private schools). The products of major public schools such as Eton, Harrow, and Winchester form the largest proportion (and usually the majority) of all British political elites—parliamentary, civil service, judicial, military, and financial.

Assessment has, until very recently, been a major factor in maintaining the predominantly authoritarian atmosphere of classrooms in secondary schools. HMI (Her Majesty's Inspectorate—of schools) put it that:

> Public examinations exercise a powerful influence on the style and quality of pupils' work in the fourth and fifth years, leading commonly to an emphasis on factual recall rather than an understanding of underlying ideas and concepts. There is much over-directed teaching, particularly for the pupils who

are being entered for examinations beyond their capacity . . . there is a tendency to play safe, to fall back on the familiar and the known. It could thus strengthen the tendency to conservatism which is a built-in feature of the teaching profession. (HMI, 1981, pp. 2, 3)

Three developments in British education in the 1980s had started a cautious move away from these authoritarian teaching methods to more participant, student-centered learning. One is the move to a common examination for all pupils at the end of secondary school—the General Certificate of Secondary Education (GCSE)—which was introduced in 1986. With this has come a greater emphasis on skills such as analyzing, interpreting, doing research, etc., as well as recalling factual knowledge. Skills-based learning necessitates a wider range of teaching methods with more involvement of pupils in their own learning. Unfortunately, the introduction of GCSE was rushed, the necessary retraining of teachers inadequate and under-resourced, and took place, or didn't take place, in the middle of a major dispute between teachers and their employers. Consequently, the extent to which teaching has actually changed so far is still open to question. Moreover, there are signs that Mrs. Thatcher and others on the right of the Conservative Party are worried about the move from "facts" to skills. One indication of this was her rejection of the Higginson report, which recommended the next logical step of reforming Advanced Level ("A Level") in the same direction as GCSE.

A second change has been the move to "vocational education," in secondary schools, in the light of the collapse of the youth labor market. A major factor behind the introduction of such courses as the Certificate of Prevocational Education and the Technical and Vocational Educational Initiative was political. Jobs for young school-leavers are scarce, and there is the risk that the government will be blamed. If, however, a case can be made that youth unemployment is caused by a shortage of the desired skills in the potential workforce, then "vocationalizing" schooling has the effect of shifting the blame from the government to the individual (i.e., if pupils had vocational training, and still cannot get a permanent job, then it is their personal shortcomings that are the reason, rather than problems in the macro-economic structure. Ironically, because it is impossible to train for specific jobs within educational establishments, such courses have fallen back on developing generalizable social skills—being articulate, confident, capable of solving problems, etc., and this had led to more student-directed classrooms where curriculum is negotiated rather than imposed (Shemilt, 1987). However, such courses still exist side-by-side with higher status and more prestigious academic courses ('A' Level and GCSE), and hence are not only taken by a minority of pupils, but also tend to be taken by those pupils who would previously have done a lower qualification and left school at 16 (Evans & Davies, 1987; Brown, 1989). Moreover, the future nature and status of vocational courses is uncertain in the light of the newly imposed National Curriculum.

The third change has been the rapid growth of social education courses in the final two years of secondary schooling. This is again linked to youth unemployment—if schools no longer educated for employment, then what did they educate for? Obviously, life in general! Hence the titles of such courses as Preparation for Adult Life, Design for Living, etc. Often the hidden agenda of these courses is to help young people cope with unemployment and other social problems (drugs, parenthood, and citizenship, being a consumer, etc.), and hence not become a problem for the state. However, such courses also demanded a complete change in learning environment away from didactic methods to discussion, simulations, and projects, etc. As with vocational courses, although there are overtones of social control in the growth of social education courses, the frequent absence of formal assessment has meant that there is also the potential for some genuinely participant and democratic learning to take place. However, few teachers have been trained for such courses, and they often have lacked status in the eyes of both pupils and teachers. However, the National Curriculum makes no mention of such courses (or of any other form of social and political education), so it is uncertain what their future will be. The National Curriculum is further discussed in the final section of this paper. However, it is worth further noting here that the Secretary of State for Education has switched in-service training funds for 1989–1990 away from planning the curriculum in a multi-ethnic society, and training related to industry, the economy, and the world of work, and into training in management and assessment under the National Curriculum (*Guardian*, August 16, 1988).

As with the tentative changes in classroom atmosphere that have begun recently, the conscious consideration of political content in the classroom has also been a relatively recent phenomenon. For a hundred years after the introduction of state education in 1870, schools did very little or nothing to prepare young people for life in a democracy by providing courses in political education. Politics and education traditionally were viewed as separate realms. The absence of any major change to the political regime during this period—defeat in war, revolution, and independence, etc.,—meant that Britain, unlike many other countries, was not forced to confront the issue of preparing its citizens for a new political system. At the end of the 1960s, and during the 1970s and 1980s, the situation began to change. First, the relationship between education and politics became much clearer because education has become a major area of disagreement between the political parties. This began with the introduction of comprehensive schools in the 1960s, and its most recent manifestation is the Education Reform

Bill which became law in 1988, and that, among other things, introduces a National Curriculum for the first time, allows schools to opt out of the state sector, and introduces a national system of school tests at the ages of 7, 11, and 14.

Second, research on political socialization suggested that young people develop political values and attitudes at a much earlier age than had previously been thought—often before corresponding political knowledge—and the school was a major agency of political socialization (Dawson, Prewitt, & Dawson, 1977; Stacey, 1978). Moreover, work on the nature of school subjects increasingly called into question their neutrality in relation to social and political values (Whitty & Young, 1976; Gilbert, 1984; Tomlinson & Quinton, 1986; Harber, 1986).

Third, by the middle and late 1970s political violence on the streets of London between young people supporting the racist National Front, on the one hand, and the Anti-Nazi League, on the other, led to increasing concern that British youth might be slipping away from the mainstream political parties. Political education could provide one remedy.

Indeed, during the same period those in education were paying increasing attention to political education. In 1969, at a time when the gap between leaving school and voting was being reduced to two years, by the lowering of the voting age to 18, and the raising of the school-leaving age to 16, an increasing amount of people who had studied some politics were entering teaching and lecturing. The Politics Association was formed by such teachers in 1969, and it has pressed for more political education in schools since its inception. In particular it was instrumental in establishing work on the Programme for Political Education—a set of aims and objectives for political education developed during the 1970s. By 1987, there was considerable evidence of progress, in that political education was being taken seriously at all levels of the education system (Harber, 1987). However, in the same year a general election returned a Conservative Party to power that was committed to the idea of a National Curriculum to cover the years of compulsory schooling. This is now law, and political education forms no part of it.

SCHOOLS AND RACISM

The link between the lack of serious or widespread education for democracy in Britain, and the problems faced by black pupils, is made by Reeves and Chevannes (1984, p. 182), when they quote Entwistle (1971, p. 31) to the effect that "the government of most schools still approximates to that of a totalitarian state rather than a democratic model," and add that "the position is likely to be even worse for a minority group virtually unrepresented in the teaching profession and suffering racial discrimination at the hands of white teachers and students."

Concern with multi-cultural and anti-racist education is a relatively new phenomenon in Britain; most textbooks for teachers on the subject appeared in the 1980s. Moreover, as the back cover of one such book puts it: ". . . attempts by teachers to develop curricula that reflect the cultural diversity and confront the racial inequality of contemporary society have had a highly critical reception" (Nixon, 1985). Thus, although some teachers and teacher educators have begun to incorporate anti-racist ideas into their teaching, British education is still marred by racism and racial inequality. As with racism in general, in British society there has been much written on racism and education, so the following will confine itself to identifying three major aspects of the problem.

Among 20,246 teachers included in a survey by the Commission for Racial Equality, only 2 percent were from ethnic minority groups; yet in the eight areas where the survey was carried out, the ethnic minority population ranged from 2.4 percent to 33.5 percent. Seventy-eight percent of the ethnic minority teachers were on pay scales 1 or 2 (the lowest scales), compared to 57 percent of white teachers. Forty-seven percent of the white teachers rejected the idea that race relations had improved over the past five years, and 40 percent thought that there would not be any improvement in race relations in the United Kingdom during the next five years. The ethnic minority teachers were more pessimistic. Their figures were 55 percent and 45 percent, respectively. Nearly two-thirds of white teachers thought there was racial discrimination in schools generally, but for the ethnic minority teachers the figure was 81 percent. Over half of the ethnic minority teachers said they had personal experience of racial discrimination in their employment (*Guardian*, March 25, 1988).

Racial labeling and stereotyping of pupils by white teachers is also a problem in British schools. In particular, this has been identified as one factor in the widely discussed problem of the academic underachievement of pupils of "West Indian" or Afro-Caribbean origins. One review of the research literature, according to Pilkington (1984), put it that:

> Even if too much emphasis can be placed on teachers' attitudes in accounting for patterns of achievement, the judgement of the Rampton report that they have "a direct and important bearing on the performance of West Indian children in our schools" seems a reasonable one. In view of the extensiveness of racial prejudice in Britain, it is scarcely surprising to learn that many teachers hold "negative, patronizing or stereotyped views about ethnic minority groups." Since such views tend to affect their behavior towards members of these groups teachers must therefore be held to be partially responsible for the underachievement of West Indian children. (pp. 141–142)

School subjects and the textbooks used to teach them are often biased in omitting reference to, or using negative language and stereotypes, in discussing black people or African and Asian cultures. Klein (1985, Chapters 5 & 6), for example, reviews much of the work that has been done on this subject, especially in relation to history and geography school textbooks. However, she also provides case studies of other subjects in the curriculum. In regard to arts education, she argues that African and Asian art, when mentioned at all in school textbooks, is usually regarded as "primitive," and at a lower level of Darwinesque development than Western art (p. 76). Similarly, the *Oxford Junior Companion to Music* (1979) states: "Whether it be in the primitive rituals of a tribe, the stately patterns of an 18th century minuet, the langorous swirl of the 19th century waltz, or the jerkiness of today's popular dances (described in the preceding paragraph as nearer to the style of 'primitive tribes') you get a clear picture of the kind of life and values of the people that danced them" (p. 78).

Klein (1985) also argues that resources for teaching mathematics, science, and technology are almost exclusively ethnocentric: "Omission on a large scale can endorse a hidden curriculum that is racist and sexist, that proclaims that only white children—and in most cases only white boys—conduct experiments in physics and chemistry, make mathematical measurements or design and construct" (p. 86). Mathematics is presented in textbooks as a solely western science and the part played by India and by Arabs in the development of mathematics is ignored.

Finally, her warning about Religious Education now seems to have a prophetic ring: "Primary assembly books, like the Religious Education resources in secondary schools, can, if not predicated upon a comparative religion stance, be biased against any religion other than Christianity. There are anthologies for assemblies that are based entirely on the assumption that all children to whom it is addressed are Christians—or should be" (p. 82).

The Education Reform Act (1988) states that religious education in British schools will henceforth be mainly Christian, and collective worship or daily assemblies will also be wholly or mainly of a broadly Christian character. Although the Act is ambiguous, it does seem that children of other faiths will theoretically be able to have their own assemblies, and the right of parents to withdraw their children from lessons remains intact. However, the Act has drawn criticism from many groups of non-Christians. The Islamic Society for the Promotion of Religious Tolerance, for example, has argued that it will result in a situation whereby non-Christian students will have to leave the class and their classmates during that lesson, and that will emphasize their feelings of being "different." Those who remain in the class will be seen as privileged by virtue of being Christian, and those who are out will learn from an early age that to identify as British, one must be Christian. They have stated that this will lead to intolerance and resentment (*Guardian*, June 28, 1988).

YOUNG PEOPLE AND POLITICS

The discussion above has argued that schools reflect aspects of the British political culture—that there is no strong tradition of education for democracy, and racism is a feature of British schooling. What is the outcome of this among British young people, and what are the implications for schools?

A key idea in democracy is that of choice (i.e., between candidates, parties, and policies, etc.). Yet choice based on ignorance is no choice at all—if a voter does not possess the basic knowledge to choose between political alternatives, then no conscious choice has taken place. How informed about politics are the young people of Britain? One survey of 1,000 15-year-old school-leavers found widespread political ignorance among school-leavers. It also quoted evidence that suggests that this ignorance continues into adult life (Stradling, 1977). More recently, a summary of six research projects by the Economic and Social Research Council on 16- to 19-year-olds over a five year period, found that the overwhelming majority of young people were politically illiterate, with no conception of how Parliament, political parties, or the economy operated (McGurk, 1987, p. 6).

An inquiry into the political knowledge of 15-year-olds in 1979–1980 was one of the few in Britain that has differentiated on the basis of ethnicity, and it produced some interesting findings (Wormald, 1982). While "Asian" and "West Indian" young people were relatively knowledgeable about their parents' country of origin, on questions related to British politics, those of Asian and West Indian origin were relatively unknowledgeable compared to whites. She comments that "There appears, with this group, a clear disjuncture between interest in politics and knowledge of the British political system, a gap which parents cannot, and schools do not, fill." One example of lack of political knowledge that she gives is that of the meaning of democracy. Sixty-nine percent of "Asians," 57 percent of "West Indians," and 32 percent of "whites" said that they did not know what it meant. These are disturbing proportions for all groups. The major source of political learning was the television, while the school was only infrequently seen as an alternative source of political learning. Moreover, according to Wormald (1982):

> The "whites" were able to "test" what they learned from the media by discussion with their parents, the "Asians" and "West Indians" were not, and the picture of British society that is being presented to them on the

television may well be a prejudiced, as well as a frightening one . . . it seems reasonable that the schools should be asked to help their pupils to handle this information in a critical way, and to help them to form their own opinion, to appreciate those of others, and to give them the will and the means to participate in an effective and responsible manner. (p. 138)

Finally, Wormald quotes studies in the United States (Button, 1974; Langton, 1969) which suggest that political education courses can be of considerable value for ethnic minority pupils, among whom interest was relatively high, but knowledge relatively low. However, in the British context, and bearing in mind the evidence of political ignorance in the Stradling and McGurk surveys mentioned above, such courses would hardly seem redundant for "white" British pupils.

Indeed, the McGurk (1987) summary of six Economic and Social Research Council commissioned research projects on 16- to 19-year-old young people in the 1980s was emphatic on this, and made the connection with racism strongly: "Perhaps the most salient (theme), commented upon time and time again by the different research teams, is the political innocence, naivety, and ignorance of young people. . . . Stemming perhaps from such political ignorance is the overt racism which the research projects commonly reveal to be endemic among white youth in Britain. Political ignorance and racism are hardly the hallmarks of a healthy multiracial democracy" (p. 6).

The research found that among young whites, the only political party whose policies were well known was the National Front, and its commitment to the enforced expulsion of non-whites. Support for the National Front rose from seven to fourteen percent between 1979 and 1982. The study also found that such fascist parties presented a symbol attractive to white teenagers in the face of economic decline. Many young people conceded that with greater knowledge they would not have reached racist conclusions, and expressed regret that they had not been taught more about politics in school. McGurk (1987) concluded that:

Lacking any political education in the broadest sense, young people will continue to exist in a condition of ignorance in which simple solutions, especially racist ones, will have appeal. This is not necessarily because of their intrinsic attractiveness but because of a perceived lack of alternatives. Some of the respondents in the present study seemed aware of this danger and wanted the sort of information that would prevent them from being drawn into racist simplicities. The policy implications are clear. The current reluctance to introduce political studies into the school curriculum needs to be reevaluated. (p. 51)

POLITICAL EDUCATION

All the evidence suggests, therefore, that unlike in America, where schools are "a major, if not the major" source of political learning (Ehman, 1980), British schools need to play a much greater role in political education. There is now, moreover, a great deal in the way of published advice on aims and objectives, teaching methods (including teaching controversial issues), and classroom resources. The authoritative Swann Report on multi-cultural education (Department of Education and Science [DES], 1985) put the case for political education for democracy as a way of combatting racism:

> If youngsters are led to reflect critically on the political framework of life in this country, this should involve a consideration of how particular structures and procedures have evolved and their appropriateness to today's multiracial population. Learning how some long-established practices were originally developed to cater for a relatively homogeneous population should lead youngsters by extension to consider whether such practices are still appropriate to the changed and changing nature of British society today. It should also lead them to consider whether some can now be seen to operate against the interests of certain sections of the community, especially the numerically smaller ethnic minority groups, by depriving them of equality of access to the full range of opportunities open to the majority community. In thus learning how racism can operate, youngsters from both minority and majority communities may be better able to understand and challenge its influences and to consider positive and constructive changes to reflect the values of a pluralist democracy. This process should not be seen as in any sense posing a threat to democratic principles but rather as a reaffirmation of these principles in response to changing circumstances.

The aim of such a political education is the creation of citizens who are capable of active participation in a political arena in which skin color or cultural background (or gender or social class) is not an immediate and serious handicap.

Political education must itself espouse democratic principles. As one book on multicultural education puts it: "Anti-racist education is political in its commitment and teachers who are committed to striving for equality in school and society must be prepared to change their style to one which is non-authoritarian" (Straker-Welds, 1984, p. 6). Indeed, the major reason why political education courses in schools have had little impact on pupils in the past, is the didactic, descriptive, passive, and non-controversial nature of the courses concerned (Stacey, 1978, pp. 67–68). The Programme for Political Education, the set of aims and objectives devised during the 1970s, does, on the other hand, have an underlying democratic ideology which is expressed in its procedural values. These are, according to Porter (1979):

1. Willingness to adopt a critical stance towards political information,
2. Willingness to give reasons why one holds a view or acts in a certain way and to expect similar reasons from others,
3. Respect for evidence in forming and holding political opinions,
4. Willingness to be open to the possibility of changing one's own attitudes in the light of evidence,
5. To value fairness as a criterion for judging and making decisions,
6. To value the freedom to choose between political alternatives, and
7. Toleration of a diversity of ideas, beliefs, values, and interests.

However, "toleration" does not mean toleration of racism. Racism is not just another political issue where there is a case "for" and "against." Racist opinions and comments assume that people are unequal on the irrelevant basis of skin color, and, therefore, contradict the notion of equality of opinion that is a key aspect of the procedural values that go to make up the democratic learning environment necessary for political education. Political education for democracy must, therefore, be opposed to racism, although being prepared to use an open classroom style to analyse racism as a social and political phenomenon. Moreover, one of the key aims of political education — the ability to detect political values and bias—is an important skill in identifying racism in such sources of learning as textbooks and the media.

Encouragingly, there are findings from research on political socialization which suggest that using an open and democratic classroom environment to discuss political issues helps to foster a range of more democratic political orientations, such as greater political interest, less authoritarianism, greater political knowledge, a greater sense of political efficacy and trust, and less political cynicism and alienation (Ehman, 1980). Button (1974) showed that a program of study of models of political change, along with political socialization self-analysis, could benefit all pupils, but in particular those from minority groups. The clear aim of her teaching was that "education must promote belief in the basic democratic values (political participation, majority rule with minority rights, human brotherhood and concern for community, and the right of dissent)—and the behaviour that is consistent with these beliefs."

The spread of such values is even more important among young white people in Britain, if black people are not to be denied access to power and policy making in the future. At the moment, there is evidence that young black people are less willing to use the institutionalized routes for access to the political system, to a large extent because they have little reason to have much confidence in them (Wormald, 1982; Reeves & Chevannes, 1984). The education system, therefore, must not only develop more democratic political values in all young people, it must also help to create a climate in the future where black people will actually feel able to use existing political machinery, because those who control political institutions have begun to reform their operation in a more democratic direction.

POLITICS AND POLITICAL EDUCATION

Political education for democracy is, however, not likely to be a feature of British schools in the foreseeable future. The reason for this lies within the politics of the Conservative Party. In the debates about political education during the late 1970s and early 1980s two party political views emerged. The Conservative Party saw political education in terms of system support. It was necessary only to present the world as it is, and explain the system whereby formal politics are administered. One senior Conservative member of the House of Commons, for example, said, "It is right that all young people should be made aware of the British Constitution, the British form of democracy and our parliamentary system." Labor Party politicians, on the other hand, tended to stress a more active role for political education in creating a society that is more democratic and more participant. One member of the Labor shadow cabinet stated that: "There ought to be attempts by every school to make youngsters aware of the full responsibilities of the citizen in a democracy. Political education promotes the idea of rights and responsibilities and embraces something much wider than what people generally understand to be politics: a respect for truth, discernment, and judgement" (Evans, 1982, p. 28).

This party political difference was not difficult to explain. The dominant messages and assumptions transmitted by schools in Britain favor center-right political values rather than center-left ones. Schools not only tend to be authoritarian, ethnocentric, and racist, as has been argued above, but they are also predominantly competitive, sexist, and socially divisive. Teachers themselves have consistently favored the center-right in electoral terms, rather than the center-left. Therefore: "Conservative resistance to newer approaches in political education are not about a threat from the left but about a threat to their own hegemony" (Harber, 1984, p. 119). Only isolated individual Conservative politicians, usually on the right of the party, were opposed to the whole idea of political education.

Since then, the Conservative Party has won two further elections, and the right wing of the party has been increasingly influential in educational policy making. Publications emanating from right wing groups have sought further to enhance the conservative nature of schools, and to eliminate any informed discussion of politics, by repeatedly attacking the whole idea of schools being involved in taught courses of political education (Scruton, Ellis-Jones, & O'Keeffe, 1985; O'Keeffe, 1986). In the conclusion to a critique of the latter of these two books (*The Wayward Curriculum*), which focused on the lack of evidence used, the unsubstantiated statements and the overwhelming evidence to the contrary, Harber and Brown (1986) stated that:

> We do not suggest a conspiracy against social science but we do think it necessary to alert social science teachers to what appears to be a quickening of right-wing sniping at the teaching of anything that does not reinforce conservative concepts of society and educational practice. *The Wayward Curriculum* is a good example of the intellectual poverty of the right-wing critique; it is also a reminder of its dangers. (p. 6)

Since writing this, it has become more difficult to dismiss conspiracy, as there is both evidence of an informal network of individuals and small organizations which seek to influence policy at the highest levels, and evidence that they are successful. The National Curriculum, which is now law, includes no reference to any subject—politics, sociology, or even economics—that directly addresses the nature of society. One right-wing group, for example, the Campaign for Real Education, opposes the teaching of sociology, politics, peace studies, world studies, and political education, is critical of anti-racism and anti-sexism, and claims to have been influential in the framing of the National Curriculum (Hempel, 1988).

CONCLUSION

There are a number of points that, therefore, need to be borne in mind when considering the British experience, in relation to the issue of education for democracy in a multiethnic society. The first, is that it must not be assumed that existing political structures are the most open and democratic that can be achieved. Second, there is the need to examine the extent to which the major obstacle to greater democracy is the "white" power holders. Third, there is the need to make educational structures as democratic as possible. Fourth, is the need to insure that political education for all young people not only involves knowledge, but political skills and democratic values as well. Finally, political education must be clearly anti-racist in nature.

It is, however, not easy for someone concerned about greater democracy in Britain to be optimistic about the future. The signs are that early progress in political education and anti-racist education will now be reversed as schools are increasingly forced to concentrate on mathematics, science, technology, and English. This will do nothing to combat racism among white young people, and alienation among black young people. Some teachers and schools will do their best to maintain a concern with democratic values, but this will be difficult and outside of the mainstream of schooling for technocracy.

REFERENCES

Almond, G. A. & Verba, S. (1963). *The civic culture*. Princeton, NJ: Princeton University Press.

Brown, C. (1984). *Black and white in Britain: 3rd PSI survey*. London: Heinemann.

Brown, C. (1989). Democratic practice and CPVE. In C. Harber & R. Meighan (Eds.), *Democratic practice and educational management*. Ticknall: Education Now Publishing Cooperative.

Button, C. B. (1974). Political education for minority groups. In R. Niemi et al., Politics of future citizens. New York: Josey Bass.

Commission for Racial Equality (1987). *Living in terror*. London: Commission for Racial Equality.

Dawson, R., Prewitt, K., & Dawson, K. (1977). *Political socialization*. Boston: Little, Brown.

Ehman, L. (1980). The American high school in the political socialisation process. *Review of Educational Research*, 50.

D. E. S. (1985). *Education for all* (The Swann Report). London: HMSO.

Entwistle, H. (1971). *Education in a democracy*. London: Routledge & Kegan Paul.

Evans, R. (1982, September 17). Teaching about politics. *Times Educational Supplement*.

Evans, J. & Davies, B. (1987). The social context of educational opportunities in new vocation education initiatives. In D. Gleeson (Ed.), *T.V.E.I. and secondary education: A critical appraisal*. Milton Keynes: Open University Press.

Fletcher, C., Caron, M., & Williams, W. (1985). *Schools on trial*. Milton Keynes: Open University Press.

Gilbert, R. (1984). *The impotent image*. Lewes: The Falmer Press.

Harber, C. (1984). Politics and political education in 1984. *Educational Review*, 36(2).

Harber, C. (1986). Schools and the political socialisation of young people. *Social Science Teacher*, 15(3).

Harber, C. (Ed.) (1987). *Political education in Britain*. Lewes: The Falmer Press.

Harber, C. & Brown, C. (1986). Sociology, politics and the wayward curriculum. *Social Science Teacher* 16(1).

Harber, C. & Meighan, R. (Eds) (1989). *Democratic practice and educational management*. Ticknall, Education Now Publishing Cooperative.

Hartmann, P. & Husband, C. (1974). *Racism and the mass media*. London: Davis-Poynter.

Her Majesty's Inspectorate (H.M.I.). (1981). *Teacher training and the secondary school*. London: Department of Education and Science.

Kavanagh, D. (1981). The decline of the civic culture? In M. Burch & M. Moran (Eds.), *British politics: A reader*. Manchester: Manchester University Press.

Klein, G. (1985). *Reading into racism*. London: Routledge & Kegan Paul.

Langton, K. (1969). *Political socialization*. London: Oxford University Press.

McGurk, H. (Ed.) (1987). *What next?* London: Economic and Social Research Council.

Nixon, J. (1985). *A teacher's guide to multicultural education*. Oxford: Basil Blackwell.

O'Keeffe, D. (Ed.) (1986). *The wayward curriculum*. Exeter: The Social Affairs Unit.

Pilkington, A. (1984). *Race relations in Britain*. Slough: University Tutorial Press.

Porter, A. (1979). The programme for political education. *Social Science Teacher, 8*(3).

Richardson, J. & Lambert, J. (1985). *The sociology of race*. Ormskirk: The Causeway Press.

Reeves, F. & Chevannes, M. (1984). The political education of young blacks in Britain. *Educational Review, 36*(2).

Ridley, F. (1987, August 10). At the bottom of the democracy league. *The Guardian*.

Scruton, R., Ellis-Jones, A., & O'Keeffe, D. (1985). *Education and indoctrination*. Harrow: Education Research Centre.

Shemilt, R. (1987). The politics of political education in 16–19 vocational preparation. In C. Harber (Ed.), *Political education in Britain*. Lewes: The Falmer Press.

Shipman, M. (1971). *Education and modernisation*. London: Faber and Faber.

Smith, D. (1977). *Racial disadvantage in Britain*. Harmondsworth: Penguin.

Stacey, B. (1978). *Political socialization in western society*. London: Edward Arnold.

Stradling, R. (1977). *The political awareness of the school leaver*. London: The Hansard Society.

Straker-Welds, M. (1984). *Education for a multicultural society*. London: Bell and Hyman.

Tomlinson, P. & Quinton, M. (1986). *Values across the curriculum*. Lewes: The Falmer Press.

Whitty, G. & Young, M. (1976). *Explorations in the politics of school knowledge*. Driffield: Nafferton.

Wormald, E. (1982). Political education and ethnic minority groups. *Teaching politics, 11*(2).

Young, J. & Lea, J. (1982). Urban violence and political marginalisation. *Critical Social Policy, 1*(3).

4

The Integration of Second Generation Immigrants in Germany: An Explanation of "Cultural" Differences

Hartmut Esser

I. INTRODUCTION: COMPETING MODELS OF INTEGRATION

It is an old assumption that the integration of migrants requires the course of generations before it is complete. Such an assumption, however, is not universally accepted by migration sociologists. In fact, two rather different models exist within this field of study. One (the so-called *assimilation model*) is based on the traditional hypothesis that actual assimilation is only a question of time, and as such is inevitable. The other, and more strongly supported model (the *segmentation model*), posits that ethnic orientation and segmentation remain, and even increase over generations. Both models have their supporters. The assimilation model is backed by such West German research as that of Schrader, Nikles, and Griese (1976, 66ff), and the American work of Alba (1986). The segmentation model, on the other hand, is supported more by various studies on the "multicultural society," and on internal integration (for West Germany, the studies of Wilpert 1980, 11ff), and Elwert (1982).

Over the years, migration sociology has been the forum in which these models have been challenged and refined. In the United States in the 1920s and 1930s, the hypothesis of progressive assimilation was advanced primarily through models of a "three-generation assimilation cycle" (cf. Price, 1969, p. 204). In this variation, first generation immigrants adopted only those new behavioral patterns necessary to meet basic needs, while simultaneously forming homogeneous and cohesive ethnic groups. Such arrangements protected new immigrants from the most drastic culture shocks, but also restricted members to informal and primary contacts with their own ethnic groups. The second generation bore the full brunt of the conflicting cultures, as they were caught between the socializing traditions of the first generation, and the aspirations of the new culture. Such a dual normative, and cognitive orientation frequently gave rise to marginality, a condition and conception introduced in the work of Park (1928). Marginality produced two alternative consequences—mobilization or disorientation—which appeared in both increasing rates of interethnic contact, and various forms of delinquency (see, among others, the contributions of Whyte, 1943, and Child, 1943). In the third generation, the original culture was totally discarded, resulting in complete integration into the new culture with few remnants of ethnic identification (Parsons, 1975).

The three–generation–assimilation model has not gone unchallenged. Criticism has been based mainly on observations of constancy in intraethnic marriage rates, ethnic resistance to change, and intergenerational adherence to ethnospecific religious rituals. The third generation, in particular, displayed certain resegmentation tendencies in ethnic identification and social relationships, and subsequent generations showed a revived interest in traditional religious practices (Kennedy & Reeves, 1944, 1952; Gordon, 1964, pp. 122ff).

Hansen (1938) and Herberg (1960) were particularly important in challenging the intergenerational assimilation model. According to them, resistance to assimilation appears in the third generation or, as Hansen concluded, "What the son wishes to forget, the grandson wishes to remember." Segmentation thus reappears as a reorientation toward the ethnic origin of the grandparents, and a counterreaction to the disorientation of a universalized world, or to the imperviousness of an ostensibly open system to immigrants. Most research suggests that ethnic segmentation appears to result more from limited possibilities for immigrants (education, interethnic experiences), than from persistent ethnic peculiarities or characteristics (language or social habits).

An especially interesting case of assimilation differences has appeared in West Germany. Migrants began to arrive in force in the early 1960s, in response to labor shortages and the closing of the Berlin border, and continued to come into Germany through 1973. During that period 2.6 million foreign workers were recruited, and a total of 4 million foreigners entered the country. Significantly, Germany contended from the start that foreigners were to be temporary residents, and assumed that they would not remain long enough to establish second generations. That expectation was never met. Although recruitment of foreigners stopped in 1973, the overall size of the non-German population continued to grow. More important, the proportion of the foreign population who were working dropped

TABLE 4.1

Percentage of foreign pupils in 1987 attending schools providing a general education, divided according to nationality and type of school

	Foreign pupils			German pupils
	Total	Turkish	Yugoslav	
Primary School	39.3	40.3	37.7	30.0
Secondary	30.8	33.8	29.4	13.5
Special School	5.8	6.9	4.2	3.1
Secondary Mod.	8.5	6.8	13.5	12.6
Grammar School	9.1	4.9	11.0	22.7
Comprehensive & Rudolf Steiner Schools	4.4	4.9	3.1	3.1

Source: Bundesminister für Bildung und Wissenschaft, Ausgabe 1988/89, p. 60; own calculations

from the initial 65 percent to under 40 percent by 1978, due to the influx of family and a relatively high fertility rate among immigrants. Turks emerged as the single largest immigrant group, establishing itself permanently within the social system of the Federal Republic of Germany as a distinct minority with its own ethnic infrastructure.

The significance of the foreign population for the German educational system is aptly reflected in the share of foreign pupils attending Comprehensive Schools (Table 4.1). In 1965 only 6 percent of the school population were non-German. Since then, the increasing numbers of foreign children

TABLE 4.2

Percentage of foreigners attending Comprehensive Schools for different years

Year	In percent	Absolute figures (in 1000)
1965	.6	54
1970	1.7	186
1975	3.7	451
1980	6.4	747
1982	7.7	855
1983	7.9	840
1984	7.7	791
1985	8.0	789
1986	8.5	811
1987	9.1	848

Source: Bundesminister für Bildung und Wissenschaft, Ausgabe 1988/89, p. 10; own calculation.

TABLE 4.3
**Language skills and interethnic friendships in comparison,
according to rationality and generation**

| | | Language skills | | |
Groups*	Mean values	eta (generation)	eta (nationality)	n
T1	6.60	.57		461
T2	11.56		.38	460
Y1	9.80		.42	476
Y2	14.34	.56		430

| | | Interethnic friendships | | |
Groups*	Mean values	eta (generation)	eta (nationality)	n
T1	1.32	.14		346
T2	1.55		.22	394
Y1	1.72		.46	378
Y2	2.64	.37		389

*T = Turks; Y = Yugoslavs; 1 = first generation; 2 = second generation.

combined with a receding German birth rate were to produce a foreign student proportion of 9 percent. Moreover, the data in Table 4.2 indicate that the balance between German and foreign pupils varies according to type of school. Foreign pupils are clearly underrepresented in secondary schools, and Turkish students are especially underrepresented.

Esser and Friedrich conducted an extensive study of assimilation differences among Turkish and Yugoslavian students (1986). Given the importance attributed to language and social relations in the literature, this study investigated these two factors for their role in defining assimilation.[1] As Table 4.3 indicates, the pattern of language learning supports an assimilation model for both groups, even though Turks lag behind, even after two generations. On the other hand, although there are no major differences between the two ethnic groups in their first generation pattern of interethnic friendships, the second generation Yugoslav group was distinctly more likely to form interethnic relations (eta = .46).

Differences between integration experiences of different second generation ethnic groups are examined in this chapter. We first develop a

---

[1] Language assimilation was measured by a 15-level scale indicating the respondent's command of the German language. The extent of interethnic friendship was measured by a four-level index (and mean values where appropriate) of the ethnic composition of the respondent's friendship networks.

theoretical model in Section 2 which outlines the preconditions for inter-ethnic learning (measured by language), and social behavior (measured by friendship patterns). Section 3 develops empirical indicators and variables for the language and friendship constructs outlined in the model for first and second generations. Differences between generations for both ethnic groups are examined in Section 4, and Section 5 proceeds to examine whether the remaining cultural differences concern only the *distribution* of the respective variables in the groups or whether these variables also show different *effects* in the respective groups (and in their characteristic situational contexts). Finally, these empirical analyses are then reintegrated into the initial theoretical model for some conclusions on the process of intergroup and intergenerational assimilation.

II. A THEORETICAL MODEL OF INTERETHNIC RELATIONSHIPS

The following theoretical model refers to all possible aspects of interethnic relationships. Acquiring skills (for example, mastering a language), performing certain actions (retaining cultural traditions), and entering into relationships (forming interethnic friendships), are in principle dealt with in the same manner. These are labeled *interethnic reactions*.

Two main factors form the basis of the theoretical model advanced here to explain differences in interethnic relationships. Interethnic reactions are the combined result of (latent) *interest* in such reactions and the (actual) *effort* necessary to satisfy this interest by means of certain reactions. The interest stems either from a broad range of personal motives to regard certain reactions (including the acquisition of dispositions and entering into relationships) as worthwhile, or from the resources or opportunities available to effect reactions. Both may vary greatly from individual to individual.

In general, the actual interest in a given reaction (acquisition of a skill, performance of an action, entering into a relationship) increases or decreases according to the amount of effort necessary to realize the interest by means of that reaction. However, we must stress the fact that the interest function has a negative slope independent of the actors' individual motives. This is due to the fact that the actors' preferences for the reaction or relationship may vary, or that the actors have limited resources available to them. If more and more effort is necessary for acquiring a disposition, performing an action, or entering into a relationship, it is inevitable that with limited resources, inclination (or interest) will diminish. Thus it is possible to visualize the curve (or negative slope) of the function, but not its concrete position, even without further data on special motives or other factors. Similarly, it is possible to visualize the slope without knowing

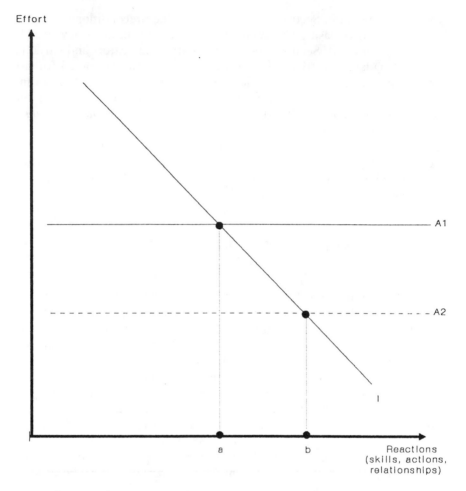

FIG. 4.1. The consequences of a decrease in effort for the extend of interethnic re-actions. (Acquisition of skills, taking actions, entering into relationships).

whether the respective reaction is effected intentionally, coincidentally, or habitually (for a general overview see Becker, 1976; for personal relation-ships in particular, see Esser, 1988).

These considerations suggest a simple correlation between the effort required for a reaction, and the extent to which the reaction can be realized (cf. Figure 4.1). A reduction of the necessary effort from A1 to A2 (for example, by increasing opportunities for interethnic contacts) automati-cally leads to an increase in the inclination toward this reaction. This is, of course, a direct consequence of the shape of interest function I.

For purposes of simplicity, we assume that the shape of the interest function is the same for all groups studied. We must consequently assume that differences in interethnic relationships are explained exclusively by differences in effort that the groups confront. It is, of course, necessary to determine empirically in each case whether there actually are differences in necessary efforts between the groups under study.

It is first necessary to define as precisely as possible the basic concepts involved in our investigation. Empirical studies of the integration of the second generation (Rogler, Cooney, & Ortiz, 1980; Miller, 1987; Michalowski, 1989; de Jong, 1988) primarily posit four dimensions in the process. One is the whole set of actual or perceived *opportunities* (O) of a group with respect to interethnic reactions (for example, educational opportunities, possibilities for making contacts). A second includes the individual possibilities with regard to acquiring knowledge and taking actions that vary according to the respective *individual dispositions* (a) such as the greater susceptibility to language learning at younger ages. A third dimension includes the dissonances which arise as a result of ties with the culture of the country of origin (b). Finally, there is the inherent restriction of interethnic reactions where external social dissimilarities are obvious (c). Integrational differences may arise as a result of various factors, which nevertheless have similar effects: they are either differences in general opportunities or individual dispositions (which are likely to account for a part of the general effect), or differences in existing ties or social dissimilarities (which are, at first glance, likely to account for cultural differences).

The model outlined in Figure 4.2 illustrates minimum and maximum levels in the extent of interethnic actions (positions "a" and "b," respectively) by indicating maximum effort (line A) and maximum effort (M). The difference between "a" and "d" represents the increase of interethnic reactions in case of an elimination of internal ties and external social dissimilarities; the difference between "c" and "b" indicates the respective rise in the case where integrational opportunities are considerably enhanced.

The conceptual differentiation of the notion of "effort" facilitates the identification of relevant empirical indicators. It also makes it possible to distinguish between the various functionally equivalent social mechanisms that could lead to the extent of interethnic reactions being widened or restricted. Interethnic relationships can only develop if there are opportunities for learning or acting. Such relationships also presuppose certain capabilities on the part of the individual (such as the ability to learn a new language). In the presence of strong internal ties or external similarities, the "cost" of interethnic relations may be so high that they are entered into even in the presence of the respective opportunities and dispositions.

The variables "nationality" and "generation" are assumed to include the theoretical constructs outlined above, meaning that statistical analysis would lead to a disappearance of differences between nationalities and

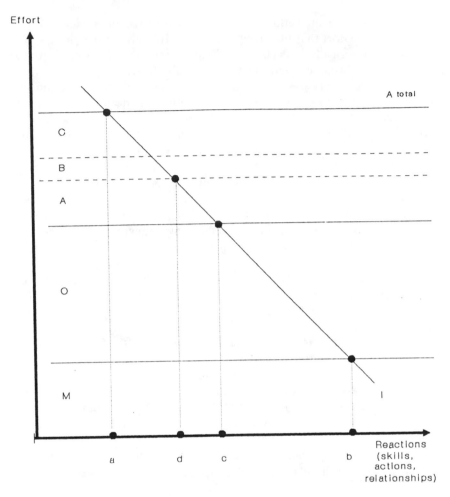

FIG. 4.2.   Individual dimensions of effort with regard to interethnic reactions.

generations. Any further differences would then have to be interpreted as genuine, non-reducible differences (such as cultural differences). For example, one of the major differences between the first and second generations included in our study was the age at the time of immigration (with an average of 26.9 years for the first, and 8.6 years for the second generation). If one proceeds from the assumption that higher age at immigration leads to a reduction in both opportunities, for both interethnic reactions and susceptibility (to language learning, or entering into interethnic relationships), a statistical evaluation of age at immigration would result in a disappearance of generational effects. On the other hand, since they are likely to be influenced by other variables, nationality effects would

TABLE 4.4
Group differences in language skills and interethnic friendships
when taking age at immigration into account

	Language skills		
Groups	Deviation of mean (without covariate)	Age at immigration as covariate	n
Turks	−1.45	−1.35	908
Yugoslavs	1.45	1.36	903
eta	.32	.30	
1. Generation	−2.28	−.72	931
2. Generation	2.41	.76	880
eta	.53	.16	

	Interethnic friendships		
Groups	Deviation of mean (without covariate)	Age at immigration as covariate	n
Turks	−.38	−.36	729
Yugoslavs	.36	.34	766
eta	.34	.32	
1. Generation	−.29	.10	721
2. Generation	.27	−.10	774
eta	.26	.09	

remain perceptible. In fact, an analysis of variance confirms this pattern (Table 4.4). The generational differences with respect to both command of language (SUB) and interethnic friendships (FDE) nearly disappear, while differences between nationalities remain stable.

III. COORDINATING EMPIRICAL INDICATORS AND THE MODEL

The effort associated with interethnic reactions may vary according to existing (objective) opportunities, individual dispositions, internal cultural ties, and external social dissimilarities. In developing empirical indicators for these constructs, we present a general model on integration of immigrants, in which the following factors are distinguished: (a) factors stemming from macrostructural conditions in the country of origin; (b) factors based on individual experiences in the country of origin; (c) peculiarities in the courses of migration inasmuch as they are relevant to subsequent behavior; (d) factors existing or emerging in the host country; and (e) factors associated with the acquisition of resources and qualifications in the host country (Esser, 1980, 1982).

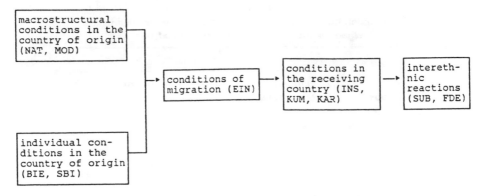

FIG. 4.3.   General model on the course of migration and integration.

The study presented here utilized several indicators of the aspects of migration and integration, which are integrally related to the four dimensions outlined above. First, macrostructural conditions in the country of origin (that is, those related to the acquisition of individual dispositions, or to the development of ethnic ties) are assumed to vary according to the respective nationality (NAT) and level of modernization (MOD). Next, individual experiences—also linked to individual dispositions and cultural ties—are likely to vary according to the educational level of the parents (BIE), as well as that of the country of origin (SBI). Age at the time of migration is assumed to be particularly significant to the migration and integration experiences. In the receiving country, the extent of ethnic institutionalization and the degree of cultural traditionalism (KUM, limited to the second generation), are likely to reflect differences in opportunities, ties, and social dissimilarities there. In addition, the acquisition of resources and qualifications are related to educational career in the host country (KAR, especially for the second generation), as well as to command of the language (SUB). Among these indicators, educational career refers primarily to the opportunities (for interethnic contacts), and to the acquisition of individual dispositions (of which command of the language is fundamental for entering into interethnic relationships). The model including these variables is presented in Figure 4.3. The variables account for variation in acquisition of language skills (SUB), and in entering into interethnic friendships (FDE), which, in turn, are hypothesized to help explain cultural differences.

One qualifier should be noted. Identifying the empirical effect of a certain indicator allows us to confirm abstractly that the effort linked to interethnic relations does vary according to the respective indicator. How-

dimensions

indicators (abbreviations)*	objective opportunities	individual dispositions	internal ties	external dis-similarities
MOD		x	x	x
BIE	x	x	x	
SBI	x	x		
EIN	x	x	x	x
KUM			x	x
INS	x		x	x
KAR	x	x		x
SUB		x		x
NAT	x	x	x	x
GEN	x	x	x	x

* explained in the text

FIG. 4.4. Allocation of the empirical indicators to the dimensions of effort with regard to interethnic reactions.

ever, only in exceptional cases will it be possible to correlate unequivocally this indicator with one of the four dimensions discussed above, and thus to identify precisely the mechanism by which variation occurs (for example, why parental education facilitates language acquisition by the children). In order to illustrate this inevitable vagueness, indicators are allocated to respective dimensions in Figure 4.4, but note that it is not possible to allocate an indicator to a particular dimension (and thus to a particular social mechanism) exclusively and unequivocally. The correlation between statistical effect and social mechanism is thus necessarily tentative.

IV. THE EXPLANATION OF "CULTURAL" DIFFERENCES IN THE INTEGRATIONAL PATTERNS OF THE FIRST AND SECOND GENERATIONS

The generational effects observable in Table 4.1 can be almost completely accounted for in Table 4.2 by controlling for age at immigration (accepting that the precise mechanisms have to be left open as a number of social processes and conditions are related to age). Nationality effects, however, still need explanation.

Our general model indicated that since the first and second generations differed markedly in some aspects (education in the country of origin and host, for example), the generations should be analyzed separately.[2] Our

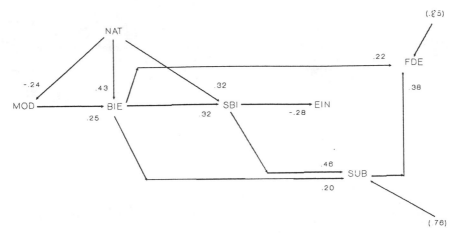

FIG. 4.5. Determinants of the integration of the first generation.

generation-specific causal models of the processes of migration and integration only included correlations in which beta > .20. For both dependent variables (command of language and friendship choice) unexplained variances were indicated by residual arrows. Any remaining nationality effects were included in the model, especially in order to be in a position to reconstruct existing and indirect relationships. The coefficients in the model were computed together with the "nationality" variable (coded as a dummy variable in which Turks were set to "0" and Yugoslavs set to "1"). The causal models were therefore constructed from the remaining relevant variables for a statistical explanation of language learning and friendship choice. In order to examine nationality effects, covariance analyses (with nationality as a factor) were added, successively introducing individual variables as covariates.

IV.1 Nationality Effects in the First Generation

The results of empirical analyses of the migrational and integrational model for the first generation can be easily summarized in Figure 4.5. There is a chain of direct correlations between the degree of modernity of the region

---

[2] The variable "school education in the country of origin" causally precedes the variable "age at immigration," whereas the age at immigration for the second generation can be important to the definition of educational career in the receiving country. Thus school education in the country of origin (SBI) is distinguished in the general model from school education in the receiving country (KAR). Moreover, the "cultural" environment variable was included only for the second generation, since it was assumed to be negligible for the first.

of origin (the only exogenous variable), parents' level of education, education in the country of origin, and the age at immigration.

Three of the variables showed pronounced nationality effects. Turks come predominantly from modernized and urbanized regions, but both they and their parents have considerably lower levels of education. This pattern is easily explained by the fact that from the early 1960s the Turkish government allowed concentrated recruitment in urban areas where a higher level of education was assumed. The Yugoslavian government, on the other hand, made sure that recruitment was focused primarily in rural areas.

Not surprisingly, among first generation migrants the acquisition of language is primarily dependent on the individual's level of education (beta = .46), and that of his or her parents (beta = .20). The explained variance for this relationship is relatively high (R^2 = .42).

Entering into interethnic friendships is also mainly determined by two factors: the individual's command of language (beta = .38) and, somewhat surprisingly, education level of the parents (beta = .22). It is possible that this correlation is due to the cultural atmosphere in the home, especially the receptivity to new friendships, which relates to parental education. As the cultural environment was not measured for first generation respondents, the direct correlation between parental education and command of language may possibly be a reflection of this unmeasured environment. The explained variance with regard to interethnic friendships is relatively low among first generation respondents (R^2 = .27).

Virtually no significance can be attached to national background in determining command of language or interethnic friendships (Figure 4.5). Age at immigration is also not related to either dependent variable for first generation respondents.

The covariance analyses also note the decrease in nationality effects from the differences that initially prevailed (Table 4.5). Differences between the groups on language decrease to .25 (from .38) when parental education is taken into account, to .17 if the individual's level of education is included, and to .13 if both covariates are jointly considered. Similarly the relatively low group difference with respect to interethnic friendships (beta = .22) almost disappears when parental education is added.

As a whole, virtually all cultural differences (measured as nationality effects) observed in the first generation disappear when controls are introduced. From a theoretical standpoint it is interesting to note that the variables which explain national differences among first generation immigrants are all *individual qualifications*. It thus appears that initially observed "cultural" differences between first generation Turks and Yugoslavs were due to differences in the distributions or qualifications and opportunities. There was no indication of any environmental or dissimilarity effects, even taking into consideration the fact that parental education may have been influenced by environmental factors.

TABLE 4.5
Nationality differences with regard to language skills and
interethnic friendships after incorporation of covariates
(first generation)

	Language skills				
	Deviation of mean (without covariate)	*covariate BIE*	*covariate SBI*	*covariate BIE, SBI*	*n*
Turks	− 1.62	− 1.07	− .74	− .57	453
Yugoslavs	1.55	1.06	.70	.55	474
eta, beta	.38	.25	.17	.13	
R		.53	.63	.64	

	Interethnic friendships				
	Deviation of mean (without covariate)	*covariate BIE*	*covariate SBI*	*covariate BIE, SBI*	*n*
Turks	− .21	− .07	− .04	.02	337
Yugoslavs	.19	.07	.04	− .02	340
eta, beta	.22	.08	.04	.03	
R		.41	.48	.54	

IV.2   Nationality Effects in the Second Generation

Nationality effects on language learning (beta = .42), and the formation of interethnic friendships (beta = .46) were particularly pronounced among second generation migrants (Table 4.7). Applying the causal model of integration to this generation (Figure 4.6), it becomes evident that again only two variables are noteworthy. The school career in the receiving country (KAR, beta = .33) and the age at immigration (EIN, beta = .26) are both significant for language. Language (SUB, beta = .31) and social environment in the home (KUM, beta = .32) are both relevant for the formation of interethnic friendships. In both cases the explained variances are very high (R^2 = .43 in language, and R^2 = .41 in interethnic friendships).

The remaining correlations are also of interest. Parental education increases with modernity of the region (beta = .24), as was the case in the first generation. Age at immigration decreases with an increase in parental education (beta = − .27). The cultural environment in the home is decisively related to parental educational level (beta = .38). It is of particular interest to note that age at immigration has a drastic influence on school career (beta = − .61). Thus age at immigration both directly and indirectly affects language (and also indirectly affects friendship structure). Similar to the pattern in the first generation, nationality correlates primarily with

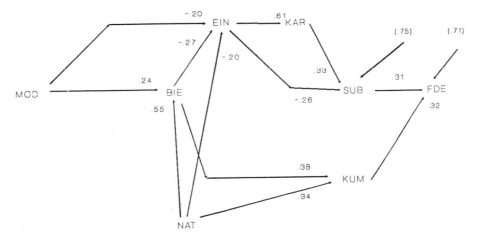

FIG. 4.6. Determinants of the integration of the second generation.

parental education level but, contrary to the pattern of the first generation, bears no relationship to age at immigration.

With regard to the *theoretical* issue of special social mechanisms, the explanation of language learning and friendship choice is more complex than was the case with the first generation. As in the first generation, *language learning is exclusively a matter of individual disposition and op-*

TABLE 4.6
Nationality differences with regard to language skills and
interethnic friendships after incorporation of covariates
(second generation)

	Language skills				
	Deviation of mean (without covariate)	covariate EIN	covariate KAR	covariate EIN, KAR	n
Turks	−1.36	−.93	−.81	−.77	451
Yugoslavs	1.43	.98	.77	.72	428
eta, beta	.42	.29	.24	.23	
R		.61	.62	.65	
	Interethnic friendships				
	Deviation of mean (without covariate)	covariate SUB	covariate KUM	covariate SUB, KUM	n
Turks	−.54	−.34	−.26	−.13	392
Yugoslavs	.55	.34	.26	.13	388
eta, beta	.46	.29	.22	.16	
R		.58	.57	.64	

portunities, with the critical determinants rooted in age at immigration and school career. Those, in turn, are influenced by parental education. Environmental effects and external dissimilarities have no effect on language learning in the second generation.

The situation is different for *interethnic friendships*. If the cultural environment of the home is an index of the effectiveness of ethnic ties, friendship choice (in conjunction with the "individual" factor of language command) is clearly determined by such ties. Possible opportunities for entering into interethnic friendships are utilized to a considerably lesser extent. The possibility cannot be dismissed, however, that external dissimilarities (between potential German interaction partners and migrant families) play a role in suppressing such interactions.

Contrary to the pattern in the first generation, nationality effects do not disappear when other factors are controlled (Table 4.6). School career remains the single strongest correlate of language command (beta = .24). Even when school career and age at immigration are considered together, a group difference of beta = .23 remains. The cultural environment in the home leads to the strongest reduction of the nationality effect on friendship choice·(beta = .22). Even when command of the language is joined with environment, the group effect remains (beta = .16).[3]

To summarize our analyses, our inclusion of individual variables has largely caused national differences to disappear in the first generation and to diminish to a great extent in the second. Only when interethnic friendships are being explained culturally determined mechanisms are significant. In this context the home environment assumes some importance, along with opportunities for interaction, and individual dispositions and qualifications for learning the language and forming interethnic friendships.

V. TWO UNANSWERED QUESTIONS

The analysis to this point has not accounted for two factors: the incomplete reduction of group effects in the second generation, and the strength of

---

[3] A partial explanation of the remaining differences can be accounted for by a variable called "institutional completeness of the ethnic environment," which is not included in the models. This variable showed a significant correlation only to nationality. First and second generation Turks (both with beta = .37) exhibit a stronger tendency to live in ethnic colonies than Yugoslavs. However, this factor remains largely without consequence when the effects of other variables are taken into consideration. If the relatively restrictive exclusion filter of the beta > .20 is widened, it becomes obvious that there is only a "ghetto effect" when it comes to friendship choice (beta = − .13). If this variable is included as an additional covariate for the explanation of friendship choice, the nationality effect falls to a negligible level (beta = .11).

social mechanisms in explaining the results reported above. With respect to the latter factor, we might ask: assuming that age at immigration and command of the language can be regarded respectively as individual dispositions or qualifications, what effects do these features have in specific social contexts, characterized by different opportunities, ties, and dissimilarities?

Two extremes are conceivable. In one the effectiveness of both variables would remain the same in all contexts, implying an additivity to individual disposition and context. In the other, the slope, and thus the effect of the variables display differences. In the latter case, either systematic or unsystematic differences would have to be investigated.

The case of systematic differences would be particularly interesting as the variables only function in conjunction with one another. The statistical consequence of this case would be that results of multiple regression and covariance analyses would have to be regarded with reservation, since these methods assume a similarity of slope among subgroups. The theoretical consequence would be that the simple model developed in Section 2 would no longer make sense, as it only accounts for linear and additive differences in language learning and friendship choice resulting from appropriate unit changes in each. In other words, since the model cannot explain complex, context-specific relationships, it could not be used further.

Both questions are approached in two steps. First, the theoretical model is modified in order to account for differences in effects. Then the modified model will be tested empirically and its results assessed.

V.1 Explanation of Differences in Effects by the New Model

In both the theoretical and statistical models developed here certain effects were explained as the result of (latent) interests and (actual) efforts. Individual dispositions, opportunities, internal ties and external dissimilarities were dealt with as dimensions of the "constraints" of actions (or of the acquisition of skills and knowledge). The question now arises as to whether certain social factors result in those constraints having effects on the dependent variable.[4] One can also assume that action environments modify the effects of the constraints. It is conceivable, for example, that given a strong traditional ethnic environment in the home, even a good command of the language may not result in the formation of interethnic

---

[4] Technically speaking, the question is whether "contexts not only affect the axial section of the regression but also its slope." The effect on the axial section can easily be integrated into a simple linearly additive model, referring to differences in the distribution of the constraints, which, according to the functional dependency assumed in the model, affect the examined dependent variables in any context in the same manner.

friendships. External social dissimilarities could function in a similar manner. From a technical point of view such differences in effect would be reflected in contextual differences in the slope of the effort function (assuming that the shape of the interest function were left unaltered).

These considerations lead to a differentiation of the concept of "reactions" (as a collective expression for learning, taking actions, or entering into relationships), and of their explanation in the model. On the one hand, there are actions or reactions that exist relatively independently of agreement by a third party. Friendship choice, as opposed to language learning, is dependent not only on the availability of opportunities and individual dispositions, but also on the agreement of third parties, and their readiness to take action to develop the relationship. As a consequence, the extent of constraints does not remain constant over the total number of friendship choices, but rather varies according to the extent of reactions. If one assumes the simplest case, a linearly increasing distribution of constraints (in a population of potential interaction partners), there would accordingly be a linear increase in the constraint function (Figure 4.7). The consequence of a linear increase in constraints is thus illustrated by a decrease in the number of realizable actions.

What effects does an increase in constraints have on the impact of a given variable? Let d be the decrease in constraints at a specific rate (for example, as a result of the availability of individual dispositions such as language facility). Where the function is constant, such a reduction in constraints would lead to the reactions increasing from a to b; where the function increases, the increase would be from a' to b', with $(b - b')$ being considerably lower than $(a - a')$. In other words, the difference in diminished constraints is considerably less effective in the case of relational reactions.[5]

Before empirically analyzing potential interaction effects, a more precise statement of our theoretical argument is in order. Most important is our distinction between two types of reaction alternatives—absolute and relational—within a social context. *Absolute reactions* may occur independently from certain dispositions, and from actors' characteristics (for example, from learning processes that are dependent only on opportunity, or from purely instrumental actions which are independent of the private motives of third parties). If the reactions increase, there is no systematic increase in constraints. In our case, language learning would have to be regarded as such an absolute reaction, for which we would not expect any interaction effects in different social contexts.

---

[5] In statistical terms differential effects of variables may be modeled as interaction effects. A statistical interaction effect, observable in certain contexts, would serve as an indication that the shape of the constraint function differs from context to context.

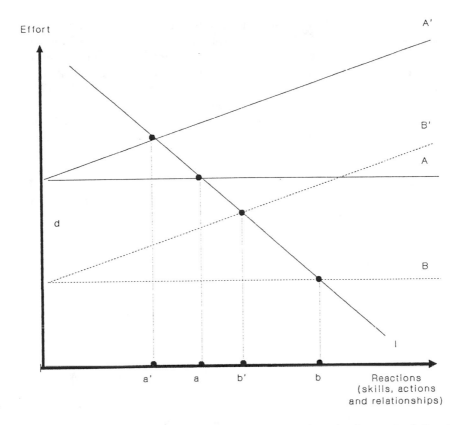

FIG. 4.7.   Different effects of reduced effort with regard to absolute and relational reactions.

Relational reactions, on the other hand, are not only dependent on the presence of opportunities, but also on reactions in the environment. In this case one would assume variable constraint functions — in the simplest case a linearly rising function. If the constraints increase at different rates in the various contexts, one would expect statistical interaction effects between the individual independent variables in conjunction with the context variable, and the observed reaction. In our case, interethnic friendships would have to be regarded as relational reactions. Inasmuch as certain social contexts (nationality, cultural environment in the home, and school environment) lead to an unequal distribution of relevant constraints, statistical interaction effects would be expected in friendship choice.

V.2   An Empirical Analysis of Differences in Effect

Our first task is to specify the contextual conditions which are assumed to effect a change in the constraint function (that is, contexts in which the constraints for the same dependent variable either remain constant or increase systematically). Three contexts are examined here: nationality, school environment, and the cultural environment in the home. With respect to relational reactions, it is assumed that (a) Turks will be confronted with stronger constraints than Yugoslavs; (b) constraints will be higher where disadvantageous school conditions exist (in this case, a high percentage of foreign pupils); and (c) relationship reaction will be more pronounced in traditional home environments. For absolute reactions, it is assumed that the constraints—in our case for language learning—only influence the reaction level (the respective mean value and axial section). Constraints for relational actions (in our case friendship choice) also determine the impact of the individual variables (and, in turn, the increase in the context-specific regression function).

TABLE 4.7
The effects of age at immigration (EIN) on language skills (SUB) under various contextual conditions (school career (KAR)* and cultural environment in the home (KUM)**)

	a	b	ß	Mean values		n
				EIN	SUB	
Turks	14.75	−.31	−.46	10.1	11.6	451
Yugoslavs	16.11	−.25	−.53	7.0	14.5	428

	a	b	ß	Mean values		n
				EIN	SUB	
Turks						
KAR 1	13.53	−.29	−.40	11.4	10.3	211
KAR 2	14.89	−.14	−.26	6.9	13.9	146
Yugoslavs						
KAR 1	15.18	−.26	−.46	10.3	12.5	108
KAR 2	15.79	−.12	−.32	5.6	15.1	274

	a	b	ß	Mean values		n
				EIN	SUB	
Turks						
KUM 1	14.54	−.32	−.47	10.4	11.2	306
KUM 2	15.20	−.26	−.46	8.4	13.0	97
Yugoslavs						
KUM 1	15.24	−.21	−.37	8.6	13.4	93
KUM 2	16.12	−.21	−.51	6.4	14.7	303

* KAR = school career; 1: worse, 2: better.
** KUM = cultural environment in the Home; 1: traditional, 2: less traditional.

These assumptions produce the following statistical hypotheses: (a) the increase of the regression line will remain constant when examining language learning in different contexts; and (b) the increase for friendship choice will be systematically higher in the case of Yugoslavs, due to more advantageous conditions in the school and less traditional home environments.

In the case of language skills, home environment and age at immigration were highlighted as central determinants. The context variables have been dichotomized and analyzed separately for each nationality group (Table 4.7).

As the table indicates, language learning under more restrictive conditions (among Turks, in a disadvantageous school environment, in traditional homes) occurs at a lower level. However, age at immigration had a relatively *strong* effect, even under these conditions. This pattern runs counter to our theoretical assumptions. However, the fact that an advantageous environment does not enhance the effect of individual disposition, and that a disadvantageous environment does not reduce the effect, substantiates the assumption that language learning has to be regarded as a largely *absolute* reaction. This conclusion is supported by the observation that above a certain level there is no longer a difference between rates of

TABLE 4.8
The effects of language skills (SUB) on interethnic friendships (FDE) under various contextual conditions (school career (KAR) and cultural environment in the home (KUM))

	a	b	ß	SUB	FDE	n
Turks	−0.24	.11	.44	11.6	1.55	392
Yugoslavs	−1.25	.21	.41	14.5	2.64	388
	a	**b**	**ß**	**SUB**	**FDE**	**n**
Turks						
KAR 1	0.26	.08	.33	10.4	1.35	192
KAR 2	−1.03	.16	.40	14.0	1.92	128
Yugoslavs						
KAR 1	0.36	.09	.25	12.7	1.88	94
KAR 2	−1.34	.22	.31	15.2	2.92	255
	a	**b**	**ß**	**SUB**	**FDE**	**n**
Turks						
KUM 1	0.08	.09	.38	11.3	1.40	272
KUM 2	−0.53	.15	.42	13.2	2.07	86
Yugoslavs						
KUM 1	−1.49	.20	.46	13.5	2.01	84
KUM 2	−0.42	.17	.28	14.9	2.83	276

increase. Moreover, there is no indication of any relational effects in language learning. Any other effect will require additional and different conceptualization. Finally school career (a context variable) and command of language (an individual variable) are relevant determinants of friendship selection (Table 4.8).

The findings presented here unequivocally substantiate our assumption that interethnic friendships are not solely dependent on individual dispositions and skills. School situation appears to be the most important contextual factor. Particularly noteworthy is the fact that command of language is equally ineffective among both nationality groups where school conditions are disadvantageous. Better conditions, however, prove to be more beneficial for Yugoslavs than for Turks ($a = .16$). Only among Turks does a traditional environment have restrictive effects on command of the language. Otherwise, the regression function increases are very similar.

VI.   THREE CONCLUSIONS

Our findings shed light on the theoretical model, on the evaluation of the statistical results presented in Section IV, and on the interpretation of nationality effects.

With respect to the theoretical model, two findings have been especially useful: the distinction between absolute and relational reactions, and the explanation of learning processes, actions, and relationships as functions of latent interests and actual constraints. The findings on the context-specific conditions of language learning do, however, imply that the *shape* of the interest function may be relevant. A linearly falling function may not necessarily be the most appropriate approach. There appear to be reactions which—given a decrease in constraints—show a more rapid increase at a lower level of realization, hence illustrating saturation effects. If the cause of this pattern is more related to organismic-psychological conditions of learning processes (and less to an increasingly restrictive environment), the linear structure of the interest function would have to be modified for such processes. A negative increase of the interest function appears to be adequate in modeling this modification (Figure 4.8). A similar reduction of the constraints leads to a reduction in the difference in accordance with the extent of the reactions: $(a - a') > (b - b')$. This would allow the negative interaction effect statistically determined for language learning to be theoretically integrated into the general model.

With respect to friendship choice, no modification of the interest function is necessary. Although the empirical effect could also be modeled via a hyperbolically shaped interest function, it is difficult to imagine that the interaction effects of the relational actions have to be seen in conjunction with organismic-psychological processes. It appears more plausible to posit

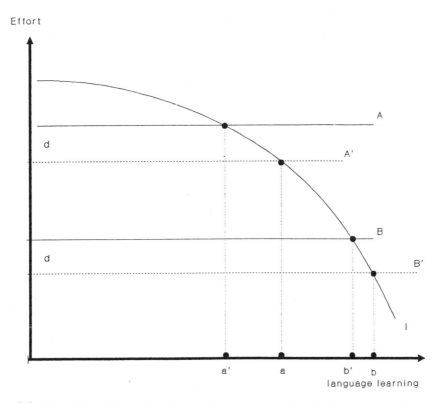

FIG. 4.8. A possible explanation for the saturation effect in language learning.

that environmental conditions are involved exclusively, and have to be modeled via the constraint function. An increasing rise in the constraint function would be a simple way of including this fact in the model, and would be supported by the result of Table 4.8.

Ascertaining interaction effects in both variables may have consequences for the evaluation of data examined in the covariance analysis. Given an inequality in the increase, misconceptions sometimes ensue when the effects pertaining to group differences are considered (Schuessler, 1970 p. 201ff). On checking these distortions in these data, it became obvious that in language learning the adjustment of the mean value was hardly influenced by the different rates of increase. With regard to friendship choice, an adjustment of rates of increase resulted in a lower adjustment to the total mean value among the Turks, than among Yugoslavs. The group difference, however, remains practically unaffected. In other words, taking the lower susceptibility of Turks for interethnic friendships into consideration when analyzing group differences, the result of the overall covariance analysis does not change.

The consequences can be summarized as follows. For neither language learning nor interethnic friendships (in both generations) are there any direct cultural effects that are significant. However, indirect nationality effects should not be dismissed entirely, since nationality determines to a certain extent the initial conditions of migration as well as prevalent conditions and the processes of integration. Very few variables are important for interethnic friendships in this process, for the second generation: age at immigration, school career for language learning, the cultural environment in the home, and command of the language.

Cultural differences lose their direct impact step-by-step during the integrational process. This is particularly evident when examining the consequences of a relatively advantageous situation at school. Given improved educational conditions, the age at immigration has almost the same impact on language learning for both Turkish and Yugoslav youngsters. However, given relatively disadvantageous conditions in the school, the age at immigration is nearly equally unimportant for both groups. School career therefore has a threefold effect: (a) it constitutes a strong factor in and of itself in the improvement of command of the language; (b) through these language skills it improves the possibilities of entering into interethnic friendships; and (c) an advantageous school climate increases the positive effects of language skills.

Age at immigration plays a central role for the second generation—almost exclusively determining the course of the school career and, in turn, its consequences. Age at immigration itself depends on immediate conditions of the whole process, conditions related to nationality. Overall, however, the integration process is mainly influenced by prevalent structural possibilities in the receiving country.

The findings presented in this study have shown unambiguously that differences between Turkish and Yugoslavian pupils cannot be attributed to different cultural orientations, but rather to differences in the economic and material conditions, as well as to more accidental differences in migration situations. This conclusion has obvious implications for the political assessment of this situation. Views frequently voiced in Germany assume that it is impossible to establish a conflict-free coexistence between culturally distinct groups. Our findings dispute such views. The second generation shows clear indications of an increasing cognitive adaptation, and an increasing political participation, while retaining cultural characteristics. Given the stability of the foreign population in Germany over the past thirty years, there is little evidence to dispute our findings that successive generations will integrate into German society.

REFERENCES

Alba, R. D. (1986). *Italian-Americans: Into the twilight of ethnicity.* Englewood Cliffs, NJ: Prentice Hall.

Becker, G. S. (1976). Irrational behaviour and economic theory. In G. S. Becker (Ed.), *The Economic Approach to Human Behaviour* (pp. 153–168). Cambridge & London: University of Chicago Press.

Child, I. L. (1943). *Italian or American? The second generation in conflict.* New Haven: Yale University Press.

Elwert, G. (1982). Probleme der Ausländerintegration [Problems of integration of immigrants]. *Kölner Zeitschrift für Soziologie und Sozialpsychologie, 34,* 717–731.

Esser, H. (1980). *Aspekte der Wanderungssoziologie* [Aspects of immigration sociology]. Darmstadt und Neuwied: Luchterhand.

Esser, H. (1988). *The substitution of complete networks: An "economic" explanation of the development and change of friendship networks.* Unpublished manuscript.

Esser, H. & Friedrichs, J. (1986). Schlußbericht zum Forschungsvorhaben *Kulturelle und ethnische Identität bei Arbeitsmigranten im interkontextuellen, intergenerationalen und internationalen Vergleich.* Essen & Hamburg:DGG-Schlußbericht. [Cultural and ethnic identity in employment exchange in intercontextual, intergenerational, and international comparison].

Gordon, M. M. (1964). *Assimilation in American life: The role of race, religion, and national origins.* New York: Oxford University Press.

Hansen, M. L. (1938). *The problem of the third generation immigrant.* Rock Island: Augustana Historical Society Publications.

Herberg, W. (1960). *Protestant-Catholic-Jew.* Garden City, NY: Anchor Books.

Jong, M. J. de (1988). Ethnic origin and educational careers in Holland. *The Netherlands Journal of Sociology, 24,* 65–75.

Kennedy, R. & Reeves, J. (1944). Single or triple melting pot? Intermarriage trends in New Haven 1870–1940. *American Journal of Sociology, 49,* 331–339.

Kennedy, R. & Reeves, J. (1952). Single or triple melting pot? Intermarriage trends in New Haven 1870–1950. *American Journal of Sociology, 58,* 56–59.

Michalowski, M. (1987). Adjustment of immigrants in Canada: Methodological possibilities and its implications. *International Migration Review, 25,* 21–31.

Miller, P. W. (1987). Aspects of occupational mobility and attainment among immigrants in Australia. *International Migration Review, 21,* 96–109.

Park, R. E. (1928). Human migration and the marginal man. *American Journal of Sociology, 33,* 881–893.

Parsons, T. (1975). Some theoretical considerations on the nature and trends of change in ethnicity. In N. Glazer & D. P. Moynihan (Eds.), *Ethnicity, Theory, and Experience* (pp. 53–58). Cambridge, MA: Harvard University Press.

Price, C. A. (1989). The study of assimilation. In J. A. Jackson (Ed.), *Migration* (pp. 181–237). Cambridge: Cambridge University Press.

Richmond, A. H. (1986). Ethnogenerational variation in educational achievement. *Canadian Ethnic Studies, 18,* 75–89.

Rogler, L. H., Cooney, R. S. & Ortiz, W. (1988). Intergenerational change in ethnic identity in the Puerto Rican family. *International Migration Review, 14,* 193–214.

Schrader, A., Nikles, B. W. & Griese, H. M. (1976). Die zweite Generation: Sozialisation und Akkulturation ausländischer Kinder in der Bundesrepublik. Kronberg: [The second generation: Socialization and acculturation of foreign children in the Federal Republic]. Athenaeüm Verlag.

Schuessler, K. (1970). *Analyzing Social Data.* Boston, MA: Houghton Mifflin.

Whyte, W. F. (1943). *Street corner society: The social structure of an Italian slum.* Chicago, IL: University of Chicago Press.

Wilpert, C. (1980). *Die zukunft der zweiten generation,* Königstein. [The future of the second generation]. Athenaeüm Verlag.

5 The Development of Democratic Culture in a Society with Powerful Traditional Forces: The Case of Israel

Israelit Rubinstein and Chaim Adler

THE DEVELOPMENT OF A DEMOCRATIC POLITICAL CULTURE IN ISRAEL

Democracy as a political culture[1] generally implies the simultaneous operation of several elements, two of which are fundamental: government by the majority (either directly or through its representatives), and the protection of individual and minority rights. When Israel was founded in 1948, its founders aimed to create a democratic state. Several social institutions were called upon to promote democracy in the newly-born society. Needless to say, education was visualized as one such system. In this chapter we shall comment at length on those social factors in the nation's development which have posed particular problems, as well as challenges for the educational system as it dedicated itself to preparing youth for democratic citizenship.

The next chapter will discuss how the schools went about discharging this function, and what still needs to be done. In a current effort to enhance

---

[1] The concept political culture, coined by Almond (1956) and Almond and Verba (1963) is applied here in a broad sense. It refers to individuals' behaviors, to organizational arrangements, and to the types of communication between citizens and various forms of political organization (see also Kavanaugh, 1972).

democratic values, the authors and a number of other colleagues are in the process of developing a new educational program known as the "Rules of the Game," on which we shall comment in that chapter. The need for developing such a program is acute, we believe, because Israeli society today is composed of several groups who have their origins in non-democratic societies, and whose allegiance to democratic values, therefore, cannot be taken for granted, and might have to be cultivated. In general, we may state that in this relatively new and multi-ethnic society, it is not always clear which political norms and "rules of the game" command the widest social consensus.

Within this diverse, multi-ethnic society, three main cleavages are relevant for the discussion at hand. The main cleavage is between the Jewish majority (about 83%), and the Arab minority (about 17%).[2] The latter are Arab citizens of Israel. Many of their relatives, however, do not live in Israel, but in neighboring countries. That fact, as well as the recurrent wars in the Middle East, have created in these two ethnic-national groups a history of distrust and antagonism.

But there are also cleavages within the Jewish majority. Two especially deserve mention. One cleavage is essentially non-ethnic. It is the conflict between the religious Jews and the secular ones. Although the majority of Jews are secular, they, too, are not a homogeneous group but include small anti-religious groups, as well as—at the opposite side of the secular continuum—traditional Jews, i.e., Jews who have an attachment to religion, and practice some of its rituals, but subscribe to the idea of a secular state. The religious groups also present a wide spectrum, from the ultra-orthodox, who refuse to recognize the modern Jewish secular political system of the democratic state, to the modern religious, who are moderates, and seek ways of co-existing with the secular state.

The second intra-Jewish cleavage is that between "Eastern" and "Western" Jews. The term "Western" Jews refers to those who themselves, or whose families, had emigrated from European countries, while "Eastern" refers to those who had emigrated from Asian and African countries (mostly from the Near and Middle East). This cleavage relates to different value orientations, especially democratic values. It is further complicated because it is highly correlated with social class as well.

These differences notwithstanding, social integration of the various Jewish sub-groups was always high on the society's agenda. When Israel was created (and in many ways before that), a process of nation-building was launched in which social integration was a major element. Although, as we have shown, the Jews were divided among themselves with respect to religious outlook, and by country of origin, they nonetheless exhibited very

---

[2] The Arabs are subdivided by religion but the majority is Muslim.

powerful integrative tendencies. To begin with, the very desire and commitment to build a new nation was based on the acceptance of ancient common identities. Even the most secular groups, and all religious groups (except for a tiny splinter one), identified themselves as being part of the Jewish nation. Modern Hebrew, as the language originally imposed quite aggressively upon new immigrants, never became a divisive factor, but actually served as one of the main tools of nation-building. It thus never became the source of educational conflict that it has become in some of the other countries discussed in this volume. Education also became an important factor in the formation of the nation's old–new identity.

Behind the various efforts at nation-building lay the conviction of the earlier, largely European, immigrants, that even the more recent immigrants would share their value system, and would consequently integrate quickly and smoothly into the new society. After all, many of the founders also had not experienced democracy in their countries of origin, but nonetheless became deeply and unequivocally committed to it, convinced that it was the only type of regime possible for the new society and state. So deep was their commitment, that they were sure the masses of new immigrants from the Arab Near and Middle East (the Eastern Jews) would acquire a similar commitment by merely living in Israel, participating in the institutional framework, and by attending the same classes in school that everyone else did. It is only recently that Israelis have begun to question these assumptions.

In the case of the cleavage between Arabs and Jews, which, of course, is the major cleavage in Israel, integration takes on an entirely different meaning. In this case, neither group intended to relinquish its separate religious, linguistic, historical, cultural, and political identity. Nor was it the intention of the majority to encroach upon the Arabs' separate identity. All that the majority expected of the Arab minority, was loyalty to the state. Interestingly, all that the minority, which cherishes its separateness, expected was equality. It is to this expectation of equality that we can trace the commitment to democracy which began to evolve in this community— a community which lacked almost entirely a democratic tradition and experience with democratic institutions.

These and other cleavages have lead to a growing awareness, unanticipated by the founders, of the potential fragility of the democratic system. In order better to understand what threat they might pose for the survival of democracy, we shall in the next section offer an overview of the nation's recent history.

HISTORICAL BACKGROUND

Pre-Statehood and Early Statehood.   To understand today's development, especially as it is relevant for democratic citizenship education, one must know something about the nation's founding fathers, who they were, their definition of a democratic government, and how that affected their policies and plans for the new state.

When we speak of founding fathers, we have to bear in mind that the term is all but synonymous with founders and leaders of the Labor Party. While this chapter certainly is not intended as a history of Israeli parties, it is important to realize that it is next to impossible to talk about the first four decades of Israeli statehood without focusing on the role the party played in shaping the characteristic features of the young democracy.[3] (Horowitz and Lissak, 1978; Yatziv, 1978.)

The roots of Israel's unique political system lie in the pre-state period when the Labor Party succeeded in rallying the resources needed for immigrant absorption, economic growth, and the establishment of a complex defense machinery (Eisenstadt, 1967; 1981). The core force responsible for bringing this about, and forging a democratic political culture, was a relatively small group of young visionaries of mostly Eastern European origin. A majority of them were young men of middle class backgrounds, who came to Palestine out of an ideological commitment to create a new and different revolutionary Jewish society. One that would be modern, democratic, socialist, and politically independent, as well as economically and culturally creative. The main components of this revolutionary commitment were the following:

1. Establishment of a Jewish nation state.
2. Promotion of socialism.
3. Loyalty to the Jewish cultural (as opposed to religious) tradition.[4]
4. Commitment to democracy.

For Israel's founding fathers this commitment to democracy was a commitment to the principle of majoritarian representative rule, which they stressed far more than they did the principle of individual and minority rights. We may thus conclude that the political culture of the pre-state Jewish community of Palestine was a combination of the following features: hegemony of one political party; a lack of alternative competing political forces; lack of organized mediation between the citizen and the official

---

[3] From the early 1930s through 1948, the Labor Party controlled the internal governing organizations of the Jewish community in Palestine. From 1948 to 1977, it constituted the largest bloc in the parliament (Knesset), forming ruling coalitions through collaboration with a number of smaller, mostly religious parties.

[4] Unlike most Western democracies, Israel did not succeed in separating the process of nation-building from the common religious heritage and tradition. Despite their mostly socialist backgrounds, Zionists did not deny their Judaism, even though it proved to be impossible to define Judaism without the religious factor (Schweid, 1973; Shapiro, 1977).

organizations that commanded power; strong emphasis on nation-building, and collectivism within the framework of the Jewish heritage, rather than on individual liberties and minority rights.

Recent Developments. In the last two decades the political culture has undergone significant changes (Arian, 1985; Galnoor, 1977, 1982; Kimmerling, 1985). These changes have been based on two models. The first reflects a growing emphasis on social welfare. The second, based on the United States political model, represents a growth in citizen and group participation, individual entrepreneurship, and widespread political consensus concerning at least a few national symbols. They represent a departure, or at least a modification, from the earlier socialist, collectivist, and largely non-participatory mode, to a more individualistic and consumption-oriented one. In the last two decades, Israeli democracy has developed a growing commitment to the libertarian version of democracy (Avineri 1983; Yishai, 1987). Nevertheless, as will be shown, both the nationalist and the religious elements of Israel's political culture have not always lived in harmony with these libertarian principles of democracy, and at times have clashed with them.

The trauma of the 1973 Yom Kippur War accelerated the changes, resulting in the 1977 political upset in which the Labor Party lost the election to the right-wing Likkud Party. It symbolized and accelerated the change from a collectivist-socialist culture, to a more individualistic-libertarian one. Nonetheless, although Israel is certainly fully democratic in the formal structural sense, the status of various libertarian aspects of Israeli democracy is still in flux. We shall claim that parallel with the process of ongoing improvement of the democratic system—mostly in the realm of greater libertarianism—there have emerged groups that serve as countervailing forces. The three groups on which we focus in the following section share a lack of democratic traditions and institutions in their history, or an ambivalent approach to contemporary democracy. The incorporation process of these three groups into the center of Israeli society will be traced, thus showing the impact this process has had on the nature of Israeli democracy.

THE RELIGIOUS GROUPS

One of the most interesting groups, in the context of our analysis is the religious Zionist one or, more specifically, its ultranationalist "Gush Emunim"[5] sub-group. An examination of its integration into society, and

---

[5] Gush Emunim (literally "block of the faithful") is an ideological-political movement based on a fundamentalist interpretation of Jewish national elements.

its attitude towards the State of Israel may illuminate a number of important general trends in the contemporary society.

Religious Zionist groups have consistently represented an important component of the central value system (Aran, 1985; Rubinstein, 1981). The religious Zionist groups, more than any other, have rejected the notion of a separation between state and religion (Samet, 1979). In the view of many analysts, their attitude presents a serious obstacle to the development of a fully democratic, libertarian system, since it excludes an entire area of public issues from the agenda of democratic decision-making (Liebman & Don-Hehiya, 1985). Because Jewish law, though not intrinsically anti-democratic, is built around a set of regulations and behavioral prescriptions, which must not be questioned, it essentially obviates democratic discourse and practice. In fact, some religious theorists—including a number from Gush Emunim—argue that the democratic system so limits the arena for the operation of religion, that religion itself becomes almost obsolete. In short, the relationship between religion and democracy is extremely complicated in Israel.

The emergence of Gush Emunim as part of the Israeli socio-political scene can be related to a general weakening of Zionist fervor beginning in the mid-1960s. The secular Zionist revolution, as represented by the founding fathers, was both a reaction against the Eastern European "ghetto" structure and mentality, as well as a movement opposed to Jewish assimilation into the bourgeois culture and life styles of Western Europe. This reaction notwithstanding, Zionism has to date failed to forge an alternative secular and modern Jewish culture. Thus the groundwork has been laid for a re-emergence of traditional Jewish values and culture among many secular Israeli Jews. It should be pointed out that this return does not generally entail a rejection of modern modes of behavior and cultural styles. Rather, it stresses the incorporation of traditional Judaism into elements of modern society (Avineri, 1983; Eisenstadt, 1983; Shaked, 1983; also Werblovsky, 1983).

Gush Emunim likewise adopted secular tactics (e.g., interest group mobilization, propaganda, and demonstrations) to implement its deep-seated religious commitments. Such commitments, in their view, legitimized their use of the political arena, the army, and youth groups, in order to gain support and membership. As second- and third-generation Israelis, the members (unlike previous religious elites) were familiar with these institutions and knew how to use them, notwithstanding their basic ambivalence about the democratic, secular system.

The rise of Gush Emunim, as well as its loss of impact in the more recent past, symbolizes some of the most serious dilemmas of the Jewish national renaissance, the philosophy of exclusiveness and separateness of the "chosen people," as opposed to the philosophy of the openness and normalcy among fellow citizens and participation in public affairs, as advocated by secular democratic theorists (Raanan, 1980; Rubinstein, 1982). In sum, we may state that Gush Emunim does not display an unequivocal commitment to democracy. There is in their philosophy a yearning to replace the democratic regime with one of Jewish religious law.

In certain essential respects, the analysis of Gush Emunim illustrates some of the fundamental problems confronting Israeli democracy—in particular the issue of the role played by religion in Israeli politics (Aran, 1987). The most essential problem for democracy in this respect is that of freedom. The principle of individual freedom constitutes a fundamental element in any democratic system; it draws its legitimation from the concept of man's sovereignty over transcendental forces. Jewish law, which is an all-embracing set of prescribed behaviors, by contrast, draws its legitimacy from the concept of God's superiority and sovereignty. It would seem that this contradiction can hardly be bridged, especially in a system that does not clearly distinguish between the religious and the political realms (Avinar, 1982; Sprinzak, 1984).

EASTERN JEWS

Another group whose devotion to democracy might be problematic, is the large group of Eastern Jews who came from Moslem countries in the Middle East and North Africa. This migration reached its peak in the 1950s and early 1960s. In contrast to the founders and early settlers, who mainly came from Europe, and brought with them an understanding of the principles of democracy and, in some cases, experience in living in a democratic regime, Eastern immigrants generally lacked such knowledge and experience.

Not sufficient attention was perhaps paid during the years of mass immigration to the problems these differences might create. Instead, the prevailing approach to cultural diversity was that of "absorption." The idea was that full assimilation into the mainstream would be both the most equitable arrangement for immigrants, and the most beneficial one for society (Bar-Josef, 1968). The "melting pot" ideology was preferred, since it rejected the suppression of minorities, their isolation, or their exclusion. The idea of having "separate but equal" cultures was seen as unjust, since any institution, geographical region, or role that might be assigned to the minority was likely to be perceived as being inferior. A few intellectuals expressed both reservations about the desirability of rapid assimilation, and warned that it might lead to the loss of the new immigrants' own unique cultural heritage. Absorption policy continued to be based on heritage. Nevertheless, absorption policy also continued to be based on the goal of complete integration, as expressed in such slogans as "absorption of immigrants," "social and cultural change," "modernization," and "nation-building" (Frankenstein et al., 1951–2). Both the practice, and the debate on the topic, mirrored in many ways the experiences of many other, especially Western countries, and is also reflected in several chapters in this volume.

Unlike some of the groups discussed in this volume, the second generation of Eastern immigrants was indeed gradually becoming integrated into the life of society. By 1970, Eastern Jews began to show a distinct preference for the more conservative and nationalistic policies represented by the Likkud party, and to reject certain democratic aspects of the more "Western-oriented" parties, such as Labor and other left-wing groups.

This voting behavior had led Israeli social scientists to study the phenomenon as representing an ethnic, rather than a cultural or social class gap (see Smooha, 1984, 1987). Peres and Shemer (1974) found that only among university graduates of Eastern origin does the correlation with right-wing voting behavior weaken; but the latter constituted merely a small fraction of the sample studied. In any event, the ethnic polarization in voting behavior has clearly increased over the past twenty years.

In some analysts' (Herzog, 1984; 1985) view, this fact seems to refute the claim that most Eastern Jews identify themselves primarily as members of the Israeli collective—i.e., as "Israelis"—rather than as members of an ethnic group (Ben Rafael, 1982). Thus, the sense many Eastern Jews have of still being relatively peripheral in the economic and social spheres has not contributed to the development of a separate ethnic identity (Bernstein, 1976; Deshen, 1980).[6]

On the whole, however, it is safe to state that in spite of some major differences between the western and eastern groups, the notion and politics of the "melting pot" seem in the final analysis to have been relatively successful. Eastern Jews have become participants in the Israeli social, political, economic, and cultural systems.

The integration of Eastern immigrants into Israeli political life, however, has had other consequences as well. It may well be true that their lack of prior experience with democracy has impeded the enhancement of Israeli democracy, constituting a kind of "Achilles heel" for the system.

THE ARAB SECTOR—A PERMANENT MINORITY

The Arab minority (those Arabs who are Israeli citizens) poses yet a different challenge for multi-ethnic, democratic education. Not only do they

---

[6] A few recent public opinion polls and attitude studies point to a somewhat lower degree of commitment to democratic values and principles among Eastern voters. These data, however, remain inconclusive because the samples were small.

constitute a permanent minority but, needless to say, the political development of the Arab minority has taken place in a country with a distinctly Jewish-Zionist culture. Almost all Israeli institutions are exclusively, or almost exclusively, Jewish, be it the Jewish Agency, the leadership of the major political parties, collective and cooperative rural settlements, the army, etc. In addition, the essentially Jewish nature of the state is expressed in a number of fundamental ways ("the Law of Return,"[7] the legal currency featuring Zionist leaders, etc.), and most importantly, in the everyday culture of the Jewish majority. This emphasis on the Jewish character of the state has made for a distinct separation between Israeli Jews and Arabs, with only a few cultural and political organizations common to both groups (Al-Haj, 1988).

The coexistence of Jews and Arabs in Israel has been enforced by historical developments (Lustick, 1980; Mansur, 1981; Smooha, 1985). For the first two decades of statehood both looked upon the other as a passing, insignificant phenomenon. For the Jews, the Arabs were part of the Arab geo-political region (to be ultimately absorbed by it). For Israeli Arabs, the Jewish state was an ephemeral episode. Only since 1967 have the two communities begun to relate to each other, not only as participants in a regional conflict, but as two distinct entities—citizens of the same state who are bound to remain as such (Benvenişti, 1988; Cohen, 1985; Landau, 1971).

Thus there remains a gulf between the everyday status of the Arab, and his legal one. Israel's fundamental constitutional document—the Declaration of Independence—specifically declares that the Arab minority is to enjoy full civic, political, and social equality. Indeed, since the foundation of the state, Israeli Arab minority rights have been recognized in terms of language (e.g., separate Arabic broadcasts are provided on national radio and TV), culture (a separate Arab educational system), and religion (freedom of worship and the granting of authority to Moslem and Christian religious courts to deal with matters such as marriage and divorce). However, as long as the state of war between some Arab nations and Israel continues, certain inequalities in rights and obligations probably will continue, notwithstanding the constitutional provisions.

---

[7] The recent appearance of a new political party ("Shas"), sponsored by the Ashkenazic ultra-orthodox elite, is a particularly interesting phenomenon. This party addresses itself to a new ultra-orthodox group, drawn mainly from a lower-class Eastern population. In the last few years this population has expressed increasing disenchantment with the Zionist consensus, by voting for ethnic and/or religious non-Zionist parties. It is beyond the scope of this paper to deal with the semi-legitimation accorded to non-Zionist parties in recent elections (Shokeid, 1984).

The treatment of the Arab minority can be seen as a test case for the strength of Israeli democracy; i.e., the extent to which political freedoms and equality are being preserved by the dominant majority vis-a-vis this permanent minority (which, of course, is at the same time an historical, cultural, and religious part of a regional majority that is hostile to Israel's existence). With this in mind the question arises: how do Israeli Arabs feel about the Jewish state?

The first survey of Israeli Arab attitudes towards the state was performed in the summer of 1976 (Smooha and Cibluski, 1978). This study established that Israeli Arabs are in the midst of a process of politicization that has three related themes:

1. While Jews were found to be committed to the Zionist ideology, the Arabs were, to different degrees, wary of it.

2. Most Israeli Arabs tended to accept their own status as a minority in Israel while advocating Palestinian independence for the West Bank and Gaza (a state they themselves would choose *not* to become citizens of).

3. Israeli Arabs professed a growing sense of incorporation into Israeli society. Their future was seen as being linked to the well-being of the state of Israel and its development, rather than to the rest of the Arab world.

An analysis of the 1980 and 1984 voting patterns of the Israeli Arab minority in both local and national elections (Cohen, 1985; Lahuni, 1983) shows the following characteristics:

In local elections, family and extended family ties play the most crucial role. The mayor (or chairperson of the municipal council) will usually come from the biggest and strongest extended family.

On the national scene, family and traditional factors play a minor role only. Two contrasting concerns determine the direction in which the Arab national vote is cast:

1. pragmatists, concerned mainly with physical improvements tend to vote for one of the major (Zionist) political parties;

2. ideologues tend to vote for either the Israel Communist Party (which has both Jewish and Arab members, and is non-Zionist), or for a newly-formed leftist party, the Progressive List for Peace (similarly bi-national and anti-Zionist).

The Israeli Arab sector professes a growing degree of commitment to democracy. The main reason for this development may be that the Arab minority has increasingly resorted to the democratic process, in order to protect its rights and interests. The treatment of the Arab minority can be seen as a test case for the strength of Israeli democracy, i.e., the extent to which political freedoms and equality are being preserved or violated by the dominant majority vis-a-vis this permanent minority. On that topic, the jury is still out, and opinion in Israel remains divided.

CONCLUSION

The three groups dealt with in this analysis are all basically committed to participating in the Israeli democracy, albeit with certain qualifications at times. Gush Emunim, for example, takes part in the democratic order, but does not maintain an unconditional commitment to it. As with many other religious Jewish groups, it displays reservations about democracy in all those areas in which Jewish religious law comes into conflict with the Israeli civil law. The Eastern sub-group within the Jewish majority, on the other hand, is unconditionally committed to the democratic order, and has essentially not altered the character of Israel's political system, despite the fact that the first generation of Eastern immigrants came from non-democratic backgrounds. Finally, the Arab population has increasingly used the rules of the democratic game for the preservations of its rights as a minority, without jeopardizing its distinctness and separateness as a community.

The Israeli political culture has been experiencing improvements in its democratic regime, mostly in the realm of civil rights. At the same time, we cannot be oblivious to the fact that Israel has reached a stage at which a few fundamental ideological conflicts are causing a serious split in the polity. Such conflicts may have far-reaching impact upon the future political character of the society. The status of religion, as we indicated earlier, is one such source of conflict. Another is the very status of democracy itself. There are in Israel those citizens who see democracy as a fundamental feature of Israeli society that has to be unconditionally accepted. On the other hand, are those who perceive contradictions between the democratic order and some other ultimate value (e.g., religion, or territorial rights). They are thus not as totally committed to democracy as are its staunch defenders. In this potentially divisive situation, the educational system has become increasingly involved in efforts to strengthen democracy against the danger of its erosion. This is the first time in Israel that it was felt necessary to launch an institutionalized effort to promote a universalistic value such as democracy.

DEMOCRACY AND EDUCATION IN ISRAEL

The developments analyzed in this chapter represent powerful social processes that are anchored in cultural and religious traditions. As such, they seem to overshadow the formal educational system's prevailing investments in the nurturing of democratic commitments among students of all backgrounds.

Israel has two major types of educational investments that deal with the development of democratic commitment. The first is curricular in nature. All students are required to take a civics course in 10th or 11th grade, in which they study the history of modern Israel with an emphasis on the evolution of its democratic order. High school students also study world history, especially those aspects dealing with the essence and emergence of democracy. Second, familiarity with democratic procedures is also promoted by the organization of student elections and debates, as well as by lectures given by visiting political leaders.

However, these and other educational practices do not appear to be potent enough to fully counteract the previously described forces that may act to constrict the enhancement of Israeli democracy. Israel's geo-political situation also complicates efforts to educate students for democracy. In the face of continuous external Arab hostility, significant numbers of Israeli Jewish youths have developed anti-democratic sentiments concerning the rights of the Israeli Arab minority. Similarly, there are those young Israeli Arabs who profess varying degrees of sympathy for the Palestine Liberation Organization (PLO), whose proclaimed goals and terror-based methods contradict a number of very basic democratic principles.

It is against this background, that the authors have been involved over the past 4 years in the introduction of a new curriculum designed to develop in young people commitments to democracy. The following chapter deals with that project.

ACKNOWLEDGMENTS

This paper was first presented in October 1988 at a workshop sponsored by the Spencer Foundation of Chicago, Illinois, which was held at Rutgers University. We wish to thank Professor Roberta Sigel who chaired the workshop, as well as the other participants, for the opportunity to present and discuss this paper. We also gratefully acknowledge Professor Sarane Boocock, the discussant for this paper, whose remarks were taken into account for the revision of the original, as were comments made by other participants.

We would like to thank Ms. Laurie Fialkoff for making stylistic improvements in the final version. The authors, of course, bear sole responsibility for the contents of this work.

REFERENCES

Al-Haj, M. (1988, April 17–18). *Israeli Arabs between citizenship and nationalism.* Paper presented at the conference on Crystallization of Israeli Citizen, Beer Sheva, Ben Gurion University. (Hebrew).

Almond, G. A. (1956). Comparative political systems. *Journal of Politics, 18,* 391–404.

Almond, G. A., & Verba, S. (1963). *The civic culture.* NJ: Princeton University.

Aran, G. (1985). *Eretz Israel between politics and religion: The movement to stop the withdrawal from Sinai* (No. 18). Jerusalem: The Jerusalem Institute for Israel Studies. (Hebrew).

Aran, G. (1987). *From religious Zionism to a Zionist religion: The origin and culture of Gush-Emunim messianic movement.* Unpublished doctoral dissertation. The Hebrew University, Jerusalem. (Hebrew).

Arian, A. (1985). *Politics and government in Israel.* Tel–Aviv: Zmora, Bitan. (Hebrew).

Avinar, S. (1982). We were true to your covenants. *Arzi, 1,* 38–39. (Hebrew).

Avineri, S. (1983). Political perspectives. In A. Hareven (Ed.), *On the difficulty of being an Israeli* (pp. 289–295). Jerusalem: Van Leer Foundation. (Hebrew).

Bar Josef, R. (1968). Desocialization and resocialization. *International Migration Review, 2,* 27–43.

Ben Rafael, E. (1976). *The emergence of ethnicity—Cultural groups and social conflict in Israel.* London: Glenwood.

Benvenisti, M. (1988). *The sling and the club: Territories, Jewish and Arab,* Jerusalem: Keter. (Hebrew).

Bernstein, D. (1986). *The black panthers of Israel 1971–1972: Contradictions and protest in the process of nation building.* Unpublished doctoral dissertation; University of Sussex, England.

Cohen, R. (1985). *The processes of political development and electoral pattern of Israeli Arabs.* Unpublished Master's thesis. University of Tel–Aviv. Tel–Aviv, Israel.

Deshen, S. (1980). Political ethnicity and cultural ethnicity in Israel during the 1960s. In E. Krausz (Ed.), *Politics and society* (pp. 117–146). New Brunswick: Transaction Books.

Eisenstadt, S. N. (1967). *Israeli society: Background, development and problems.* Jerusalem: Magnes. (Hebrew).

Eisenstadt, S. N. (1981). Cultural traditions and political dynamics: The origins and modes of ideological politics. *British Journal of Sociology, 32,* (2), 155–181.

Eisenstadt, S. N. (1983). Summary: Central problems. In A. Hareven (Ed.), *On the difficulty of being an Israeli* (pp. 294–306). Jerusalem: Van Leer Foundation.

Frankenstein, K., Simmon, P. A., Rotenstriech, N., Grol, M., & Ben–David, Y. (1951–1952). Arguments on the problem of ethnic dissimilarities. *Megamot, 2–3.* (Hebrew).

Galnoor, I. (1977). Transformations within Israel's political system since Yom Kippur. *State Regime and International Relationships, 1,* 5–25. (Hebrew).

Galnoor, I. (1982). The participation of citizens with Israeli democracy." *Mollad, 4,* 71–87. (Hebrew).

Gutman, A. (1987). *Democratic education.* Princeton: Princeton University.

Herzog, H. (1984). Political ethnicity in Israel. *Megamot, 28* (2–3), 332–351. (Hebrew).

Herzog, H. (1985). The ethnic list in election 1981: An ethnic politic identify. In E. Krausz (Ed.), *Politics and society* (pp. 245–269). New Brunswick: Transaction Books.

Horowitz, D. & Lissak, M. (1978). *The origin of the Israeli polity.* Chicago: The University of Chicago.

Kavanaugh, D. (1972). *Political culture.* London: MacMillan.

Kimmerling, B. (1985). The reopening of the frontiers, 1967–1982. In E. Krausz (Ed.), *Politics and society* (pp. 81–116). New Brunswick, Transaction Books.

Lahuammi, M. (1985). *The development of municipalities in the Israeli–Arab sector 1948–1978.* Unpublished Master's thesis, University of Haifa, Haifa, Israel. (Hebrew).

Landau, Y. (1971). *The Arabs in Israel: Political orientation.* Israel: Maarchot. (Hebrew).

Leibman, C. D. & Don-Yehiya, E. (1985). The dilemma of reconciling traditional culture and political needs: Civil religion in Israel. In E. Krausz (Ed.), *Politics and society* (pp. 196–209). Brunswick: Transaction Books.

Lustick, I. (1980). *Arabs in the Jewish state: A study in the control of a national minority.* Austin: University of Texas.

Mansur, A. (1981). Integration, equality and co-existence. In A. Hareven (Ed.), *One out of every six Israelis: On relations between the Jewish majority and Arab minority in Israel* (pp. 77–97). Jerusalem: Van Leer Foundation. (Hebrew).

Peres, Y. & Shemer, S. (1984). The ethnic factor in the elections to the 10th Knesset. *Megamot, 27,* (2–3), 316–331. (Hebrew).

Raanan, T. (1980). *Gush–Emunim.* Tel–Aviv: Sifriath–Hapoalim. (Hebrew).

Rubinstein, A. (1981). *A movement in a period of transition: A chapter in the history of Mizrahi in Poland.* Ramat–Gan: Bar Ilan University. (Hebrew).

Rubinstein, D. (1982). *Gush–Emunim: With God and me.* Tel–Aviv: Hakibbutz Hameuchad. (Hebrew).

Samet, M. (1979). *Religion and state in Israel: The conflict of the institutionalization of the Jewish values in the state of Israel.* Jerusalem: The Hebrew Univeristy. (Hebrew).

Schweid, E. (1973). What it means to be a Jew? In M. Samet (Ed.), *State and religion,* (pp. 68–87). Jerusalem: Academon. (Hebrew).

Shaked, G. (1983). In praise of secularization and in disgrace of immigration and "returning." In A. Hareven (Ed.), *One out of every six Israelis: On relations between the Jewish majority and the Arab minority in Israel,* (pp. 45–63). (Hebrew).

Shapiro, Y. (1977). *The Israeli democracy.* Ramat–Gan: Massada. (Hebrew).

Shokeid, M. (1984). Precepts versus tradition: Religious trends among Middle Eastern Jews. *Megamot, 28* (2–3), 250–264. (Hebrew).

Smooha, S. (1984). Three perspectives in the sociology of ethnic relations in Israel. *Megamot, 28* (2–3), 169–206. (Hebrew).

Smooha, S. (1985). Existing and alternative policy towards the Arabs in Israel. In E. Krausz (Ed.), *Politics and society* (pp. 334–361). New Brunswick: Transaction Books.

Smooha, S. (1987). *Social research on Jewish ethnicity in Israel 1984–1986: Review and selected bibliography with abstracts.* Haifa: Haifa University Press.

Smooha, S. & Cibluski, O. (1978). *Social research on Arabs in Israel, 1984–1977.* (Ramat–Gan: Turtledove. (Hebrew).

Sprinzak, E. (1984) Gush Emunim—iceberg model of political extremism. In *State, regime and international relationship, 9,* 22–49. (Hebrew).

Yatziv, G. (1979). *The class basis of party affiliation—The Israeli case.* Jerusalem: The Hebrew University. (Hebrew).

Yishai, Y. (1986). *Interest groups in Israel: The test of democracy.* Tel–Aviv: Am-Oved. (Hebrew).

Werblovski, H. J. Tz. (1983). What distinguishes inter–relations between the religious and the secular in Israel in contrast with other countries. In A. Hareven (Ed.), *On the difficulty of being an Israeli* (pp. 201–202). Jerusalem: Van Leer Foundation. (Hebrew).

II EDUCATIONAL INSTITUTIONS AND THEIR RESPONSES

The three essays in this section provide direct responses to the question of how well educational institutions perform in designing and modifying citizenship education. All three discuss specific curricula efforts, which were designed to help both minorities and hosts to understand the need to accept and, ideally, to cherish, cultural diversity in a democracy. The three essays are relatively pessimistic in their assessment of the ability of the school to carry the sole responsibility for resocializing minority children and their native-origin peers.

The chapter on the Israeli curriculum reform experience introduces our discussion of structural attempts to vitalize instruction in citizenship and politics. Ilana Felsenthal and Israelit Rubinstein hold that, up to now, the schools in Israel have not been able to carve out either a process or a curriculum which translates into an effective medium for teaching democratic citizenship. In fact, school material itself is not retained for very long, suggesting that it is neither terribly poignant to students, nor seen as relevant to their lives outside the classroom. The two authors then proceed to describe an experimental program designed to diffuse inter-ethnic tensions, and to promote democratic citizenship in Israeli schools. It is too early at this point to decide whether such a curriculum, were it to be adopted nationally, could produce a more unified, or even a more tolerant, yet diversified, public.

In analyzing the experience of the Netherlands, Hans Hooghoff describes how a lengthy period of inattention to minority concerns was followed in 1986 by a relatively straightforward national policy of government design and control. Its National Curriculum of Political and Social Education is comprehensive and universally administered, apparently without major resistance. Still, here too the goal of mutual adaptation has been muted in its implementation by a curriculum in which religion and morals are acceptable components of political education courses. His conclusion is that despite genuinely liberal goals, actual political instruction is quite limited.

In Britain, on the other hand, areas of agreement are dwarfed by those of controversy. As in many nations, ideological differences have emerged over the relative desirability of maintaining cultural and ethnic diversity, with the result that political debate has limited the ability of any government to husband a national curriculum. Ian Lister's chapter notes the atypical pattern in which attempts to reform a traditional and outdated approach to political education were answered almost immediately by a Conservative reaction. As a result, efforts to provide liberal experiences to supplement the learning in vocational, traditional, and elitist educational programs have been mired in conflict and resistance. Not surprisingly, major change has been slow. Although there is some support for efforts to establish prototypical courses in global and international education, he is cautious about projecting success in implementing such programs.

A substantial body of research, conducted in the period between 1960 and 1980, argued consistently that schools were essentially conservative institutions, in which discussions of any type of controversial topics were routinely avoided. In many ways, these chapters describe schools which reiterate that conclusion. Even when the real or potential sources of conflict are vividly present in the schools themselves, curricular responses are relatively timid and constrained by all the forces which have traditionally shaped the content and process of public education. We return to that theme in the final sections of the volume, when we assess the ability of other governmental programs to provide additional or complementary support to integration goals.

6 Democracy, School and Curriculum Reform: "The Rules of the Game" In Israel

Ilana Felsenthal and Israelit Rubinstein

The previous chapter by Rubinstein and Adler introduced the reader to the complicated nature of Israeli democracy, and to the problems it encounters. Israeli political culture, while striving to maintain its democratic tradition amid internal division and external strife, is under constant strain. Rubinstein and Adler, although mostly focusing on socio-political problems, also pointed out the shortcomings of prevailing curricular and pedagogical practices. They questioned (at least cast a doubt on) the adequacy of current civic education curricula for preparing youth for democratic citizenship in adulthood.

This chapter tells the story of an innovative venture in curricular reform, in which Adler, Felsenthal, and Rubinstein have been involved since 1986. The main objective of this project, entitled "The Rules of the Game," was to design (and later put into practice) a civic education curriculum, which would help students develop a genuine comprehension of basic democratic values and principles, and to encourage attitudes and behaviors conducive to the practice of democratic citizenship during their adult years. Given the diversities and strains in Israeli culture, the curriculum had to be designed in such a way as to present democracy as a set of principles in which Jewish and Arab Israelis, as well as religious and non-religious Jews could find a common denominator.

Liberal democracy, we claim, evolves around two basic principles: majority rule and the protection of human and minority rights. Although the relationship between these two components may at times be strained, the former must never be allowed to impinge on the latter. Democratic regimes establish and maintain various institutional arrangements, in order to regulate the delicate balance between the two elements. These institutional arrangements are best served by a political culture, which is supportive of an informed and highly involved citizenry. "The Rules of the Game" curriculum seeks to convey these messages.

In this chapter we describe the lengthy process through which this curriculum evolved. At the outset we must point out that "The Rules of the Game" constitutes a joint venture of practicing high school teachers and academics, in which both groups became actively engaged in curriculum development. Another unusual feature is its step-by-step decision making process. We shall outline this process as a set of junctures, at each of which we had to make some major decision, and at which we had to make up our minds and decide which road to take.

Developing a new curriculum means that a decision was taken to use schools as the arena. This immediately brings us to the first crossroad or "red traffic light" on our decision making path. We had to ask ourselves: *Why the school?* The first reason is very simple and straightforward: schools are there, and they are probably here to stay. Schools have been criticized endlessly during the last three decades, but they are still with us. Despite the radical education reform movement of the sixties and slogans calling for "deschooling" society (Illich, 1970), schools retained most of their structural characteristics and also most of their traditional functions (Carnoy & Levin, 1985). Together with the family—another persistent institution which was predicted to become extinct by the end of the century— schools retain much of their socializing power. Almost every youngster is shaped by family and school, aided or impeded by the mass media.

In addition, schools are not just there, they also are highly accessible to experimental intervention, unlike the family, which as a socializing agency is almost immune to such outside intervention. Liberal democracies in particular—due to their credo of respect for individuals' right to privacy— are certainly hard put when planning any family intervention programs— a problem which is well documented by the difficulties encountered in protecting maltreated children from their own parents. Even non-democratic states find intervention in the private domain of the family almost impossible—short of using brutal measures. Most schools, on the other hand, tend to be considered to belong to the public domain, and as such are more likely to be accessible for experimental intervention for a variety of purposes, among them attempts to provide for effective civic education and political socialization.

Moreover, the steady growth in high school enrollment constitutes an educational fact which cannot be ignored. In Israel, about 80 percent of the 16–18 age cohort spends at least six hours daily, six days a week in this "place called school" (Goodlad, 1984). Under these circumstances, could we, as educators, afford the luxury of "letting schools be," and allow a whole new generation to be exposed to an inappropriate civic studies' curriculum (compiled mostly twenty years ago), which stresses the formal aspects of democratic government but tends to ignore built-in complexities, dilemmas, and potential conflicts?

THE NEED FOR CURRICULUM REFORM

Yet it is precisely the poor quality with which the schools discharge this responsibility that has come under frequent attack. Schools, it seems, are nowadays considered by many prominent psychologists and sociologists as being notoriously unsuitable settings for such education, and particularly for democratic education (Massialas, 1976; Patrick, 1977; Battistoni, 1985).

What are the reasons for this critique? A close inspection of the structure and functions of schools in modern society reveals some of the bases for the indictment of the schools.

We shall be stating the obvious if we say that the school's main preoccupation—at least in terms of manifest goals—is merit and academic achievement. This contention is easily verifiable. One has merely to examine the amount of resources: money, space, equipment, but especially teacher and pupil time and energy, directed towards generating "better" grades in certain academic subjects, ensuring that those students who "do well" in these subjects are accepted into "better" institutions of higher learning, that shall then channel them to "better" positions in society (Turner, 1960).

While stressing academic achievement—either for the many, or for the few—the educational system, supported on the one hand by state apparatuses, and on the other hand, by the family and the community, is operating according to a simple rational principle: investing the largest "slice" of the available "pie" of school resources in producing more of this desirable commodity—student achievement—as measured by teachers' grades and scores on standard tests, and manifested in various diplomas (Collins, 1979). Claiming that schools are achievement-oriented does not necessarily mean that they provide equal opportunity to all the competitors. It does mean though, that one is considered a "failure" according to the school's formal norms, if one does not do well academically. Informal norms, supported by the peer group, might, of course, reflect a very different attitude towards the prevailing merit system. This, however, does not contradict the fact that educational credentialization is legitimized by the credo of individual achievement (Yogev & Shapira, 1987). Certain groups—women, blacks, Arabs, and ethnic minorities, may have less of a chance to "make it," but in most cases, they do accept the rules of the competitive academic game (Bashi, Cahan & Davis, 1981).

Given this meritocratic emphasis—so characteristic of Israeli education—, it becomes clear to the observer that any messages that are non-achievement-oriented are doomed to become peripheral to the school's main agenda. Thus, it should come as no surprise that the messages of civic and political socialization, which some educators try to relate through the schools, tend to get lost amidst the ever-present stress, on academic achievement.

Meritocratic orientation is not confined to the manifest functions of school. It also dominates other, more latent dimensions of the process of schooling, like the organization of time and space, and the social relations in the classroom, all combining to defeat schools as socio-political educational agents. One such structural component is the norm dictating school and classroom behavior role definitions. While inside the school, the youngster has to adapt and to behave according to certain role expectations, which stem from a broadly accepted definition of "the pupil" or "the student" roles. One of the main features of this definition is that it places the student at the passive end of the student-teacher interaction. The student is expected to "behave"—that is, according to school expectations, to sit quietly, not to move around without permission, not to make unauthorized noises, and to listen and to answer only if addressed. Jackson (1968), in his well-known description of classroom norms, speaks about the effect of "crowds," "distraction," "denial," and "delay," upon the student; of being in a subordinate position in an asymmetric relationship, constantly judged and "pecked-at" by teachers and peers.

The picture Jackson paints—if a bit exaggerated—is still essentially true. Despite changes brought about by the radical educational movement, the student's role is still defined along these traditional lines, i.e., stressing passivity and subordination. In his classical, well-known analysis of school norms, (Dreeben, 1967) claims that the messages transmitted by the school's structure are essentially aimed at integrating pupils into the competitive and individualistic modern society. This is certainly true for some of the economic roles adults are supposed to undertake. But is it also true for the citizen's role, which the very same adults are anticipated to fulfill in democratic societies? Is not the educational system expected to prepare its clients successfully to exercise the citizen's role? And if so, what does it imply vis-a-vis schools' overt and covert messages? To what extent is the student's role relevant to the learning of the citizen's role? Under any kind of definition, the citizen's role in a democratic society entails a combination of elements stressing information, critical thought, some degree of scepticism about authority, involvement and active participation. Even under the most minimal definition, educational systems are expected to imprint in the future citizens some notion of potential participation in the collective decision-making process, as an undeniable prerogative of the individual. Thus, anticipatory socialization for the role of citizen entails an emphasis on processing varied and sometimes conflicting information; the ability to question prevailing attitudes, and the will to defend a non-conformist idea; the capacity to evaluate complex situations, to apply critical thinking, and act on the basis of autonomous deliberation and decision. Clearly, such role-socialization stands in complete contrast to the standard definition of the student's role, which leaves a very narrow margin for manifest articulation of criticism of school regime, and no room at all for actual demonstration against decision of the school's staff. Thus, any generalization from the role of the student to the role of the citizen can hardly be seen as a simple task.

Another obstacle to civic education is posed by the schools' evaluation system. From his or her very first steps in elementary school, up to the moment of graduation, the student is being constantly evaluated and graded relatively to his or her fellow students. What is the message carried by these evaluation procedures? If one looks at the world from the student's point of view, it certainly seems that people are constantly "rank-ordered" according to merit. Moreover, a certain moral significance is attached to better grades, as if being "better" in math lends you some kind of moral superiority or virtue. A low-achiever is considered "bad," and has to be "reformed" or dropped out of the system.

Through its evaluation system, the school transmits a very strong message of inequality, of some people being worth more than the others. This notion of inequality is not confined to the academic realm, but has been diffused into other domains.

The basic logic of the democratic state is, of course, the absolute opposite. All human beings are considered equal in those attributes relevant to political participation. This is the axiom which lends legitimation and justification to the democratic idea. Clearly, schools' grading systems do not contribute much to fostering the idea of the equality of human beings as such (Bowles, 1988).

The frequent use schools make of grading and rank-ordering is, of course, by no means accidental, but is closely related to one of their most important functions in modern societies: allocating students into differentiated and stratified social positions. Even the most ardent functionalists (Parsons, 1959; Turner, 1960) do not deny the major role schools play vis-a-vis stratification. Jencks (Jencks, et al., 1972), observing the wide-spread correlation between parents and offsprings' socio-economic status, argues that schools do not do much to eliminate social inequalities, while neo-marxist scholars (Bordieu, 1973) claim that schools contribute more to the reproduction of existing social differences than to their elimination. According to this school of thought, the educational system in modern societies, although manifestly meritocratic, actually legitimates existing power structures. Behind the myth of individual achievement hides the reality of unequal chances. Students from certain social groups are, according to this theory, predestined to fail in the presumably meritocratic open-to-all, school system, thus ensuring the preservation of elite positions in the same hands, and passing them on from one generation to the other. Ability grouping, tracking policies, and the differentiated statuses attached to different curricular subject matters, all define schools as "gate keepers" in the lengthy social selection process. Thus, while schools in modern societies have become an essential device for social differentiation and stratification, civic education in the very same schools is supposed to address the societal goals of solidarity and integration. Here again, as in the case of the student's versus the citizen's role, there is an inherent contradiction between the messages transmitted by the school's structure and social relations on the one hand and those suggested by the content of the civics curriculum, on the other.

So, taking into consideration the limitations of schools and schooling, we made our decision to focus on the school and proceeded with the task of developing a school curriculum. It should be pointed out here that "The Rules of the Game" does not propose any organizational or structural changes in schools or in classrooms. In fact, it has so far been introduced, with similar rates of success, in both very traditional and less traditional schools. We accept the structure of the school as a given, and then proceeded to turn to our advantage exactly those characteristics which are so often seen by educators as disadvantages.

First, with respect to the inherent contradictions in role definitions between the student's and the citizen's roles (Almond & Verba, 1965), we rejected the common assumption of role-transfer. We are suggesting that in order to learn a certain role, one does not have to exercise this role alone, to the exclusion of all others. Clearly, most children seem to be doing quite well in fulfilling two extremely contradictory roles—that of a son, daughter or sibling at home, and that of a student at school. Different roles, based on a widely differing set of expectations, seem to become operative at the right time and place, without necessarily impinging on each other.

As people grow up, new role-opportunities unfold and they acquire, in a variety of ways, the knowledge and the skills relevant to each new social role. Does this mean that one has to exercise a role fully before one actually "takes it on?" In other words, do schools have to become democratic institutions in order for youngsters to learn democratic citizenship? We feel that trying to simulate democracy in the classroom and thus train young people for citizenship while in a student's situation, might create such an artificial experience; that wrong, misleading messages, might be transmitted, and cause more harm than good by creating an illusory effect. School is actually a "Hot-House" society, and not an experimental laboratory for reality—and this may be the only way to create a proper environment for learning and development. Thus, we chose to make the best out of the students' role the way it is, and to utilize it to our project's advantage, i.e., to develop a curriculum in civic education which shall be congruent with the structural components of schools. Much of school-knowledge is future-oriented—why should not civic education be the same?

Even the most ardent and aggressive critics of school acknowledge its unique capacity to expose students to critical philosophies and alternative frames of reference (Bowles & Gintis, 1976). The fact that schools have, generally speaking, failed in achieving this goal, may be attributed not so much to their lack of power, but to their lack of will and, in certain areas, a dearth of "know-how."

After carefully studying the cons and pros of schools as the proper or improper environment for political socialization, we reached the conclusion that a certain type of program can be most effective in the milieu of the school, without actually claiming to change either its social functions, or its traditional structure and social relations.

Bowles and Gintis have pointed out the central contradiction assailing schools in modern societies—the fact that, on the one hand, they are a subsystem of the state, which is legitimized in terms of "persons rights," but on the other hand, they serve the interests of the economic system and the labor market, which are regulated in terms of "property rights." Bowles and Gintis go on to argue that the characteristic form of discourse—as against the form of social relations—in American schools, is that of liberal-democratic discourse . . . "the educational system cannot be cited as the source of the near universality of liberal discourse. Yet it certainly has played a central role in its reproduction" (Bowles, 1988, p. 28). In the previous chapter we have cast some doubt as to whether this statement is also true for schools in Israel today. We argue the need to enhance such discourse in our schools, for without this liberal terminology, the articulation and understanding of minority rights and civic freedoms shall be severely hindered.

GENESIS OF THE PROJECT

"The Rules of the Game" is not just a high school curriculum like any other. It is also what we shall designate as a "grass-roots" or "bottom-up" curriculum, developed with the full cooperation of teachers. In November, 1987, a group of about twenty high school teachers was brought together in order to cooperate in the task of developing a curriculum that would foster the understanding of democratic principles in our high schools. These twenty teachers came from five different schools in the northern part of Israel. Half the participants in this first group were Jewish, the other half, Arabs. In the course of a single year of heated debates and intensive workshops, an outline of the curriculum has emerged. The range of relevant topics, was mapped out, and then narrowed down through a lengthy screening process, to six major subjects. Only then did the actual writing and re-writing commence. By September 1988, the first version of "The Rules of the Game" was introduced in eight 11th grade classrooms. The curriculum is a bilingual one—in Hebrew and Arabic, and is identical in content for Jewish and Arab students. The process of developing and modifying the curriculum in teachers' workshops has been continuing for the fourth year, with new teachers involved each year. A group of teachers from the Jewish religious sector joined us last academic year. Participating teachers and students provide feedback that has led to some major revisions in the material. In 1988–1989, the curriculum has been taught in 20 classes, and a third version was prepared for the 1989–1990 academic year, and is now being taught in 25 classes.

RATIONALE FOR ADOPTED PROCEDURES

Why did we decide to take this lengthy road, paved with ideological disputes and strewn with organizational obstacles? Why did we choose to invest so much effort in coordination and cooperation—when it would have been much simpler to put together a group of academic experts and let them produce a coherent, well-informed and scholarly new curriculum?

Here again our decision rests on several lines of reasoning. First, there is an almost total agreement among experts on curriculum development and implementation (Connelly, 1972; Silberman, 1978)—that the curriculum which has the best chance of being successfully implemented, and accepted by teachers and students alike, is that which involved teachers from the very beginning. If this seems to hold true for most curricular innovations, even for those emerging from a long tradition of instruction, and stemming from a well-crystallized body of knowledge, it should be even truer for such a fluid and sensitive field as political socialization. Empirical evidence supporting this claim is presented by Young (1985).

Research findings in the social psychology of groups and organizations established long ago the difficulties encountered by change agents when trying to introduce innovations into a group through an outsider. Changes are less prone to be rejected offhand, and innovations are best accepted and implemented, when initiative and ideas come from within (Katz &

Lazarsfeld, 1955). The same, of course, holds true for schools as social organizations. Any reform, curricular or otherwise, which had been introduced into the school system without first securing the commitment of teachers, was deemed from the outset to fail. A "grass roots" curriculum, introduced by the very same teachers by whom it was developed, might secure the goodwill and cooperation that are so direly needed in order to overcome negative attitudes and resistance to change.

Another major reason for the importance of teachers' participation in the development of "The Rules of the Game," is its interdisciplinary nature. The curriculum constitutes an attempt to observe "Democracy" from the points of view of several disciplines—history, philosophy, psychology, sociology, logics, political science, communication, and legal studies. The only way to weave together all these variegated bodies of knowledge into a coherent curricular statement, is through the cooperation of teachers who are able to see the classroom situation beyond their own disciplinary expertise. Indeed, the contribution of the teachers' workshops was twofold: First, was the actual development of a curriculum not confined to a single, well-defined discipline, and second, was the molding of the different points of view represented by the variety of disciplines into an integrated, non-fragmented curriculum. At the same time, these workshops constituted a teacher training arena, in which people trained in different disciplines learned from each other through constant feedback. Moreover, considering the many kinds of expertise the participants brought with them, we saw to it that each teacher comes out of our workshop equipped with the information necessary to teach the new course. Thus, during the workshops, the teachers were exposed to the best available experts in each of the relevant fields of study.

Keeping in mind the fact that the curriculum is still at the experimental stage, and that the "next generation" of its teachers might want to exercise their own discretion as to the content and structure of what is being taught, the curriculum is also of a modular design. This fact both enables and encourages each teacher to change the order of the subjects, to omit what he or she considers redundant, or to enrich the texture of the instruction by adding new materials—thus once again becoming a creative partner to the development of the curriculum.

Yet another set of considerations that suggested to us a "grass-roots" curriculum stems from sociological theory. For the last three decades, sociologists of education, mainly from the neo-marxist school, have been underlining the reproductive function of schools in modern societies, alerting us to the fact that school curricula tend to mirror certain group or class preferences, and to preserve the interests of these groups and classes (Whitty, 1985; Apple, 1985). Involving teachers from diverse backgrounds in curriculum development, while not completely eliminating such self-serving interests from coming to bear on the process of selection and presentation of the material, does widen the range of the interests represented. We don't claim to be able to create an objective, interest-free curriculum, but we felt that the least we could do was to try to involve in the process the most heterogeneously composed group of educators.

The result of this conception was indeed a group of teachers representing almost all different types of high schools existing in Israel: academic, comprehensive, and vocational. The intention was not to produce two kinds of curriculum: one aimed at the "better" students in the academic stream, and a diluted version for the less prestigious streams. We are well aware of the stratified nature of school knowledge (Young, 1985; Apple, 1989), and of the tendency of school systems to expose students in the more prestigious streams to more sophisticated information and knowledge, and we deliberately tried to avoid this kind of subtle discrimination. Although every high school student in Israel is expected to "take" a certain amount of "civics," regardless of "stream" and type of school, one should also consider the possibility that students in the less prestigious "streams" and schools will be exposed to a curriculum stressing a passive definition of citizenship, while more academically oriented students will be trained for active participation in the decision-making process. This danger our curriculum seeks to avoid. Thus, the only modifications we might consider in the future in order to adapt "The Rules of the Game" to different populations, will be strictly confined to the didactic side, and in no way to the content.

DEVELOPMENT OF THE PROJECT

"The Rules of the Game" is, we have said, a "grass roots" curriculum because of the unusual procedure for its development. Let us now elaborate a little on the process through which the curriculum of "The Rules of the Game" was developed. The initiative for the project came from a team of sociologists of education, who, following a graduate research seminar dedicated to the close examination of existing curricula, reached the conclusion that "something has to be done" about the state of civic education in Israel. None of the participants in the original team has had any previous experience in classroom instruction (other than teaching sociology to college students). The participants, therefore, decided that they needed partners with extensive public school teaching experience—high school teachers from both the Jewish and the Arab sectors. The recruitment of the participating teachers was done mostly through the "grape vine" method— one school principal led to another. In November, 1986 the first group of twenty teachers met, and the first workshop took place. As far as we know, it was the first time such a diversified group of teachers met for such a broadly defined task: rethinking high school civics curriculum. The first step was, of course, defining the "mandate" of the group. We soon discovered that while some of us were talking liberal democracy: i.e., minority rights and civic liberties as the foundations for coexistence, others were talking coexistence in terms of "know thy neighbor" strategies. It took several months and many heated discussions for the group to agree on a common theme. During those first months, the initiating team had to overcome several barriers. First, belonging to the academic community obviously put us in a somewhat humble position vis-a-vis our partners. No one doubted our theoretical knowledge, but the prevailing feeling was that we do not know as much about "real schools and real classrooms." This feeling was, of course, quite understandable, as it is very common for university staff to get into the "deep and sometimes cold waters" of reality where practitioners rule. At all times, we never claimed to know more than the teachers about schools, didactics, and teaching strategies. Whenever arguments such as "our students cannot cope with the material" or, alternatively "this form of presentation is apt to be considered childish by our students" were voiced, they were taken seriously and appropriate changes were introduced. At the same time, being sociologists of education proved to be an important asset in our complex net of interactions with our partners. They very soon discovered that some theoretical understanding of the school and classroom as social systems, as viewed through the eyes of a sociologist, can lend them fresh insights about these too-familiar frameworks. In time, a feeling of mutual respect between the initiating team and the teachers-partners evolved, each appreciating the contribution of the other to the common project in terms of knowledge and expertise.

Belonging to the academic community carried other advantages. In Israel today this community is still considered to be somewhat removed from the political, especially partisan, arena. While nobody is naive enough to suppose that academics do not have political opinions, they are not yet completely identified with either the political—and educational—"establishment," nor with what is considered the "leftist" attack on government policies. This relative distance enabled us to function as mediators or "ideological brokers" between different sub-groups of teachers—Jews and Arabs, religious and non-religious Jews.

Of course this advantage was at times turned into a disadvantage, and "The Rules of the Game" curriculum was attacked both as being too liberal, and as not being liberal enough. Despite such criticism originating from both poles of the political spectrum, we found that the advantages of the situation offset the disadvantages. The only way of dealing with some of the very sensitive topics we tried to tackle, was by creating an atmosphere of impartiality—which was not, at times, easy to maintain. Being a bit beyond and above partisan disputes made the existence of the group as a working team possible in spite of the "Intifada" and the deepening cleavages in Israeli society.

In spite of the fact that the groups of teachers we worked with, both in the first and during the two consecutive years, were defined strictly as task-oriented groups—the task being the development and modification of a civic curriculum—each group developed its own social pattern.

While we, at first, recruited teachers along the Jewish-Arab classification, it very soon became clear that, by and large, the line between Arabs and Jews overlaps the line between the sexes; most of the Jewish teachers in all our workshops were, and still are, females, while all Arab teachers (except one) in these workshops were males. Politically speaking, on the other hand, the groups of teachers are much less uniform. Each group represented almost the full political spectrum in the sector it comes from— except some very extremist political manifestations, such as anti-Zionist parties—both on the right and on the left of the political spectrum, and extreme nationalistic groups, like the one advocating the "transfer" of Arabs from Israel, the West Bank and Gaza, or its equivalent militant anti-Israel groups within the Arab sector. Navigating such a colorful group of educators was, of course, not an easy task—but a very gratifying one. Although we never intentionally used any group dynamics strategies, the network of interactions and relationships that evolved between the initiating team and the teachers, and between the teachers themselves, is unusually broad, warm and steadfast.

The workshops became a meeting ground for different social cultures, a fact that both enriched and deepened our conceptions of each other, and the complexity of the task before us. The often heated debates taught us more than volumes of learned works about mutual tolerance and understanding. The quiet talks in the evenings, after long days of hard work, brought us closer together than any artificial encounter would have. It took time for both the Jewish and the Arab groups to open up and share their feelings, attitudes, and opinions with each other. This was a lengthy and delicate process, demanding a lot of perseverance and optimism, but as mutual trust increased, the united front each group presented at first crumbled, and people emerged as individual persons. We assume that the success of the Jewish-Arab encounter in this case—as against many instances in which it led to negative, even disastrous, results—can be explained by its unique context and content. As the encounter itself was not the main objective for the groups getting together, social interactions were defined as secondary to the main task, and thus were left to develop slowly and naturally. Moreover, while most Arab and Jewish groups usually get together in order to discuss issues pertaining to the "Arab-Israeli conflict," which are, by definition, divisive, our groups focused on common, integrating themes such as democracy, human rights and civil liberties. It should not come as a surprise that in this context the participants, instead of growing apart, moved more closely together, sharing their common interest in democracy and in a democratic political culture.

After the first year of intensive work, a tentative version of the curriculum was put to the test in the schools by the same teachers who took part in its development. Since then, three additional groups (including a group of teachers from the religious Jewish section), became involved in the development, enrichment, and modification of the curriculum, each group adding its own point of view and its unique flavor. A complex feedback system is constantly at work—team members visiting and observing classrooms, "veteran" teachers meeting less experienced ones, and everyone getting together for intensive, three-day workshops. The textbooks and teacher manuals which are currently used for instruction are the product of many layers of original material, changes, modifications and new contributions.

During the present academic year, a more structured evaluation study was set in motion utilizing the "before and after" design. Questionnaires, checking both information, understanding, and attitudes were administered to experimental and control classrooms. The same questionnaires will be administered again by the end of the school year.

We were not interested only in what the students learn—but also in how they learn it. Here the contribution of our partners, the teachers, was of the utmost importance, and the combination of experience and creativity they brought with them became indispensable.

FROM PROCEDURE TO CONTENT

"The Rules of the Game" is a curriculum which emphasizes a cognitive approach. Its main plea is to human reason—as against sentiments and gut feelings. It is aimed at helping the student to distinguish empirical findings from value judgments, eye-witness evidence from hearsay, and a logical argument from an emotional one.

Here, for sure, we arrive at a most important juncture. Why take the cognitive, rationally oriented path? We certainly recognize that the rational component is but one of several that make up a person's value judgments, norms, attitudes, and behavioral manifestations. Our choice is rooted in theory and practice. First, despite the diversified social arrangements and particular institutional forms which democracy could and does take empirically, ethically it is a universalistic idea, founded on logical thinking and rational deliberation.

Recent survey data (Tzemach 1986, 1987) have shown that quite a few young Jews in Israel claimed to be prodemocratic, while at the same time denying equal rights to Arab citizens. Clearly, these young people did not have positive feelings towards the Arab minority, but even more clearly, they did not possess the faintest idea about the most basic principles of democracy, at least not how to apply it. Certainly, without this vital information, the concept of democracy is but an empty vessel—and here is where "The Rules of the Game" comes in. In the Rubenstein and Adler chapter, Israel was described as a democratic state, with a strong commitment to the formal aspects of democracy, but with a very thin layer of liberal tradition in its political and civic culture. Thus, in "The Rules of the Game," the liberal aspects are heavily underlined, some might say, overrepresented. The curriculum contains a great deal of information pertaining to human and minority rights, and the limitations on majority rule, which a true liberal democracy must exercise. Another unique feature of the curriculum lies in its emphasis on the development of critical thinking in the students. While most curricula in civic education are blamed for being either one-sided, or, alternatively, shallow and diluted, so as to appeal to the widest common denominator, "The Rules of the Game" points out the dilemmas inherent in democratic orders, and the potential conflicts which are inevitable to them. In this way we hope to avoid students' customary reactions to civic curricula reported in the literature— i.e., the tendency to reject the messages as unreliable and irrelevant to "real life," which they notice is far from being well ordered and consentual!

"The Rules of the Game," while pointing out the democratic state as the only known political arrangement allowing the individual the full exercise of his or her human and civic rights, does not avoid an open discussion of the costs inherent in this arrangement. At the same time, let it be stressed, the curriculum does not take the defensive point of view—it does not present the quite common argument that people should adhere to democratic principles, in spite of the ineffectiveness of democratic regimes. On the contrary, we argue that democracy is not just morally right, but also socially and economically worthwhile from a utilitarian point of view.

Our main message is that democracy, in its actual institutional manifestations, is never perfect, but that it is the only political order which has built-in mechanisms for self-improvement through the cooperative efforts of its citizens.

Another reason for choosing to emphasize logical argument and rational thinking was of a more pragmatic nature. We chose the cognitive approach since this is the realm in which schools seem to have a relative advantage. Schools—and teachers—are certainly better equipped to deal with intellectual issues than with emotional ones. Here again, taking the nature of schools as a given, we unabashedly utilize the prevailing credit system, in order to reach the widest possible student audience. True, it is in a sense a "captive audience"; but one ought to face the realities of a situation and make the best of it.

We have now to face the question of the way through which the educational process is supposed to link the individual to the body politic. Certainly, the role of the citizen is an empty concept without such linkage. Individuals connect to collectivities through several associative mechanisms which create commitment. Commitment means that the individual is willing to allow the collectivity the use of a certain amount of his resources, such as time and energy.

The educational system in Israel tended, and still tends, to rely heavily on negative associative mechanisms for the recruitment of its youngsters' commitment. This tendency is articulated by the utilization of symbols, such as the falling of Massada on the one hand, and Aushwitz on the other, on top of accentuating the very real survival problems that beset the State of Israel. "The Rules of the Game" takes another path—we try to make use of positive associative mechanisms for recruiting students' commitment. We believe that commitment can flourish in an atmosphere of tolerance, mutual respect, and individual freedom.

At a time when the Berlin Wall crumbles, such a credo is self-explanatory.

REFERENCES

Almond, G. & Verba, S. (1965). *The civic culture*. Boston: Little, Brown and Co.

Apple, M. W. (1989). How equality has been redefined in the conservative restoration. In W. G. Secada (Ed.), *Equity in education*. New York: The Palmer Press.

Bashi, J., Cahan, S., & Davis, D. (1981). *School achievements: Elementary Arab school in Israel*. Jerusalem: The Hebrew University.

Battistoni, R. M. (1985). *Public schooling and the education of the democratic citizen*. Jackson: University Press of Mississippi.

Bourdieu, P. (1973). Cultural reproduction and social reproduction. In A. Brown (Ed.), *Knowledge, education and cultural change*. London, Tavistock.

Bowles, S. & Gintis, H. (1976). *Schooling in Capitalist America*. New York, Basic Books.

Bowles, S. (1988). The politics and economics of educational reform: The correspondence principle reconsidered. In E. B. Gumbert (Ed.), *Making the future*. Atlanta: Georgia State University.

Carnoy, M. & Levin, H. (1985). *Schooling and work in the democratic state*. California: Stanford University Press.

Collins, R. (1979). *The credential society*. New York: Academic Press.

Connelly, F. M. (1972). The function of curriculum development. *Interchange, 2,* 161–177.

Dreeben, R. (1967). The contribution of schooling of the learning of norms. *Harvard Educational Review, 37*(2), 238–249.

Goodlad, J. I. (1984). *A place called school*. New York: McGraw–Hill.

Illich, I. (1970). *Deschooling society*. New York: Harper and Row.

Jackson, P. W. (1968). *Life in classrooms*, New York: Holt, Rinehart and Winston.

Jencks, C., Smith, M., Edland, H., Bain, M. J., Cohen, D., Gintis, H., Heyns, B., & Michelson, S. (1972). *Inequality: A reassesssment of the effect of family and schooling in America*. New York: Basic Books.

Katz, E. & Lazarsfeld, P. H. (1955). *Personal influence*. Glencoe, IL, Free Press.

Massialas, B. G. (1976). Some propositions about the role of the school in the formation of political behaviour and political attitudes of students: Cross-National perspectives. *Comparative Education Review, 19*, 169–171.

Meyer, J. W. (1977). The effects of education as an institution. *American Journal of Sociology, 83*, 55–77.

Patrick, J. J. (1977). Political socialization and political education in schools. In S. A. Renshon (Ed.), *Handbook of socialization: Theory and research*. New York: The Free Press.

Parsons, T. (1959). The school class as a social system: Some of its functions in American society. *Harvard Educational Review, 29*, 297–318.

Sewell, W. H. & Houser, R. M. (1975). *Education, occupation and earnings*. United States: Academy Press.

Silberman, M. (1978). Is the implementation of curriculum an integral part of its development? *Studies in Education, 17*, 77–88.

Turner, R. H. (1960). Sponsored and contest mobility and the school system. *American Sociological Review, 25*, 855–867.

Tzemach, M. (1986, 1987). *Sociological and political attitudes of youth*. Israel: Dachaf & Van Leer. (Hebrew).

Whitty, G. (1985). *Sociology and school knowledge*. London: Methuen.

Yogev, A. & Shapira, R. (1987). Ethnicity, meritocracy and credentialization in Israel: Elaborating the credential society. In Robinson (Ed.), *Research in social stratification and mobility*, (6). Greenwich, CN: JAI Press.

Young, J. H. (1985). Participation in curriculum development: An inquiry into the response of teachers. *Curriculum Inquiry, 15*, 387–413.

ACKNOWLEDGMENT

The "Rules of the Game" project is funded by the Samuel Warshauer Memorial Endowment Fund and by the Ford Foundation, U.S.A.

7 Government Policy and Curriculum Development With an Intercultural Perspective: The Netherlands, A Multi-Ethnic Society

Hans Hooghoff

1. INTRODUCTION

Since the Middle Ages national states have developed in Europe. Within these states national cultures have developed. However, in Europe it has not been possible in the past to let political boundaries correspond with cultural boundaries. As a result of this there exist substantial cultural minorities within most European states. Besides, migration has always been a common feature in Europe: Danes went to France, French Huguenots to The Netherlands, East European Jews to Western Europe, Greeks to Germany, etc. Moreover, several West European states have taken part in a period of expansion outside Europe. In this period there was an 'encounter' of European and non-Western cultures. But as a result of this expansion large groups of people from outside Europe have emigrated to European states. Increasing employment in Western Europe in the sixties and seventies led to a wave of migration both inside Europe and from Turkey and Morocco.

In Europe cooperation is growing. Moreover, particularly in Western Europe, societies have become more intercultural and contacts between larger and smaller sectors of the population with a culture of their own have increased substantially over the last decades.

Broadly speaking, three (im)migration movements can be distinguished in the Netherlands after the Second World War. First, the Netherlands was confronted with a large-scale, fairly heterogenous, late colonial and post-colonial influx from its (former) colonies overseas (repatriates from

Indonesia, Moluccans, Surinamese and Antilleans). In addition, the Netherlands, like almost all the countries of Western Europe, has been faced with immigration based primarily on economic motives, mainly of workers from the Mediterranean with their families. Finally, the Netherlands has received quite a few political refugees, and granted political asylum to many.

Immigration is not a new phenomenon. Through the ages, foreigners have settled in the Netherlands. However, the structure of society, having its basis in the values of Christian Europe, was such that newcomers were left no choice but to assimilate into this society. Even today, ethnic groups tend to adapt themselves to the prevalent standards and values and to subscribe to democratic principles. Apart from this, though attention is devoted to the newcomers' own identity and culture.

In countries like the United States, Canada, and Israel, the numbers of immigrants have always been higher than in the Netherlands, and, in addition, immigration was an instrument in the development of a new nation. This starting point to a large extent determined the priorities: a strong emphasis on acculturation and assimilation, in which political assimilation played an important role. The immigrants were to become Americans or Canadians as soon as possible. It is in this respect that the Netherlands differs from the above mentioned countries (expressed in percentages of the total population [± 4.5%], the scale of immigration is relatively small). In the Netherlands, there is no "examination" one must pass to gain citizenship, nor does one require knowledge of Dutch history or the political system. However, countless (state) subsidized social organizations offer courses and informative meetings for ethnic minorities. On the one hand, these are focused on teaching them the Dutch language, on the other hand, they are meant to help them find jobs, housing and suitable education. There are no special courses to inform the newcomers of the rights and duties of citizens in the Dutch constitutional state, but information on "what is done and not done" has a high priority.

Not until the late seventies did the realization dawn that most of the members of allochtonous ethnic groups were in the Netherlands to stay. The Netherlands is a multiethnic, and consequently also a multicultural, multilingual, and multidenominational society.

The political recognition of a multi-ethnic society led to a governmental policy (1986), aimed, on the one hand, at improving the social position of allochtonous ethnic groups. On the other hand, this policy was (and is) focused on mutual adaption of the "Nederlanders" and the "medelanders," the native and nonnative inhabitants of the Netherlands. In an earlier stage, the Dutch government already stimulated education for pupils belonging to ethnic minority groups on their own language and culture. More and more, this aspect of education is aimed at strengthening the separate identity of pupils from other cultures. This development was followed by "intercultural education," intended to grant pupils insight into one another's cultures and backgrounds, in order to enable them to function together in Dutch society on equal terms.

Besides intercultural education as a "principle," the Dutch school system also has "social and political education" as a compulsory subject. This subject teaches pupils the basics of politics and democracy, and prepares them for their future roles as citizens in a participatory democracy.

By means of education in minority languages and cultures, intercultural education, and social and political education, the Dutch government tries to keep the field of tension between allochtonous pupils' own culture, and the attainments of democracy in equilibrium. The dual aim is for newcomers to retain their own identity, while conforming to the rules of society.

This paper goes into the social positions of the ethnic minorities. Then a brief description is given of the government's role, and, more specifically, educational policy in a multiethnic society. Results and possible effects of the policy pursued until now are scrutinized.

In view of the importance of the compulsory school subject "social and political education," especially when it comes to becoming familiar with, and learning to apply democratic principles, a detailed discussion is given of the developments, objectives, and content of this subject. Indeed, this subject, about which there is a broad consensus in the Netherlands, is focused on living together critically, in the democratic and humane sense of the word. This goes for both autochtonous and allochtonous pupils.

Finally, a number of conclusions and recommendations are brought forward.

2. ETHNIC MINORITIES IN THE NETHERLANDS—
A DESCRIPTION OF THE CONTEXT

2.1. Development of the Social and Ethnic Position of Minorities

In terms of labor, the social position of groups labelled minorities in the Netherlands has deteriorated dramatically in the past 15 years. Considering the importance of labor and income as factors determining the place of groups in the layers of society, and the negative effects a setback in this field has on housing and educational opportunities, this trend must be viewed with great concern.

Judging by the level of secondary education, children from minorities enter after primary school, and by the level on leaving school, education for these groups has hardly improved. However, there are hopeful signs for the future: immigrants' children born in the Netherlands do more or less as well as autochtonous children. The terms "deterioration" or "improvement" should here be understood as the widening or narrowing of the original gap between the minorities' position, and that of the autochtonous population as a whole.

The ethnocultural position of minorities in the Netherlands—that is, the extent to which members of a group see themselves primarily as members of their own group, or are seen as such by (major sections of) society—has developed differently. In the seventies, Dutch society was faced with a number of infavorable developments, which were also reflected in a policy emphasizing the separate and temporary position of immigrants. In the same period, politics mobilized against immigrants, their image in the press became increasingly negative, and the climate of public opinion towards foreigners and minorities became chilly. In some neighborhoods this led to interethnic tensions, and in a few cases to group confrontations.

In the seventies, the minorities themselves did little to actively assert their ethnocultural identity. The recent immigrants do see themselves primarily as members of a separate group, and try to recreate in their own immigrants' world, the familiar world they have left behind, but this cannot be seen as assertion of ethnocultural identity; it is inherent in migration.

In the eighties, the negative developments outlined above came to a halt, or took a turn for the better. In minority policy after 1980, minorities have been given an equal place in society, in principle at least. Strong counterforces also have arisen opposing the antiimmigrant (political) movements, and discrimination in general. The climate of public opinion has become somewhat milder. Newcomers and residents are getting used to each other, and in neighborhoods, people find ways of living together, or at least side by side peacefully. The minority groups show no strong tendency towards ethnization; the formation of groups is hardly used as an instrument to gain a better position in the labor market, the housing market, or education, if at all. Assertion of ethnocultural identity is therefore seldom directly exploited to climb the social ladder. To a certain extent this is achieved via the bodies organizing participation, acting as spokesmen for immigrants and protecting their interests, mostly stimulated and financed by the government. Politically speaking, the formation of specific groups asserting their own identity is largely embedded in the general political structure of Dutch society. The formation of groups and ethnization seem to take place chiefly in recreation and private life.

The groups generally labelled as minorities in the Netherlands are small in number. The largest group, the Surinamese, constitutes 1.3% of the total Dutch population, and all the target groups of minority policy taken together constitute 4.6 percent (see Survey below in Table 7.1). Although formally, these groups have (been given) opportunities for political participation, at least at the municipal level, it must be observed that in reality

TABLE 7.1
Survey: Minorities in the Netherlands and Their Identifiability in National Data Bases

Nationality	Number on January 1, 1988
Turks	167,325
Moroccans	130,054
Spaniards	17,528
Italians	15,850
Yugoslavians	11,717
Portugese	7,706
Cape Verdeans	2,045
Greeks	3,953
Tunisians	2,600
Surinamese	203,030
Antilleans	60,745
Moluccans	40,000
Fugitives	18,000

Source: CBS/ISEO-EWR, The Hague, 1989.

they have no direct, effective political influence, even in those places where stronger concentrations exist.

2.2   Ethnic Minorities in the Netherlands

The position of *Turks* and *Moroccans* is one of great social disadvantage. Both the first and the "one–and–a–half" generation are low on the social ladder. An adult second generation, whose social position could be compared to that of the parents and autochtonous peers, does not yet exist. The ethnocultural position of these groups is strongly determined by the first generation, which is busy providing the immigrant community with its own social infrastructure. For the "one–and–a–half" generation, especially the girls, this entails a substantial amount of social control. However, partly due to the heterogeneity within the groups, and a certain scattering of housing patterns, no closed systems seem to be developing. Within Dutch society, on the other hand, there are considerable forces stressing the separate ethnocultural position of these groups, and perhaps making it permanent in the future. In the eyes of a great many Dutch people. Turks and Moroccans have been made the prototypes of a minority group.

The *Surinamese* in the Netherlands are a heterogenous category. Their social position is not homogenously low, although on average they have a disadvantage compared to the total Dutch population, especially when it comes to jobs. Ethnoculturally, they are also a heterogenous category lacking internal unity, divided along ethnical, religious, and linguistic lines. However, this internal heterogeneity is not always reflected in the image the Surinamese have in Dutch society. At least in part, this image is biased and stereotypic.

The *Antilleans* are a group of immigrants whose average stay is the Netherlands is relatively short. Even less than of the Surinamese, can it be said of Antilleans that the entire group is low on the social ladder. On the contrary, in some respects, their position approaches that of autochtones.

Judging by their position in the labor market and their housing situation, the social standing of the *Moluccans* has declined. Indeed, the second and later generation(s) have done better than their parents at school, but the little research comparing them to autochtonous pupils still proves them to be somewhat behind. The group's ethnocultural position, on the other hand, has done the opposite. Both the majority of the Moluccans themselves, and the Dutch government, have redefined the group's situation and orientation, and geared them to a future in the Netherlands. Particularism is no longer, or to a much lesser extent, the Moluccans' expression of ethnocultural identity. This is now sought mainly in private life (revival of the Moluccan language and culture), and can be combined with efforts to improve the group's social position in the Netherlands.

2.3 A Few Conclusions Concerning Social Positions

• Explicit negative ranking on the basis of one's belonging to an ethnocultural group is rare in the Netherlands. This is generally felt to be wrong and worthy of punishment when it occurs. In the Netherlands, negative ranking appears to take place indirectly, through making indirect distinctions. Moreover, there are indications that to a large extent, unequal treatment of minority members—compared to autochtones with the same relevant characteristics—is the result of unintentional effects of rules and procedures, which in themselves are phrased neutrally. Conscious, deliberate discrimination on the basis of racist ideas and attitudes certainly exists, but only accounts for part of the situations in which distinctions are—directly or indirectly—made.

• The influential role of the Dutch government has always been and still is of great importance; in the first place, when it comes to ethnocultural ranking. Before 1980, policy regarding the various groups of immigrants often stressed the separate position of these groups. Since the early eighties, the government has changed its standpoint; equal opportunities and treatment, cultural equality, and fighting discrimination have become the goals policy is aimed at. Not only does taking such a stand directly influence the distribution of vital social commodities, but it also has an important **symbolic function**, and sets an example for society as a whole (Penninx, 1988).

- The economic climate is one of the main factors which can stimulate either the formation of minority groups or their emancipation. For politicians and policy makers, this means that in times of economic stagnation or decline, when resources are low, they must take extra pains to prevent the formation of minority groups.

- An important factor influencing developments in the Netherlands was the rise of the welfare state. Within such a state, the standards of equality and equal opportunities prevail, and as a consequence, the support for equal treatment became stronger than for inequality and separation. Even distinctions which used to be important, such as alienage, become less so the longer the immigrant is in the Netherlands; as a resident, the alien then proves to be assimilated into the welfare state in all sorts of ways: as an employee, as a pensioner, as a consumer, etc. As a taxpayer, he even contributes to its continuation. The welfare state also has its drawbacks: the intensive government interference also implies more rules and obligations, and a uniformization which presupposes a certain amount of loyalty to the system.

3. INTERCULTURAL EDUCATION AS A REACTION— AN INTERIM SURVEY

3.1 The Position of Minorities With Regard to Education

To a great extent, the social position of individuals is determined by the level at which they finish their education. In studying how the position of immigrants has developed with regard to education, two facts should be borne in mind. The first is that by definition, migration has a negative impact on the immigrant's educational opportunities, due to the defective tie-up with his former schooling, and problems with language and culture. This means that there is no point in making comparisons with autochtones until the second generation. The second fact is that reaching children has two aspects to it: transfer of knowledge, and transfer of culture. For autochtones, the latter is implicit; for immigrants the latter can gain a significance all its own.

Negative ranking by exclusion from education does not exist; on the contrary, school attendance is compulsory for allochtones as well. In this decade we do see explicit positive ranking, in the sense that a fairly intensive policy has been pursued aimed at narrowing the gap between allochtones and autochtones. The education budget is by far the largest separate item in the government's minority budget. However, the school is where this policy is actually carried out.

As far as access to schools is concerned, it seems to have been of great importance that the greatest influx of allochtonous pupils took place at a time when the number of pupils in primary education was declining. At first, this led to a greater distribution over schools of various denominations, than could have been expected under other circumstances. In the second instance, however, the parents' freedom to send their children to the school of their choice gave rise to another phenomenon: the "black" or "concentration schools" (de Jong, 1987). The number of such schools has boomed and is still growing.

The factors within the school which could contribute towards ranking can be summarized as follows. The organization of the teaching, the approach, and the goals have hardly changed, if at all, under the influence of the altered ethnocultural composition of the schools. Education in the native language and culture (OETC), and Intercultural Studies, are hardly integrated into the teaching. As regards relations within the school, it appears that friction and prejudice do occur, but that in the school system as a whole, the standard prevails that pupils from minority groups should be seen and treated as equals by both fellow pupils and teachers. At primary schools, there is seldom a strong tendency to form groups, except among the older Turkish and Moroccan girls (Dors, 1987).

In searching for factors and mechanisms determining ranking, and obtaining a position in education, one is faced with a fundamental problem: education is not only a system for transferring knowledge (there is little disagreement on that point), but also an institution for transferring culture. In the educational field, and also among scientists, a debate is going on about the question of how both elements should be balanced. Obviously, being primarily staffed by autochtones, schools give priority to maximizing what is considered to be transfer of knowledge, in order to achieve equal opportunities for pupils from minority groups. Some overlook the transfer of culture, which is often implicit, others see it as an unavoidable and essential part of education.

Turkish and Moroccan parents, and OETC teachers, often see and value this transfer of knowledge and culture differently. For parents, who are at least uncertain whether their future lies in the Netherlands or their native country, teaching of the native language and culture is an important part of education. But even apart from plans for remigration, OETC can offer allochtonous parents an opening into the Dutch educational system, which they otherwise experience as inaccessible. This part of education is at least familiar to them; the teachers are members of their own group and therefore approachable, and it is in line with the standards and values of the group. It consequently becomes an ethnic symbol of identification.

3.2.   Government Policy and Intercultural Education

In the early seventies, the Dutch government introduced the possibility of teaching pupils from ethnic minorities their native language and culture (OETC). At first, the explicit objective was to facilitate reintegration into the educational system of their native country, but as the fact became accepted that many immigrants were in the Netherlands to stay, this goal changed as well. Now, the main objective of OETC is to strengthen the pupils' own cultural identity.

A subsequent logical step was the introduction of the term "intercultural education." Indeed, if immigrants are accepted as full members of Dutch society, while retaining their own identity, this should not only be reflected in the education for this particular group of pupils; the whole of Dutch education must cope with the multiform, multicultural societythat has come to exist.

Goals.   Intercultural education has its legal basis in the Primary Education Act, which says: "Education is based partly on the assumption that pupils grow up in a multicultural society." As appears from the follow-up report "Intercultural Education" of the Ministry of Education and Science of April 1986, a similar clause is to be included in the new Secondary Education Act. In the same document, the general goal of Intercultural Education is described as follows:

> "Teaching pupils to cope with similarities and differences related to ethnic and cultural background characteristics. The interaction pattern should be aimed at equality and functioning together in Dutch society."

The subgoals mentioned for intercultural education are:

- The acquisition of knowledge concerning each other's backgrounds, circumstances and culture, both by the autochtonous population group(s) and by the ethnic groups living in our country, and mutually gaining insight into the way values, standards, customs and circumstances determine people's behaviour.
- Enabling groups of various ethnic and cultural origins to live together in our country.
- Preventing and fighting prejudice, discrimination and racism based on ethnic and/or cultural differences in all sections of the population.

It is also stated explicitly that intercultural education is not a separate school subject, but must in "principle" pervade all of education.

If intercultural education is to be successful, an essential factor is changing attitudes. Prejudice and stereotypes must be opposed. This change in attitude should be based partly on better knowledge of each other's cultures and backgrounds. Therefore it is not surprising that the note of the Ministry of Education and Science puts a great deal of emphasis on increasing teachers' expertise and developing curricula. Although a lot of teaching material appears on the market—often the result of local initiatives—this often appears to be fragmentary and lacking system. Furthermore, not enough people are familiar with the backgrounds and cultures of immigrants at the moment. To break down prejudice and stereotypes, the cultures of immigrants living in the Netherlands should be studied as living cultures. Pupils must acquire knowledge of, and insight into sociocultural backgrounds, and be made familiar with the democratic principles and political rules of the form of government we have in the Netherlands.

3.3. Cultural Identity and Social Adjustment

Dilemma.   Every minority member has the right, if he so wishes, to be in his own cultural surroundings, to profess and practice his own religion and, more generally, to experience his "own identity." This basic principle can be found in clause 27 of the International Treaty concerning Civil and Political Rights, which was recently ratified by the Netherlands. In practice, this means that the government should create guarantees allowing minorities their cultural activities, without interfering with the content thereof. The Ministry of Education feels that "the limit to recognizing each separate group's own cultural identity, its own values and standards, behaviour and opinions is reached when these conflict with the values embedded in society, the Constitution and the law, which are part of our social achievements." Furthermore, that "corporal punishment, polygamy, oppression of women, marrying off minors, but also truancy, for example, may very well belong to the original cultural identity or pattern of values of some groups, within a certain social and religious context, but within the set of values laid down in the law and the Constitution by Dutch society, such practices should be neither promoted or preserved, but opposed."

The generally accepted dual aim of Dutch minority policy is (a) to offer those involved equal opportunities to participate in society, (b) while allowing them to retain their own cultural identity. The central question is: are these two subgoals compatible, and if so, under which conditions? On the basis of "study and research taking place abroad and our experience in Dutch society in the course of history with the cultural identity of religious groups, regional groups, the role of women, and similar phenomena," the government feels justified in concluding that:

> also in order to develop cultural identity, we should give priority to the removal of disadvantages. For our education, this implies that we must focus our attention and inspiration primarily on also offering these pupils from minorities every opportunity to benefit by educational facilities and obtain

qualifications, which still largely determine one's career in society. To put it somewhat provocatively: extra efforts aimed at mastering the Dutch language, at tutoring, at choosing the right type of school and at getting through Dutch school successfully, could well be more important than efforts to teach the native language and culture, especially if this actually only takes place in isolation. (Ministry of the Interior, 1983a)

The idea that native language and culture should not be taught in isolation is an obvious one. However, the overall conclusion formulated so generally here, is not only "provocative," but also unproven. These government statements (1983) are again extremely topical at the moment, in view of the nationwide debate on the necessity of bilingual education. At the same time, the suggestion is made that a unilateral adjustment of minorities to the dominant culture would offer more possibilities. This approach takes insufficient account of the inequality of power between the various groups in society. In the interest of minorities developing their own cultural identity, however, priority must be given to putting a stop to class differences.

3.4. Present Status of Intercultural Education

A study of the theory and practice of intercultural education in the Netherlands (Fase & van den Berg, 1985) yielded the following results.

An important outcome of this study is that at least half of all nursery, primary, and secondary schools does nothing at all in the way of intercultural education. There are indications that the demand for intercultural education is especially low at schools unaffected by the influx of various ethnic groups in the past years, and at schools where the researchers strongly suspect that the pupils from ethnic groups have adapted themselves to the daily school routine.

A second result of this study concerns the intercultural education offered at the other half of the schools. On average, the amount of time devoted to intercultural education is limited. The educational offering is also rather slender, if we compare present classroom practice to the quality standards formulated in theoretical contributions on the part of educational science and pedagogics. In general, schools hardly, if at all, meet the requirements regarding the school organization, the specific expertise of teachers, the quality of teaching material, etc., which increase the probability of intercultural education being effective.

The present classroom practice of intercultural education does not tally with the assumptions underlying government policy. In several consecutive notes from the central government explaining the aims of minority policy, and particularly intercultural education, it is invariably assumed that intercultural education is implemented at all primary and secondary schools. Moreover, the quality of the educational offering was also touched upon, although only in the negatively phrased condition that intercultural education must not overemphasize "folklore." Critical voices in the educational field point out that, in the absence of sound and feasible curricula, tested teaching material, special in-service training and supplementary research, classroom practice seldom goes beyond an "exotic meal" or wearing "funny clothes." A remarkable outcome of this field study is that for the most part (71%), intercultural education is given during lessons in religion and social and political education. The content is often linked with the teaching of morals, the development of values, development education (North-South issues), and human rights education.

3.5. Revision of Intercultural Education?

In the opinion of several large national organizations of ethnic groups, the government must develop a new and more effective policy. This new policy should be more focused on real participation of immigrants in Dutch society. Promoting minority interests, influencing policy, being able to function as a full and independent member of society should be primary goals. Teaching of the native language and culture, and intercultural education merely scratch the surface and are in fact monocultural (de Jong, 1987). Much more than is now the case, children of immigrants must learn basic skills enabling them to participate fully, both socially and politically, in Dutch society. In short, do not view immigrants as pathetic invalids, but as ordinary citizens, with their good and bad sides. As one representative pointed out, they are not only being "hugged to death," but also "studied to death."

4. A NATIONAL CURRICULUM FOR SOCIAL AND POLITICAL EDUCATION IN THE PERSPECTIVE OF INTERCULTURAL EDUCATION

4.1. Introduction to and Status of Political Education

In the Netherlands, there is hardly any tradition in the formal educational system when it comes to political education. Not until the end of the sixties was a new subject introduced at secondary school called "maatschappijleer" (learning about the society). The main force leading to the introduction of this new compulsory school subject was the pressure from various sectors of society to improve the social relevance of education. Another factor was that large groups of the population were striving towards a reevaluation and reformulation of our society's values and standards. In short, a demand made itself felt for explicit social and political education at school. Before, this was primarily the task of social and religious organizations (there are still a great many government-subsidized bodies active in the field of social and political education). It was made the task of education, partly through constructive government policy, to make young people aware of the possibility of giving shape to their present and future situation in life. The school subject "maatschappijleer" was to teach them the necessary social and intellectual skills (Tierolf, 1988).

The fact that, when the subject was introduced, the government had hardly indicated what its content should be (as long as it was not a pocket-sized version of sociology), had vast effects of further curriculum development. It was an impediment to the development of a broadly accepted curriculum. It prevented agreement on what qualifications teachers should have. And it also stood in the way of the establishment of good teacher training. At school, this vague subject was viewed with suspicion and some contempt. Well-meaning teachers were up against the negative image that pupils, colleagues, school management, and parents had of their subject. In the seventies, characterized by heated ideological debates (centering on German critical theories), the climate was unfavorable for reaching the desired consensus on basic content. Not until the end of the seventies, and especially the early eighties, did it become somewhat clearer what the content of the subject was to be. At the request of educational and social organizations, the National Institute for Curriculum Development (SLO) launched a six-year project, leading to the publication of a "Visie op Maatschappijleer" (View on Social and Political Education) in 1983. This was the main source of inspiration for the ministerial study groups who opened the way to an experimental final examination with their note "Naar een Eindexamen Maatschappijleer." Social and political studies made its entrance as a final examination subject in 1985, and in 1992 its status as such (either optional or compulsory) should be permanent. In 1985 the government set up a Structural Committed for Examinations in Social and Political Studies to formulate descriptions of subject matter. In May, 1987 the first examination was taken. It was received favorably by teachers and the Ministry, and moreover got a good press (which was quite unique).

The year 1987 also saw the publication of the SLO project results: a large number of documents stating basic principles, tested lesson plans, and a detailed core curriculum for social and political studies, listing precisely what pupils should at least know and be capable of.

4.2. Core Curriculum for Social and Political Education

In 1987, the National Institute for Curriculum Development produced a core curriculum for social and political education (a Maatschappijleer). This core curriculum describes not only goals and content, but also the final terms. Final terms give an unambiguous description of the minimal

DIAGRAM OF THE DUTCH EDUCATION SYSTEM

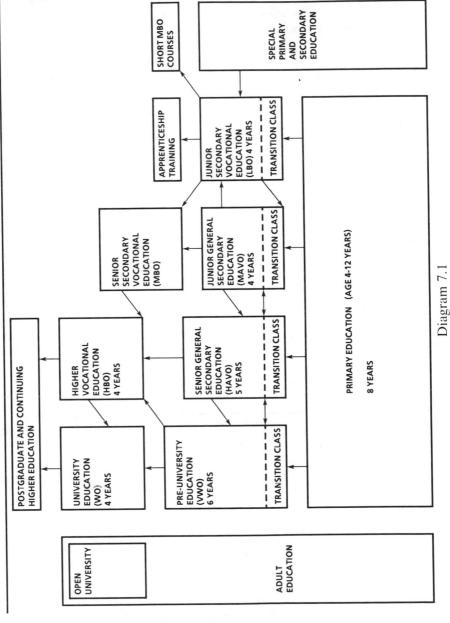

Diagram 7.1

Diagram of the Dutch Educational Support System

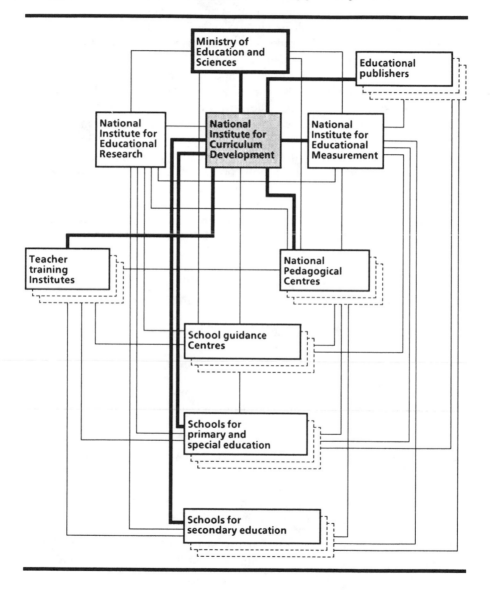

Diagram 7.2

body of knowledge in social skills all pupils are to have acquired at the end of a certain stage of education. In the centralized Dutch educational system, final terms are laid down by the Minister, and serve to enhance and control the quality of education. Quality control consists of national central written examinations (the same questions at the same moment for all pupils), preceded by examinations at school level.

The core curriculum published has been field-tested by means of concrete pilot lesson series. Among trade unions, the inspectorate, the government, and teacher training colleges, there is a broad consensus as to the way in which the identity of social and political education is formulated. The core curriculum is aimed at pupils aged 14 to 16, and is a compulsory subject within the school curriculum. The purpose of the core curriculum is to provide pupils with the knowledge, insights, and skills necessary to form a well-founded opinion about topical political phenomena and issues. Since in the Netherlands, social and political education is compulsory at school, both autochtonous and allochtonous pupils are confronted with this new subject. However, the core curriculum does not guarantee that the intended effects on pupils, such as more knowledge of the political system, taking a stand on controversial issues, the willingness to participate now or later, will actually materialize. This calls for a strategy of innovation (Kuyper, 1988) and implementation in the Dutch educational system, with the government, examination boards, the inspectorate, publishers, and teacher training colleges playing leading roles.

The current experimental examination for social and political education (1983–1992) (a government initiative) offers hopeful prospects of the actual adoption of the core curriculum.

4.3.   Elements of Content From the Core Curriculum for Social and Political Education

The aim of Social and Political Education is to develop knowledge, insight and skills in pupils, making them increasingly capable of coping critically and creatively with current social and political phenomena and problems.

Social and political education supplies pupils with the knowledge, insights and skills needed to form an opinion of their own, based on sound arguments, concerning social and political phenomena and problems. The knowledge, insights, and skills supplied by social and political education are *essential conditions* for forming an opinion as intended. This mean that:

- Knowledge of and insight into the interdependence between one's own experiences, questions, and opinions, and the structures and problems characteristic of society;
- Knowledge of and insight into one's own standards and values, views, and interests, and those of other people and groups;

- Knowledge of and insight into the changeability and stubbornness of the structure of society, and the solvability of social problems;
- Skills in gathering information on social problems and phenomena, and in applying this information, enabling pupils to be socially active if they so wish.

Social and political education is focused on the—conscious or unconscious—agreements people make or have made concerning the way they cope with social problems. For handling problems in the family, company, or in politics, there are rules of behavior and procedures. These do not come out of the blue; they are invented by people—either inspired by a political view or religion or not—and handed down to new members of this society in all sorts of educational processes. Viewed in this way, people are "products of their society." In their turn, people can also become "producers" if they question rules and procedures and are willing to change them (Slo, 1987).

The pupils' own experiences, opinions and questions necessarily entail standards, values, and interests. It is important that pupils learn to recognize these in themselves. The step towards also recognizing the standards, values, and interests of others is then a logical one. Recognizing one's own standards, values, and interests, and those of others, is important in order to gain insight into what certain groups deem desirable for society, and the solution of its problems. At least as important, is for pupils to realize that values, standards, and interests are related to various positions (of power) in society. This gives pupils a realistic view of the changeability and stubbornness of the structure of society.

The aim of social and political education is to help make pupils "increasingly capable of coping critically and creatively with current social and political phenomena and problems." Social and political education does not pretend to make pupils "critical and creative" in the course of 80 lessons over two years, but it does lay the foundation.

Coping critically means that pupils are able to look at problems and phenomena from several points of view, to analyse motives, and to distinguish facts from opinions. Social phenomena and problems are thus no longer taken for granted.

Being critical and being creative go hand in hand. If we want pupils to question things taken for granted, this implies that we also wish to stimulate them to view social phenomena and problems from different viewpoints, and to be open to various solutions before making their own choice.

The aim of social and political education is to offer pupils applicable knowledge, insights, and skills, in other words, offer them the ability to act. In the first place, this means that pupils should be able to participate in society, for example by joining a club, exercising their right to vote, etc.

Of great importance is insight into the social power structure. This allows pupils to view their own ability to act, and that of others realistically. This prevents overoptimism and undue pessimism. Often enough, pupils say "there's nothing we can do anyway," or they set their hopes regarding what they can achieve too high.

Social and political education is not about strictly *personal* or *individual problems* of people who organize their lives together as a community. If a personal or individual problem has to do with relations characteristic of society, it is a social problem. Giving shape to society and making the relevant decisions is done in different places. Sometimes people see to such matters *themselves*. They discuss things together in their social organizations, and make decisions about them. In other words, the topic is on the *social agenda*. Sometimes authority is transferred to *politics*. By politics, we mean "*government policy, its realization and its effects.*" (Hoogerwerf, 1987). If a phenomenon or problem connected with people's living together because the subject of government policy, in other words, appears on the *political agenda*, then it is considered a *political* phenomenon or problem. Politics is thus a special decision making process with regard to social phenomena and problems. Or, to put it somewhat differently; by this definition, political phenomena and problems are always of a social nature, but on the other hand, politics is not always the institution deciding on social problems. In other words, the social includes the political. The relevance of the distinction between "social" and "political" lies in the possibility of stimulating pupils to form an opinion about what should and should not be taken care of by the government.

4.4. The Object

The object of social and political education is organized in thematic fields, in which various sorts of social and political phenomena and problems are classified.

These thematic fields are:

1.	Education	Family, relations, mass-media
2.	Work and leisure	Unemployment, social benefits
3.	State and society	Parlimentary democracy, crime and criminal law
4.	Home, house, and environment	Cultural minorities, environment
5.	Technology and society	Information society, privacy

6. International relations   North-South, East-West issues, Europe

All these thematic fields are of great importance to the content of social and political education. The first three thematic fields mainly cover questions which are always and everywhere on the social agenda, whereas the latter three cover issues which are not universal, and appear on the social agenda in various forms and gradations. Social issues are presented illustratively to the pupils in a form they recognize and in a meaningful context. These thematic fields (Slo, 1987) focus on the following questions:

Education:
- *What standards, values, opinions, and beliefs does society hand down to new members, in order to guarantee its continuation (socialization)?*
- *How does this process work, which social institutions are involved?*
- *What opportunities does the individual have in this socialization process to choose his own values, standards, etc. (the so-called individuation)?*

Work and leisure:
- *How do members of society make a living? Where do they find their life fulfillment?*
- *How is this organized in society? What are the consequences for the structure of society?*

State and society:
- *How do members of society make binding agreements, consciously or unconsciously?*
- *How are these agreements carried out, observed and maintained?*
- *What structures and processes have been invented for this purpose?*

Home, house and environment:
- *What are the causes and the consequences for society of alterations in the scale of production and consumption?*
- *What are the differences and similarities between the other culture and other ways—cultures?*

Technology and society:
- *What are the social origins and consequences of the development of technology?*
- *What consequences do technologies have for the relations among citizens, and between citizens and government?*

International relations:
- *What position of power do countries have in global society?*
- *How did these positions come to exist? How are they confirmed?*

• *What tension does this give rise to within and between countries?*

These questions make it clearer what sort of phenomena and problems are covered in the various thematic fields. Perhaps other characterizing questions are conceivable. The questions function as organizing criteria, by means of which themes can be *unambiguously* classified within a particular thematic field. Take for example the question in which thematic field a theme like "foreigners" belongs; if we are mainly concerned with "immigrant workers," with the emphasis on the labor position and working conditions, such a theme belongs in the thematic field work and leisure. If we are more interested in the problems of the "second generation," for example, with the emphasis on growing up in two cultures (identity) (Gerritsen, R. & Klaassen, C., 1990), such a theme would be ranged under the thematic field of education.

5. CONCLUSIONS AND SOME RECOMMENDATIONS REGARDING THE NETHERLANDS

Not until the end of the seventies was it realized that most members of allochtonous ethnic groups were in the Netherlands to stay. The Netherlands is a multiethnic, society, and consequently also a multicultural, multilingual, and multidenominational society. In government policy, the recognition of the multiethnicity of society triggered a strategy of double emphasis in education regarding ethnic groups (1986). Besides improving the social position of allochtonous ethnic groups, the mutual adjustment of autochtonous, as well as ethnic groups was stressed. In 1988, pupils of foreign descent constituted 4.11 percent of the total number of pupils in the Netherlands: 3,314,007.

Aims of educational policy (1986):

1. Acquiring knowledge of the backgrounds, circumstances, and cultures of ethnic groups living in the Netherlands, and gaining insight into the way in which values, standards, customs, and circumstances determine people's behavior.
2. Learning to live together with groups of various ethnic and cultural origins in Dutch society.
3. Preventing and opposing prejudice, discrimination, and racism on the basis of ethnic and/or cultural differences.

Concrete action items (KOV, 1988) for the period 1986–1991:

• Promoting the realization of the necessity of intercultural education;
• Development, distribution and implementation of teaching materials;

- A strong emphasis in initial teacher training on mentality;
- National coordination and gearing of development, research, and teacher training;
- Formulating more precisely the legal obligation of schools to make education more intercultural;
- Intensifying supervision by the inspectorate;
- Teachers are hard to convince of the desirability of intercultural education "as a principle."
- There is no consistent policy guiding curriculum development, research, and implementation.

The interculturalization of Dutch education is a time-consuming process. For a more successful development and implementation strategy, it is necessary for goals to be more in keeping with practical feasibility, and consequently restricted to:

1. Increasing knowledge of and insight into ethnical relations;
2. Opposing ethnic prejudice;
3. Opposing racist behavior; and

- To give priority to intercultural education in the subjects of Religion, Geography, History, and Social and Political Education;
- To gear intercultural education to the National Curriculum Project for Development Education (1986–1992); the goal of this longitudinal project is the integration of the North–South issue into Social and Political Education, among other subjects (Slo, 1986);
- To continue working towards conceptualization of intercultural education; and
- To gradually bring about changes in the regular curriculum for the social sciences, which is of a monocultural nature (including changes in the presupposed values).

The Dutch government recognizes the need for more effective political education. This appears from its constructive policy regarding the experimental social and political studies examination (1983–1992), based partly on the core curriculum developed by the SLO. These policy measures have had a beneficial impact on the position of "Maatschappijleer" in education. The wide acceptance of the subject's "identity" has offered more support, especially to teachers.

- Setting up better in-service training courses and making teaching materials for intercultural education accessible; and
- Formulating final terms expressing the consequences of intercultural education.

Important starting points for the development and implementation of intercultural education are:

- Intercultural education must be seen as a principle determining the aspect of education as a whole, and of all its parts. It should be aimed at all those receiving education.
- Intercultural education must be prevented from becoming yet another "sort of education" like peace education, environmental education, development education, etc. (Hooghoff, 1987, 1988). It must be integrated into existing subjects such as Geography, History, Religion, and Social and Political Education.
- Intercultural education may not be limited to affective or social objectives, and may not be at the expense of good performance in basic skills. Knowledge and skills are the best guarantees for allochtonous pupils to be able to change their own position (Stone, 1981, Dors, 1984).

At Dutch schools, intercultural education is no more than a marginal activity. A few reasons are that:

- Schools assess the need for intercultural education mainly in terms of the number of pupils from ethnic minorities.
- General statements of intent, in catchwords like acculturation, functioning on equal terms, accepting differences and similarities, offer too little direction to enable effective education.
- The social basis is not broad enough, even among allochtones, who play a marginal role in the formation of opinions.

An SLO curriculum project recently started, "Social and Political Education for 16 to 19-year-olds,"offers at least some prospect of further quality improvement of this compulsory school subject in Dutch education. With a view to "Europe in 1992," more and more development and research centers in Europe will start cooperating in the field of education for minority groups. Initiatives have been, and are being taken by the Council of Europe, the European Commission, (Eurydice, 1989) and the OECD (1987) of Paris. The aim is to form a consortium in order to join forces in addressing the problems of education and integration of minorities on a European scale.

APPENDIX 1: EDUCATIONAL SUPPORT STRUCTURE IN THE NETHERLANDS

The educational support structure consists of a number of organizations designed to increase the ability of schools to solve problems they may encounter in seeking both to realize their objectives, and at the same time to systematically develop and improve education. Their work relates to all aspects of education: educational theory and teaching methods, subject content, psychology, organization, and innovation. The support organizations may be classified as providing general or specialized services. The former are concerned with improving the functioning of the school as a whole, while the latter are devoted to educational research, educational assessment, and curriculum development.

The general support organizations include the school counselling services (SBDs), and the national educational advisory centers (LPCs). There are 65 school counseling services working at local and regional level for the benefit of primary schools and certain types of special schools. Their work, like that of the LPCs, encompasses counseling and development activities, evaluation, and offering schools advice and information. Through their work they also seek to ensure that pupils make the most of their time at primary school. The three national educational advisory centers, one Catholic, one Protestant, and one nondenominational—work at a national level, mainly servicing secondary schools, but also primary schools and teacher training colleges. They have the special responsibility of coordinating national educational innovation policy, and also provide support to the local and regional school counseling services.

The specialized support organizations are the Foundation for Educational Research (SVO), the National Institute for Curriculum Development (SLO), and the National Institute for Educational Assessment (CITO). The work of all three relates to primary, secondary, and special education, as well as teacher training. The SVO promotes and coordinates educational research, grants, subsidies, and develops research programs. It performs no research of its own, however. The SLO develops national curricula, school curricula, and partial school curricula, and coordinates curriculum development in general. Its workforce is: 300 full-time employees (1989). CITO develops tests and examinations, the latter at the request of the Minister. It also processes and analyses examination results. Its workforce is: 250 full-time employees. Each of these institutions is governed by a board comprising educational experts, and representatives of the educational umbrella organizations, the Ministry of Education and Science, and the Ministry of Agriculture and Fishery.

WHO PAYS FOR EDUCATION IN THE NETHERLANDS?

Dutch education is almost totally financed from public funds, allocated to the budget of the Department of Education and Science. The total budget is 27,000,000,000 Dutch guilders, at the present exchange rate about

13,000,000,000 United States dollars. That constitutes 8 percent of Gross National Income, and about 17 percent of total government expenditure.

For primary education, parents must pay a small sum for "extras," between 10 and 200 dollars a year. In secondary education, the costs of textbooks, study trips, art materials, and etc. vary, but at most schools they amount to between 200 and 400 dollars a year. As for higher education, tuition, books, materials, etc., cost about 1800 dollars a year, but there is a rather good system of grants and loans. Roughly speaking, there are no financial barriers within the entire system.

All this money is spent on 3,300,000 pupils and students, 12,000 buildings and 220,000 teachers.

REFERENCES

Abram, I. B. H. (1983). *Intercultural education as mutual adaptation.* Amsterdam: General Educational Advisory Center.

Commission of the European Communities (1989). *Education and youth policy in the European Community.* Brussels: Eurydice European Unit.

Dors, H. G. (1987). *Friendship and social relations in multi-ethnic schoolclasses.* Amsterdam.

Dors, H. G. (1984). *About the conceptualization of intercultural education.* Amsterdam.

Fase, W. & Berg, G. van den (1985). *Theory and practice of intercultural education.* The Hague: National Institute for Educational Research (SVO).

Hoogerwerf, A. (1987). The contribution of political science to social and political education in: *Social sciences about social and political education.* Enschede: SLO.

Hooghoff, J. H. W. (1987). *New developments in the field of environmental education.* Enschede: SLO.

Hooghoff, J. H. W. (1988). *New developments on peace-education.* Enschede: SLO.

Gerritsen, R. & Klaassen, C. (1990). *Cultural differences between youth in the Netherlands. Guidelines for Teachers.* Enschede: SLO. (In preparation).

Jong, M. J. de (1987). *So many languages, so many sentences.* Rotterdam: Erasmus University.

Katholic Education Union (1988). *Effective education is intercultural.* Rijswijk.

Kuyper, W. (1988). *Implementation Study of Usability of Teaching Materials for Social and Political Education.* Enschede: University of Twente.

Ministry of the Interior (1983A). *Note about minorities. Parliamentary Papers.* The Hague.

Ministry of Education and Science (1986). *Sequel-note Intercultural Education. Parliamentary Papers.* The Hague.

Organisation for Economic Cooperation and Development (OECD) (1987). *Immigrants' children at school.* Paris: Center for Educational Research and Innovation (CERI).

Penninx, R. (1988) *Formation of minority groups and emancipation; social science research relating to immigrants and caravan dwellers in The Netherlands, 1967–1987.* Alphen aan de Rijn/Brussel: Samson Uitgeverij. *The description of the social position of ethnic minorities, chapter 2, is mainly based on Penninx' study.

Project Team for Social and Political Studies (1987). *The core of social and political education.* Enschede: SLO.

Stone, M. (1981). *The Education of the black child in Britain.* Glasgow: Fontana paperbacks.

Secretriat of the National Development Education Network (1986). *Framework plan for the period from August 1 1986 to August 1 1991*. Enschede: SLO.

Tierolf, H. & Hooghoff, J. H. W. (1983). *View on social and political studies*. Enschede: National Institute for Curriculum Development (SLO).

Tierolf, H. (1988). *Process report of the curriculum project for social and political education 1981–1987*. Enschede: SLO.

8

Civic Education for Positive Pluralism in Great Britain

Ian Lister
University of York, England

INTRODUCTION: REVIVING CIVIC EDUCATION

For political educators one of the striking features of late twentieth-century, post-industrial societies is the need for *civic education*. In the richest of these societies—the United States of America—the call for the renewal, revival, and reconstruction of civic education has grown more urgent over recent decades. In 1977, Howard D. Mehlinger was writing about "the crisis in civic education." For him, civic education was caught in a time-lag, with growing discrepancies between what people were being taught to believe about society, and their actual experience of it. "The world is different from what it was fifteen or twenty years ago" (Brown, 1977). In 1980, R. Freeman Butts was arguing for the revival of *civic learning*, and offering his *Decalogue of Democratic Civic Values* (one of which was *diversity*), as the basis for the revival program (Butts, 1980). In 1983, Morris Janowitz focused on the renovation of the concept of patriotism as the key to his reform program (which included the introduction of voluntary national service) (Janowitz, 1983). All three pointed out the inadequacies of nineteenth and early twentieth-century nationalism, and stated that global interdependence was one of the key new features which needed to be taken into account. "Global interdependence is a fact of life," wrote Mehlinger (1977). "Global interdependence or simply globalization" (was) "a concept and value which required a basic change in our historical views of citizenship," wrote R. Freeman Butts (1980). "Old-fashioned, uncritical patri-

129

otism is not effective in the current interdependent world," wrote Morris Janowitz (1983).

However, it is not only in the United States that civic educators are remarkably active. In Australia, civic education is one of three major elements of a national educational reform program—*aboriginal studies* and *Australian history* are the other two. In that country, the most soul search- ing questions about citizenship are being asked. "What is it to be an Aus- tralian today, and what will it be to be an Australian tomorrow?" asks Eric Willmot, the 1986 Boyer lecturer. He also asks whether Australia could "establish that a modern polygeneric society, a society created from people of mixed origins, can successfully exist in the midst of older indig- enous societies?" (Willmot, 1987). In Hong Kong, the introduction of a major program of civic education in the schools is part of the transition process—from being a colony to becoming a special autonomous region of the People's Republic of China in 1997 (Lee, 1987; Ting, 1987). In Canada, there have been several impressive projects in the related fields of civic education and human rights education, of which the Political Ed- ucation Project of the University of Manitoba in Winnipeg is one (Osborne, 1986, 1987). In West Germany, there is a tradition of interest in "Politische Bildung," and there has been a high level of formal support for civic education, including a national Center for Political Education and a na- tional Research Center. Even in England, where there is a whole history of formal *opposition* to civic education in schools, the national Programme for Political Education, launched in 1974, managed to establish its key concept of political literacy securely enough for it to be central to the programs for multicultural education recommended by the national com- mission chaired by Lord Swann (Lister, 1987; Reid, 1984; Swann, 1985). Even the present government, a mixture of conservative restoration, and of cultural revolution, while opposing political education in schools, ad- vocates the spread of economic literacy, and of citizenship. In the Soviet Union, the policy of *perestroika* will inevitably involve a reconstruction of citizenship. In opening itself to the world, the People's Republic of China is opening itself to other political cultures, and to developments in its own political culture.

The challenges for civic education at the end of the twentieth century arise from the nature of late industrial societies. These societies are typically multicultural and multifaith (and increasingly recognize this). They are based on industrial economics, some of whose assumptions are questioned by "Green" movements. To various degrees, they witness the assertion of women's rights. They are all, inescapably, globally interdependent. While the hope is for peaceful social development, both internally and interna- tionally, the fear is that diversity may lead to divergence, fragmentation, and disintegration. "Things fall apart . . . ." Seeking a future, to some extent, in the past, we recall that one of the prime purposes of civic education was to promote social cohesion.

CIVIC EDUCATION FOR SOCIAL COHESION

In modern society, civic education in schools has been used to overcome tribalism, localism, and transferred nationalism. In the United States— "the great experiment"—it was used to make Americans out of diverse Europeans. The theme of civic education for social cohesion runs through the works of John Dewey, Charles E. Merriam, and Morris Janowitz (all linked in their lives with that melting pot city—Chicago).

In 1916, Dewey wrote: "The intermingling in the school of youth of different races, differing religions, and unlike customs creates for all a newer and broader environment," and he went on to speak of "the assimilative force of the American public school" (Dewey, 1916). In 1931, Charles E. Merriam's work *The Making of Citizens* was a comparative study of methods of civic training in several countries, including France, Germany, and the USSR. He ventured the generalization "that the newer the regime the more vigorous the use of the educational system for civic training." He saw that there were different means to achieving civic cohesion, but he also saw civic cohesion as a major common end (Merriam, 1931). Between Dewey in 1916, and Janowitz in 1983, many things have changed, and they have changed in such a way that early twentieth-century programs are inappropriate for late twentieth-century problems. Here I mention only a few. Both Dewey and Merriam had great confidence in the school's ability to shape attitudes and to transmit values. (In Dewey's view, the school was a refinery, which established "a purified medium of action," selecting the best attitudes and values, and transmitting them to youth in a program of permanent social reconstruction. Merriam saw schools as "the organised transmitters of group tradition and of group wisdom," and believed that "on the plastic mind of youth, group characters may be written almost indelibly." Today we recognize the socializing powers of other agencies—the family, the peer group, and the media among them—and see teachers, most of whom have little to offer that their clients urgently want (Musgrove, 1971), in a weakened position. There is also now a whole literature of criticism of the previous school socialization programs, denouncing them as a kind of "internal" cultural imperialism. Such as Michael Katz, who asserted that the fundamental structural characteristics of American education was that it was "universal, tax-supported, free, compulsory, bureaucratically arranged, class based, and racist" (Katz, 1971). Such is Robert A. Carlson, with his critique of Americanization through education (Carlson, 1975). Such are Raymond E. Callahan and Joel H. Spring, who saw that the organization and management of the American public school (what we might now call "the hidden curriculum") had less to do with John Dewey (and education for democracy), than with Henry Ford and Frederick W. Taylor (standardization, mass production, and scientific management) (Callahan, 1962; Spring, 1972). The exposure of the significance and the influence of the hidden curriculum (Jackson, 1968; Snyder, 1971) has raised new challenges for civic educators, who need to shape institutions and not just plan curricula. The radical school research of the ethnographers, for example, Willis (1975), and McLaren (1986), reveal schools as contested terrain, where cultural conflict occurs, and where resistance movements develop.

While it is a fair question to ask "how to facilitate newcomers to function as democratic citizens in a post-industrial country?", any suggestion of "how are *we* to socialize *them*?" would vitiate the enterprize from the beginning.

SOME POINTERS FROM THE ENGLISH EXPERIENCE

The story of political education in England has been told, at length, elsewhere (Brennan, 1981; Lister, 1987). Leaders and followers were produced by a dual system of schools—the Public boarding schools for the chosen few, the elementary schools for the majority. The hidden curriculum of textbooks, rituals, and celebrations, and of the organization of pupils and teachers, trained the first group for leadership roles (in the government, the Civil Service, the Army, the Empire and the Church), and the second group for follower or foremen roles. Explicit political education was consistently opposed in official statements, and by those (like Sir Cyril Norwood) from the elite sector. In both the elite and the mass schools, what was offered was civic *training* without civic *education*. Education involves open-minded attitudes, an awareness of alternatives, and skills requisite for autonomous action, and its horizon is beyond the present and the particular. Education cannot be achieved by combinations of propaganda and operant conditioning. Merriam wrote, in 1931: "An examination of the English school system in its relation to civic training reveals a general denial of any conscious attempt to engender national sentiment through the agency of education. In fact, one finds an indignant repudiation of any such unbecoming purpose" (Merriam, 1931). In fact, the history textbooks celebrated Britain's power and its constitution (and the progress of other nations was measured in terms of their proximity to that constitution); the world map on the classroom wall had London at its center, and it was painted pink—showing the Empire on which the sun never set; and each year the pupils celebrated Empire Day. The prefect system in the elite schools trained the few to give orders. The factory system of teaching and learning in the Elementary schools trained the majority to take them. Whereas in the United States, civic education was used to forge a new nation (the Americans), Britain had to be wary of nationalism, as such. Britain was a multi-national state, made up not just of the English, but also of the Celtic fringemen and women—the Welsh, the Scots, and the Irish. Such particularist nationalisms were a force for division and disintegration.

The wider loyalty of the Empire provided the cohesive force, as well as ample job opportunities to all those Celtic peoples who could prove so troublesome on English soil. Britain was also a multi-faith society, but here the possible tensions were reduced by the domination of a state church which aimed to be broad, tolerant, comprehensive, and accommodating, and to take the passion out of religion. (In 1956, for example, the Royal Navy, which recorded sailors' religion on their dog-tags—presumably for burial sorting purposes—included those registering as atheists and agnostics in the Church of England group). Within the school, religious education was compulsory, circumscribed, and low-status. The pointers which I want to take from the classic English experience are not the parts that now are one with Ninevah and Tyre (although the dual school system is not one of these elements), but the parts which relate to our present need for a kind of civic education which respects pluralism, and which could facilitate democracy and human development. The question is, how might we appeal to broader loyalties and create a more over-arching concept of citizenship? Can we see a shared vision, and identify a common purpose, for humanity, for the future? And can this be done without enemies and without war?

CIVIC EDUCATION AND PARTICIPATION

Civic education has always been concerned with allegiances and loyalties. Acceptance and support of the system, and confidence that issues may be addressed and problems overcome within the democratic framework, is a precondition of democratic society. Thus, the Programme for Political Education in England argued that it was a teacher's duty to uphold democratic *procedural* values—toleration, fairness, empathy, respect for truth and evidence, and respect for reasoning. It upheld an ideal of "democratic discourse" which would underpin and characterize democratic life. The question I now raise is: how are majorities and minorities to take part in the democratic discourse of postindustrial societies?

The participation question is central for two main reasons, one political and one pedagogical:

1. The political reason is that the ideals of modern democratic society

have moved on from an ideal of *representative* democracy (where the few rule and the many occasionally vote), to an ideal of *participatory* democracy (made up of active, participating citizens who take part in democratic life on an everyday basis) (Pateman, 1970).

2.   The pedagogical reason is that it is now commonly realized (by vocational trainers and by vanguard social educators), that if people are to acquire and develop the skills necessary for active participation, they need to have opportunities to observe, acquire, and practice those skills (Webb, 1980). This has led to calls for more activity-based pedagogy—under formulae like "Education for Capability," "a skills-based curriculum," and "process-based teaching and learning."

The search for more learner-active, teacher-learner and learner-learner interactive forms of teaching and learning, is promoted both by the proponents of "the new vocationalism," and by the new social educators (those working in areas like human rights education, multicultural education, development education, peace education, and environmental education of the ecological variety—what the Germans call "Ecopedagogy" (Beer, 1984)). Both use such techniques as problem-solving exercises, role play, simulations, and collaborative learning. Both raise serious challenges for traditional teaching and learning (teacher- and content-dominated schools [cloistered environments where knowledge is quietly confined, handed out, and handed back]).

The question I raise here is: As we now (curiously) find that formal education has a major mission to perform in post-industrial society, are the educational institutions we have inherited from classical industrial society sufficiently renovated and reconstructed to carry out that mission? Put another way: How do our educational institutions, as they now are, relate to the ideals of participatory democracy, and participatory teaching and learning?

THE NEW VOCATIONALISTS AND THE NEW EDUCATORS

John Dewey argued that, apart from relating the young to the wider society (the social culture), schools should relate the young to the work culture, and to the political culture. Today, much of education is out of alignment with the work culture and with the political culture—or, more precisely, with the work culture and the political culture of emergent post-industrial society. The New Vocationalists and the New Educators are two groups attempting to achieve realignments.

The New Vocationalists in Britain have criticized schools (and universities) for being excessively and exclusively academic, remote from the realities of the world of work, and for being indifferent, or hostile, towards the vocational and the practical. Government has increased its investment in *training* and in training schemes. The national Technical and Vocational Education Initiative has been the most grandiose of many schemes. New competencies appropriate to post-industrial society (such as computer literacy) are stressed. Activity-based learning is the means, and the goals include the promotion of self-confidence, creative thinking, and entrepreneurial skills. The *new training* has asserted itself against the *old education*.

The New Educators are the promoters of "the new educations" (human rights education, multicultural education, development education, peace education, and environmental education). Butts, Mehlinger, and Janowitz would recognize them as seeking possible programs to overcome the limitations of traditional civic education as they identified them—in particular, to formulate a program of education appropriate to societies which are multicultural, multi-faith, which create, and are threatened by, supranational issues (particularly concerning resources and the environment), and which are globally interdependent. The New Educators set new, ambitious aims for civic education (Lister, 1987). The following aims, taken from the syllabus of a Leicestershire Community College, are typical.:

1. To encourage students to set their thinking about the modern world within a global framework.
2. To foster among students an allegiance to humankind in general as against an allegiance to national, local or sectional interests.
3. To help students become aware of the widening gap between the richer and poorer countries and of the consequences likely to follow if global inequalities are not remedied.
4. To encourage respect for cultural diversity.
5. To help students identify and respect those values shared by humankind in general. (Selby, 1980)

These aims are making great demands in a country where the world view of the traditional school was Anglocentric, nationalist, imperialist/paternalist, monocultural, and assumed the superiority of British values.

The "new educations" have nine important features, all of which distinguish them from conventional social education, and most of which distinguish them from traditional civic education:

1. They believe that knowledge should have a social purpose, aimed to ameliorate the human condition. (Thus, keyworks have titles like *Learning for Change in World Society* and *Teaching Geography for a Better World*) (Richardson, 1979; Fien & Gerber, 1986).
2. The curriculum should contain, and confront, major global issues—

war and peace; poverty and development; human rights; and the challenges of multicultural societies and of an interdependent world.

3. Learning must include the learning of skills (and not just knowledge content).

4. Learning needs an action dimension in order to facilitate the acquisition and development of skills.

5. Collaborative learning should be encouraged. (Manuals exist to support this—such as *The Book of Cooperative Games* and *Learning Together for a Change*).

6. Education must be affective as well as cognitive.

7. Education must recognize, respect, and celebrate pluralism and diversity.

8. The curriculum should have international and global perspectives. The ideal is that of *Global Teacher: Global Learner*—the title of a recent keywork. (Selby & Pike, 1988).

9. Education should have a future perspective (as well as a past and a present perspective). Students should be encouraged to see the present as an operational future and to consider the possibilities of "alternative futures."

A lot of the aims and features of the "new educations" are elements of, or—at least—agenda items for, a program of *Civic Education for Positive Pluralism*.

CONSERVATIVE RESTORATION AND CULTURAL REVOLUTION

In Britain now we are living in a political period which is part conservative restoration and part cultural revolution. The surprise of the cultural revolution is that the radical value-shift has come, not from the Green movement, but from the Right. The New Right was first driven by economists following the tradition of Milton Friedman and the Chicago school, and part of the radical value-shift has been the assertion of the supremacy of economics over politics (Lister, 1980). New Right economists are often libertarians. New Right philosophers, educationists, and pamphleteers are more interested in substantive questions, and in preserving traditional knowledge and "real subjects." They favor history and they oppose political education. They are hostile to the New Educators, and have sustained a consistent critique of "the new educations."

The early focus of the critique was *peace studies*. In 1982, Digby Anderson suggested that the inclusion of peace studies in the curriculum was a sign of a bad school (Anderson, 1982). In 1984, John Marks claimed that peace studies were "propaganda for defenselessness," and he argued that "lessons or courses labelled 'peace studies' should find no place in schools"; that "politically contentious subjects should normally form no part of the curriculum for pupils below the age of 16 (the school-leaving age)"; and that "public funding should be withdrawn from organisations promoting 'peace studies' or 'peace education'" (Marks, 1984). Also in 1984, Caroline Cox (now Baroness Cox in the House of Lords) and Roger Scruton asserted that "The movement for peace studies in schools is part of a trend towards the politicisation of education, involving both a lowering of intellectual standards and the assumption of foregone conclusions . . . . Peace studies . . . is all too often not an educational exercise, but an exercise in political propaganda . . . often aimed at implanting unilateralist sentiment in the minds of people young enough to receive it uncritically" (Cox & Scruton, 1984).

Thus, peace educators were presented as being pacifists, as believing in "one-sided disarmament," as introducing the Campaign for Nuclear Disarmament into schools, and into the school curriculum. Selected evidence was presented to support these arguments.

A later target of the critique was *world studies* (and *development education*). In 1985, Roger Scruton, Angela Ellis-Jones, and Dennis O'Keefe referred to world studies as "the new, highly politicised subject of 'World Studies'" (Scruton et al., 1985). They accused "the new educations" of practicing indoctrination, the features of which included the dominance of subject and method by foregone conclusions; the assimilation of those conclusions to a program of action; and the closing of the mind to argument, evidence and alternatives. Also in 1985, Roger Scruton accused world studies and development education of preaching propaganda for a cause— "the cause of Third Worldism." In his view "World Studies is less a subject than an impetuous rush to impose on children the 'global perspective'. . . ." As for its process-based pedagogy—this seeks "to replace serious knowledge with . . . infantile, manipulative games" (Scruton, 1985). It is an odd achievement of the world studies educators that they have managed to be attacked, at one and the same time, by Scruton for being part of "the Left-wing educational establishment," and by the Left for being apologists for capitalism (Hatcher, 1983).

The rhetorical debate stimulated by the critics of "the new educations" is characterized by a lot of heat, little light, and virtually no evidence drawn from observed practice. Although it may be the case that all great debates are, by their very nature, rhetorical, how the rhetoric relates to the reality is an important question. We need to be aware of the rhetoric-reality gap. For example, a researcher of peace studies in schools, working at the height of this debate, had a major problem in finding any practice to research (Green, 1986). More important politically, though, is that persuasive rhetoric influences policy, programs and practice. The New Right has accused the New Educators of lacking patriotism. They have asserted the importance of traditional subjects, and traditional forms of traditional subjects. (For example, they like history but oppose "the new history") (Beattie, 1987). The proposed National Curriculum, which is the corner-stone of the government's educational reform, is a reassertion of traditional subjects. As it stands, it is not very supportive of any proposed program of civic education for positive pluralism.

MULTICULTURALISM

It is not surprising that we should witness attempts to achieve civic cohesion through imposed uniformity in the present period. Post-industrial societies have strong tendencies towards diversity and pluralism, and towards regional and local centers of power (Toffler, 1980; Naisbitt, 1982). They are polygeneric and multicultural, and their populations are both geographically and socially mobile. They have moved beyond the separation of racial groups (reservations for Aboriginals in Australia, for Indians in North America, townships and "homelands" for Blacks in South Africa). They have moved beyond policies of *assimilation*, whereby newcomers were accepted on condition that they left their culture behind them, and took on the culture of the receiving country (or, rather, the dominant culture within the receiving society). That is not to say that in Britain now you could not find individuals and groups who would subscribe to Lord Macaulay's aim, stated in 1835, for Indian education in British India—to create people who were "Indian in blood and colour, but English in taste, morals and intellect," and use it as an aim for the education of ethnic minorities in contemporary Britain. Again, though, such people are being counter-cultural, in looking back to "Victorian values," and not looking forward to the values of post-industrial society.

Beyond *assimilation*, and beyond *integration*, a common educational policy approach in Britain now is *multiculturalism*. The National Committee of Inquiry into the Education of Children from Ethnic Minority Groups, chaired by Lord Swann, took this position. Its report, *Education for All*, included a section on political education which supported the political literacy approach recommended by the National Programme for Political Education. It advocated the encouragement of political skills and active participation, as well as resistance against some views and attitudes (including racism) which were unacceptable in a democracy (Swann, 1985). Some have criticized Swann for underrecognizing the factors of racism and of social class. Wendy Ball, for example, asserts that "the Swann Committee has ignored the material basis to racism and its relationship to class interest" (Ball, 1986). Trevor Carter, a Black commentator on Swann, writes: "*Swann* has been rejected as racist by some black individuals. I consider this view to be misguided . . . Whilst not agreeing with every word of the report, it is certainly more useful to regard its recommendations as constructive than as a slap in the face" (Carter, 1985).

It is usual for local education authorities to issue policy statements on, and guidelines for, multicultural education in their schools. (There are, of course, gaps between guidelines and practice.) Case study research in one authority suggested that it "(had) failed to consider the complex processes of curriculum innovation and (had) expected its policy and related initiatives, per se, to function as change-agents" (Troyna & Ball, 1985).

Some critics see the pluralism of multicultural education as a weak form of pluralism which tries to "do good by stealth," attempts to diffuse the significance of *race*, evades the issue of *class inequalities*, and which embeds approaches to the education of ethnic minority children in a range of "racially inexplicit" programs (Troyna, 1984).

Recently there has developed a more active approach—anti-racist education. This seeks to confront and combat racism in schools and society. It makes race issues explicit and it supports racism-awareness programs for teachers. Anti-racism (like "the new educations") has provoked critiques, and set off a backlash (mainly, but not only, from the New Right). A recent volume, *Anti-Racism—an Assault on Education and Value*, includes critiques by the philosopher Anthony Flew, and the pamphleteers John Marks and Baroness Cox (all now identified with New Right thinking), but it also includes a lament by the Socialist Tom Hastie—"the skills of the historian are being flagrantly disregarded by the race industry, skills such as the examination of evidence to ascertain (1) its authenticity, and (2) its truthfulness" (Palmer, 1986).

The debate, as with the debate about the other "new educations," is characterized by heat, not light, by assertions and counter-assertions, not by the reasoned argument and the scrupulous search, and careful display, of evidence. *Some* of the claims of both sides might be justified—for example, the claim of the anti-racists that some of the *structures* of present British society are racially biased (in education, housing, and jobs), and the claim of the anti-racists that propaganda techniques, which disregard reasoning and evidence, are commonly used.

As with the other "new educations," the government's response—with the National Curriculum: 5–13, made law by the Education Reform Act of 1988, has been to assert traditional knowledge forms (History and/or Geography) and to marginalize multicultural education. (The Education Act also appears to marginalize ethnic minority languages).

Our predicament, then, is that the more radical of the New Educators claim that our society is not positively pluralist, and the government response seems to confirm them in their belief. The problem for those arguing for positive pluralism is how *that* could become the dominant culture, and how a framework, which could facilitate peaceful social change, might be found.

SOME PLURALIST DILEMMAS

Two classic political questions about pluralism are: How far can pluralism go? and, Who runs the pluralism? However, the main problem of pluralism, as seen by pluralists such as Robert A. Dahl, is that the pluralist ideal can be undermined by the realities of structural inequalities. David Held goes as far as to assert that classic pluralism is unable to confront issues raised by the possibility of "systematic imbalances in the distribution of power, influence and resources" (Held, 1987). Such structural and systematic inequalities might relate to social class, gender, race, or location (see, for example, Harvey, 1973). Dahl has succinctly stated the need for pluralism and the problems of pluralism in a paragraph:

> In a political system as large as a country, a plurality of relatively independent organisations is necessary not only for mutual control but also for the democratic process. Applied on the scale of a country, the democratic process in turn makes relatively independent organisations both possible and inevitable. Yet a problem arises—which I have called the problem of democratic pluralism—because while necessary, desirable, and inevitable in a democratic order, organisational pluralism may also play a part in stabilizing inequalities, deforming civic consciousness, distorting the public agenda, and alienating final control over the public agenda by the citizen body (Dahl, 1982).

For Dahl, certain kinds of liberty pose more of a threat to democracy than does the demand for equality. He refers to the rise, in the United States, of "a new system of commercial and industrial capitalism that automatically generated vast inequalities of wealth, income, status and power. These inequalities were in turn a result of liberty of a certain kind—liberty to accumulate unlimited economic resources and to organise economic activity into hierarchically governed enterprises." Elsewhere, in arguing the cause of procedural democracy, he states that "many hierarchic or meritocratic arrangements would have to give way to procedural democracy" (Dahl, 1979), and, in detail, he explores the case for democracy (Dahl, 1985).

In this latter work he records: "a system of government Americans view as intolerable in governing the state has come to be accepted as desirable in governing economic enterprises." I have cited Dahl at length in order to show that one of the main proponents of pluralism is sensitively aware of pluralism's problems. We might add to the list of dilemmas the problems posed by cultural pluralism in modern societies. Theorists like Dahl, Hirsch, and Rawls are troubled by the *distribution* of wealth and power in society, and seek a moral base for the political and economic order. These are classic concerns and are worth recording at a time when "the political theory of possessive individualism," which C. B. MacPherson thought inadequate to provide a valid theory of political obligation, is now in the ascendant (MacPherson, 1962). In the UK, at least, economics now rules politics, and we are in need of a revival of civic consciousness, and a reassertion of the primacy of the political sphere. The development of a program of positive pluralism, guided by the ideals of human rights, may help us achieve these aims.

SOME HUMAN RIGHTS HOPES

Human rights have much to offer the construction of a framework for Civic Education for Positive Pluralism. They go beyond the limitations, and narrow focus, of traditional civic education (with its stresses on central and local *government, national* allegiance, and the *political* sphere), as they include *supranational* concerns for *economic* and *social* rights, and for *cultural* rights. The assertion of basic *human* rights—that is, the claim that people have rights because of their humanity (and not because they are part of any particular political, social, or legal order), helps us in a search for the kind of civic education we now need—a civic education which goes beyond nationalism. Basic rights and fundamental freedoms are one of the twin notions on which human rights are built. The other notion is fair treatment and due process. These procedural values of human rights overlap with the procedural values of democratic education—freedom, toleration, fairness, and respect for reasoning (Lister, 1984; Lister, 1986).

Human rights have the advantage that contributions to their development have come, and can come, from a range of cultures and role-models of human rights activists, and are provided by a variety of nationalities. They also offer an ideal of *humanity* (rather than the ideal of a *political* system). Sufficient pilot projects have been carried out, and adequate materials now exist, in the field of human rights education for us to be able to launch practical programs in schools.

As in many countries, some human rights are embedded in the law (either in a Bill of Rights, or in other legislation); law-related education can make a strong contribution.

CIVIC EDUCATION FOR A HUMAN FUTURE

Traditional forms of civic education have worked for uniformity and for nationalism. The school in modern society has usually promulgated national history, national literature, national language, and nationalized religion (albeit in some instances—as in the case, on occasions, of the three World Powers—as a secularized *faith*). Of the known models of political education, one—*political socialization*—is played out, and another, *liberation pedagogy*—offers long lists of complaints and few practical programs (Giroux, 1983). We are now searching for a civic education that can work for diversity and humanity (Could it work in Ireland, in Israel, in South Africa? might be an appropriate test), which is more dynamic than the old political socialization approaches, and more practical than the rhetoric of liberation pedagogy. It is the argument of this paper that only by carrying out such an ambitious enterprize can we properly answer more limited questions— like, how might immigrants from less democratic cultures be helped to function in more democratic cultures? How might the young be encouraged to espouse democratic values, when they are influenced by less democratic agencies (families, peer groups, and economic system)? And how can we, in a nonviolent fashion, confront structural inequalities (based on social class, gender, race, and geographical location) in our present societies?

RECONSTRUCTING CIVIC EDUCATION: SOME PILOT PROJECTS

It has been the argument of this paper that in our emergent post-industrial society we need civic education, and we need a *reconstructed* civic education. Some pioneers have launched pilot projects, which might be viewed as attempts to promote this reconstruction. Although these have been development areas, rather than research fields, there is some research evidence, from case studies of particular projects, which informs us about the problems, as well as the potential, of these innovatory programmes. Robert Stradling (1984) carried out a systematic study, using classroom observation and interviews, of the teaching of global issues, such as nuclear weapons and the Third World. He saw one problem, that of "capturing the interest of 14–16-year-olds on issues which they perceive as having no relevance to their own lives, and on topics such as 'The Third World' or 'North–South,' which are both geographically and conceptually remote." Judy Dyson (1986), carried out case-study research on Third World Studies in a secondary school. Her pilot project focussed on whether the demands of traditional examinations (with their stress on content knowledge) might be reconciled with the philosophy of development educators (with their stress on affective objectives, and their aim of encouraging new ways of viewing the world). Her conclusion on this question was hopeful. Some of the teachers on the project, though, saw problems: "The pupils lack a concept of the scale of the problems and issues. . . ." and "The pupils find it boring and too hard. They come with a limited set of stereotypes and keep them. It's all too distant" (Dyson, 1986).

She researched pupils' images of other countries and peoples. She reported: "In every case of people identified by the pupils as 'different from us,' comments on why they were unlike us revolved around negative perceptions of life in those areas." Overall, though she found that pupils on the project did "show a predisposition to 'a global perspective,' which the course succeeded in building on." Stephanie Duczek (1984) carried out case-study research on a pilot project on Peace Studies at Atlantic College—a Sixth–Form (16–19) college situated in Wales. She found some excellent work by the students—including the mounting of an outstanding exhibition, for the local population, on human rights. Although she discovered that some of the major issues concerned with peace, development, and human rights could have a depressing effect on students, particularly because of their apparently inaccessible and intractable nature, she also noted that students did find ways of participating in, and affecting, human rights issues, through organizations such as Amnesty International. Jeremy Cunningham (1986) carried out case-study research on a pilot project on teaching and learning about human rights in a secondary school. He found high student interest in topics like racism in South Africa; racism in Brixton, England; arbitrary arrest in the USSR; and mistreatment in Northern Ireland. Cunningham's findings concerning the possibilities and problems of this pilot project on human rights sometimes echo those of Dyson, particularly where problems are concerned:

> Interviews with those teachers who had been responsible for writing the course . . . gave some insights into its deficiencies and successes. The areas touching on torture and personal rights were seen to be very successful, generating discussion, controversy, and motivation. Racism was also successful in these terms, but a number of staff were very uneasy about the forces unleashed by open discussion. Some retreated into an attempt to teach attitudes. . . . A section on culture and religions was seen to be a failure. . . . A more general criticism was that students felt themselves bombarded with values and problems. Some actually felt guilty at their powerlessness to affect a situation like Apartheid in South Africa, and had a sense that they were being taught about it 'in order to feel responsible for it' (Cunningham, 1986).

He noted that a common criticism of this type of course is that "far too much time is spent on *problems*, without giving students the chance to think what they would *like* to happen in the future." In other words, such courses may be weakened by too much attention to problematizing and social pathology, and too little attention to positive examples of change, to skill development and the encouragement of hope.

I have selected these pilot projects as they do afford some research evidence, based upon observed practice, in fields which have been characterized more by rhetorical debates, of assertions and counter-assertions. The reconstruction of civic education is not an easy task and, like educational reform in general, it needs more practical reformers (and not so many preachers and prophets). The identification of possibilities, and problems, by researchers observing pilot projects, helps us to find a practical program for a way ahead.

CIVIC EDUCATION FOR THE FUTURE

I have tried to review what has happened in civic education in Britain in recent decades, and to analyze what is happening now. Essentially we have seen traditional provision challenged, first by the political literacy movement, and then by the avant-garde "new educations," which, in turn, have provoked a conservative reaction and an attempt by the government, through legislation, to restore the traditional knowledge forms. This action and reaction of extremes may be the educational neurosis of a society at the end of one era (classic industrial society), and struggling to adapt towards a new era (post-industrial society). The riddle for education, in general, and for civic education, in particular, is how to relate the two in a positive and productive fashion. Civic education needs to maintain social continuity, it needs to achieve social cohesion, and it also needs to facilitate social change. For me, the most necessary project now lies in the field of education for modern citizenship. Such a project needs to identify classical models of citizenship (Athens and Rome); to clarify the key elements of early modern citizenship (the American Revolution and the French Revolution); and outline the main features of modern citizenship—that is, the kind of citizenship appropriate to our own times. For the modern citizen in Britain this must include British, European, and global dimensions (with rights and responsibilities in the first two categories, and responsibilities, at least, in the third category). Because, as Howard D. Mehlinger (1977) put it, "the world is different from what it was . . . ," we need to construct a civic education appropriate to a new world, and we need to encourage a new world view, which will include the local, the national, and the international. Our relative success or failure in the key area of education for modern citizenship may well determine whether the next decade in British education, and British society, is characterized by pathology or by progress.

REFERENCES

Anderson, D. (1982). *Detecting bad schools*. London: Social Affairs Unit.
Ball, W. (1986). *Policy innovation on multicultural education in "Eastshire" local education authority*. Coventry: Centre for Research in Ethnic Relations, University of Warwick.

Beattie, A. (1987). *History is peril*. London: Centre for Policy Studies.

Beer, W. (1984). *Ökopädagogik* [in Pedagogy]. Weinheim: Beltz.

Brennan, T. (1981). *Education and democracy*. Cambridge: Cambridge University Press.

Brown, B. F. (1977). *Education for responsible citizenship*. New York: McGraw–Hill.

Butts, R. F. (1980). *The revival of civic learning*. Bloomington: Phi Delta Kappa.

Callahan, R. E. (1962). *Education and the cult efficiency*. Chicago: University of Chicago.

Carlson, R. A. (1975). *The quest for conformity: Americanisation through education*. New York: Wiley.

Carter, T. (1985). The Swann Report: A Black perspective. In B. Taylor (Ed.), *Multicultural education for all*. England: University of Exeter.

Cox, C. & Scruton, R. (1984). *Peace studies: A critical survey*. London: Institute for European Defence and Strategic Studies.

Cunningham, J. (1986). *Human rights in a secondary school*. York: University of York.

Dahl, R. A. (1979). Procedural democracy. In R. Laslett & J. Fishlin (Eds.), *Philosophy, politics and society*. Oxford: Blackwell.

Dahl, R. A. (1982). *Dilemmas of pluralist democracy*. New Haven: Yale University Press.

Dahl, R. A. (1985). *A preface to economic democracy*. Cambridge: Polity Press.

Dewey, J. (1916). *Democracy and education*. New York: MacMillan.

Duczek, S. (1984). *The peace studies project: A case study*. York: University of York.

Dyson, J. (1986). *Development education for the 14–16 age–group*. York: University of York.

Fien, J. & Gerber, R. (1986). *Teaching Geography for a better world*. Brisbane: Jacaranda Press.

Giroux, H. A. (1983). *Theory and resistance in education*. London: Heinemann Educational.

Green, K. (1986). *Peace education in the UK*. Unpublished master's thesis. Bradford: University of Bradford.

Harvey, D. (1973). *Social justice and the city*. London: Arnold.

Hatcher, R. (1983). The construction of world studies. In *Multicultural education*, 2(1), 23–35.

Held, D. (1987). *Models of democracy*. Cambridge: Polity Press.

Jackson, P. W. (1968). *Life in classrooms*. New York: Holt, Rinehardt & Winston.

Janowitz, M. (1983). *The reconstruction of patriotism*. Chicago: University of Chicago.

Katz, M. (1971). *Class bureaucracy and schools*. New York: Praeger.

Lee, S. M. (1987). Political education and civic education: The British perspective and the Hong Kong perspective. York: PERU, University of York.

Lister, I. (1980). The New Right on education: Working paper. York: PERU, University of York.

Lister, I. (1984). *Teaching and learning about human rights*. Strasbourg: Council of Europe.

Lister, I. (1986). Human rights: A case for political education. York: PERU, University of York.

Lister, I. (1987a). Political education in England: 1974–1984. In *Teaching politics*, 16(1), 3–25, January 1987, Politics Association.

Lister, I. (1987b). Contemporary developments in political education: Global and international approaches. In C. Harber (Ed.), *Political education in Britain*. Lewis: Falmer Press.

McLaren, P. (1986). *Schooling as ritual performance*. London: Routledge & Kegan Paul.

MacPherson, C. B. (1962). *Possessive individualism*. Oxford: Oxford University Press.

Marks, J. (1984). *Peace studies in our schools*. London: Women & Families for Defence.

Mehlinger, H. D. (1977). In B. F. Brown (Ed.), Education for responsible citizenship. New York: McGraw–Hill, pp. 69–82.

Merriam, C. E. (1931). *The making of citizens*. Chicago: University of Chicago Press.

Musgrove, F. (1971). *Patterns of power and authority in English education*. London: Methuen.

Naisbitt, J. (1982). *Megatrends*. London: MacDonald.

Osborne, K. (1986). A Canadian approach to political education: A working paper. York: PERU Documentation Service, University of York.

Osborne, K. (1987). Political education and participant citizenship: A working paper. York: PERU, University of York.

Palmer, F. (Ed.) (1986). *Antiracism—An assault on education and value.* London: Sherwood Press.

Pateman, C. (1970). *Participation and democratic theory.* Cambridge: Cambridge University Press.

Peters, R. (1988). *Thriving on chaos.* London: MacMillan.

Reid, A. (1984). *Curriculum development and political education.* Unpublished master's thesis. University of York, York.

Richardson, R. (1979). *Learning for change in world society.* London: World Studies Project.

Schon, D. A. (1971). *Beyond the stable state.* London: Temple Smith.

Selby, D. (1980). World studies syllabus for Groby Community College, Groby: Leicestershire.

Selby, D. & Pike, G. (1988). *Global teacher, global learner.* London: Hodder & Stoughton.

Scruton, R. (1985). *Education and indoctrination.* London: Education Research Centre.

Scruton, R. (1985). *World studies: Education or indoctrination?* London: Institute for European Defence and Strategic Studies.

Snyder, B. R. (1971). *The hidden curriculum.* New York: Knopf.

Spring, J. H. (1972). *Education and the rise of the corporate state.* Boston: Beacon Press.

Stradling, R. (1984). *Teaching controversial issues.* London: Arnold.

Swann, L. (1985). *Education for all.* London: HMSO.

Ting, A. (1987). *The implementation of civic education in England and Hong Kong.* Unpublished master's thesis. University of York, York.

Toffler, A. (1980). *The third wave.* London: Collins.

Troyna, B. (1984). *"Policy entrepreneurs" and the development of multi–ethnic policies.* Coventry: Centre for Research in Ethnic Relations, University of Warwick.

Troyna, B. & Ball, W. (1985). *Views from the chalk face: School responses to an LEA's policy on multicultural education.* Coventry: Centre for Research in Ethnic Relations, University of Warwick.

Webb, K. (1980). *Political education and the development of political skills.* Unpublished master's thesis. University of York, York.

Willis, P. (1975). *Learning to labour.* Farnborough: Saxon House.

Willmot, E. (1987). *Australia: The last experiment.* Sydney: Australian Broadcasting Corporation.

III GOVERNMENT INSTITUTIONS AND POLICIES FOR DEMOCRATIC EDUCATION

The chapters in the previous section were in substantial agreement that we should not expect schools, even when guided by national standards or curricula, to set programs which will insure the successful delivery and absorption of citizenship education. Should, or can we, then turn to government to intervene and assume this responsibility? The section which follows presents two cases, and one evaluative essay which address this question.

In the first, Charles Ungerleider traces the development of government policy in Canada: from its commitment to binational and bilingual rights, to the establishment of a National Strategy on Race Relations, to the embracing of official multiculturalism. Given the unwavering Canadian commitment to integration with diversity, this case presents an intriguing test of whether such indirect efforts are sufficient to accommodate new citizens. Although his assessment is necessarily tentative, Ungerleider suggests that their seeming successes are superficial, and not very permanent. Native populations continue to fare much better. Nonetheless, the case for consistent government support, spread over a variety of institutions, is strengthened by his research.

Taking the direction of Ungerleider's analysis one step further, is Jerome Black's study of government assistance programs. Besides providing an intriguing view into the use which minorities make of such programs, Black's investigation indicates how minimal the effects of nonpolitical services are on explicitly political behavior. However better off minorities may be for having access to bread-and-butter support, as well as some ethnic cultural activities, we cannot assume that there will be spillover into the political sphere for at least a generation.

Taken together, the two Canadian studies underscore a key role which government may, and perhaps should, play, but rarely does; namely the obvious but elusive role of assuming comprehensive leadership for programs and policies designed to promote the integration of minorities. Whatever else we might have gleaned from the research presented here, we cannot help but be struck by the pervasiveness of societal factors that contribute to the minorities' isolation—in the neighborhoods, in the churches, in the schools, in the workplace, and in politics. Looking to any one to both convey the concepts of democratic education, and combat the resistance of other forces in the society is, quite simply, unrealistic. It is too easy to pass the responsibility around, and back, so that it is never fully assumed or assessed. And, although the reversion to government as the solver of all problems is as unrealistic as the dependence on single nongovernmental institutions, it is not out of line to expect government to play a major role in coordinating efforts and expertise in implementing nationally defined programs.

Summarizing the direct challenges to government, and the indirect challenge to nongovernmental sources of education, Marilyn Hoskin's essay takes care to note that the constraints of any nation's history are major factors which are often overlooked in the quest to respond to contemporary challenges. Within such constraints as war and ethnic rivalries, governments have just as often wavered, rather than seized opportunities to define and implement multicultural policy. Perhaps because they are historically committed to be responsible to popular preferences, they have more frequently modified policy assumptions, legal directives, and socioeconomic programs only marginally and erratically; thereby proving insensitive to the needs of minorities in the short run, and to the health of democracy in the long run.

As the essay notes, however, the dominant presence of government as symbolic leader has meant that nonsupport or inconsistent support has in fact represented negative evaluations of minorities. Those evaluations, in turn, have made minorities' involvement in the democratic system understandably tepid. What continues to be central, and at this point unchanging, is the continuing reluctance of democratic governments to lead in an issue where leadership is likely to be the only real answer to a growing problem.

9 Socialization for Democratic Citizenship: the Development of the Canadian Infrastructure

Charles S. Ungerleider

CANADIAN SURVIVAL AND IMMIGRATION

From the earliest European settlement to the present, survival has been a dominant theme for Canadians. Canadians have struggled to establish and maintain community in a territory which is vast, and on a landscape which is harsh. The creation of Canada itself was difficult. Forging unity among regions with vastly different interests was an act of uncommon political compromise; maintaining it has been no less difficult. Confronted daily by the proximity of its southern neighbor, Canada has walked a fine line between resisting the United States' way of life, and being engulfed by it.

Notwithstanding the opinion of its native peoples, Canada would not have survived if it were not for immigrants. The Canadian state was forged in 1867 by immigrants from Britain and France and their offspring. Canada's growth and development as a nation is also closely linked with immigration. Canadian immigration policy has served five purposes for the past century (Harney, 1988). According to this viewpoint, Canada has used its immigrants to:

1. Occupy the country in sufficient numbers to discourage the expansionary tendencies of the American colossus.
2. Protect the Pacific Rim from heavy Asian immigration.
3. Create economies of scale and a rational East–West axis for an independent polity and viable economy.
4. Maintain a British hegemony by combating separatism, whether in its

149

Prairie Metis and Indian form of the last century, or in its Quebecian form in this one, and to counter the revanche des berceaux of the Canadiens against the British conquest.

5.   Foster an image of Canada as a new place of opportunity, a country of potential greatness, and "a land of second chance," characterized by the fairness of British institutions and now by the civility of state-sponsored democratic pluralism in the form of official multicultural-ism. (Harney, 1988; p. 53)

During the 20th century more than 4 million immigrants, accounting for approximately 21 percent of the population growth, came to Canada. The largest contribution of immigration to population growth occurred during the first decade of this century, when it rose to 44 percent.

Until the late 1960s, most of Canada's immigration came from Europe. In 1950, for example, almost 85 percent of Canada's immigrants were of European origin. But, by the 1980s, the proportion of new Canadian immigrants that came from Europe had dropped to 28.6 percent.

As immigration from European sources diminished, immigration from Africa, Asia, South and Latin America, and the Caribbean increased. Thus, between 1980 and 1986, immigration from these sources accounted for 63.43 percent of all newcomers to Canada.

Changes in immigration have been accompanied by changes in the ethnic composition of Canada. At the time of Confederation, the British and French were the numerically dominant ethnic groups, comprising 60.5 percent and 31.1 percent of Canada's population respectively. By 1981, the percentage of people tracing their origins to Britain and France had declined to 40.2 percent and 26.7 percent. The remaining 33.1 percent of the population was made up of people who were neither British nor French.

Although immigration has always figured prominently in the growth and development of Canada, recent trends have placed increasing importance upon immigration. Canada's total fertility rate is currently 1.7. This rate is too low to prevent a decline in Canada's population without continued immigration. In fact, there is growing concern that Canada's population must not only be maintained, but must actually increase if the economic and social infrastructure is to be supported. A static or declining population would result in a decrease in the standard of living for all Canadians, including reductions in the services and social programs which currently serve the population.

Statistics Canada has set an annual population growth rate of 1 percent per year as the minimum increase needed to sustain the level of services and programs Canadians currently enjoy. Assuming that the present total fertility rate continues at 1.7, the annual net immigration levels that are needed to achieve a 1 percent growth in population would be approximately

300,000 in the year 2001, 400,000 in the year 2015, and 700,000 in the year 2050 (Employment and Immigration Canada, 1987).

To some, the changing origins of Canada's immigrants challenge the survival of Canada's democratic institutions. The majority of immigrants of previous generations came primarily from sociopolitical contexts similar to Canada's. Although different in their operation, and in the evolution of their institutions, the British, French, and United States political systems trace their origins to the political thinking of the European Enlightenment of the 17th and 18th centuries. While it may prove no more difficult than the socialization of native-born Canadians, the socialization of immigrants from countries that do not share the democratic traditions of the Enlightenment is a concern for policy makers and practitioners within and outside of government, since among the prerequisites of citizenship in Canada are the requirements that immigrants have:

- An adequate knowledge of either the English or French language;
- An understanding of Canada's political systems, structure of government, history, geography, people, industries, economy, etc.; and
- Knowledge of the rights, privileges, and responsibilities of citizenship.

One of the assumptions made by those concerned about the socialization of immigrants for democratic citizenship is that the adaptation of immigrants will be impeded by dissimilarities between the civic cultures of the country of origin and Canada. Two studies by Black (1982, 1987) have bearing upon this and related issues.

Black (1982) studied the political activity levels of British and non-British immigrants by gathering comparative data on the political involvement of immigrants and Canadian-born individuals. He wanted to ascertain whether Canadian-born individuals are more politically active than British immigrants who, in turn, are more active than non-British foreign born. Black found that neither the British-born immigrants nor the non-British born immigrants lagged behind the Canadian-born, "denying the notion that immigration is debilitating for subsequent political activism." He also found "no corroboration for the idea that greater difference between systems is a penalizing factor for the non-British foreign born" (p. 14).

In another study, Black investigated the "relationship between immigrants' past political experiences and their subsequent involvement in the life of their new polity" (1987, p. 731). He questioned whether, if transferability did occur, would it be observed among those whose previous experiences had been in a polity similar to the Canadian system. He found that "not only is there substantial transference, but *transference does much to explain interest in Canadian politics among immigrants*" (Black's emphasis). Furthermore, he found that there was little distinction between British and non-British immigrants, leading him to observe that "the politically involved seem quite capable of bringing their earlier experiences to bear regardless of country of origin" (p. 745).

A second and related concern is the issue of cultural maintenance among immigrants. Investigators have used a variety of models to represent the process of adaptation of host societies to immigration. Newman (1975) distinguishes among three models. The assimilation model posits that immigrant groups will conform to the host society, shedding the identities which may have initially distinguished them from the host society. The melting pot model suggests that both the identity of the host society, and the identifies of immigrant groups are transformed into a "new" identity. The multicultural model suggests that all groups, whether they are established or recent arrivals, are able to retain their own identities (After Newman, 1975).

Berry (1984) approaches the issue of adaptation as the intersection of two questions: "Is it considered of value to maintain one's own distinctive identity and cultural group characteristics?" and "Is it considered to be of value to maintain positive relationships between my group and others within the society?" Integration is the consequence of affirmative responses to both questions. Assimilation is the consequence when immigrants who do not wish to maintain their cultural identities increasingly participate in the larger society. Alienation is the probable consequence for those individuals who wish to maintain their cultural identities but who are denied access to full participation in the larger society. And anomie is the likely result for those who do not wish to retain their cultural identities, and who are prevented from enjoying full participation in the dominant society.

There are a number of questions regarding the democratic socialization of immigrants. Two central questions are: How is it that immigrants learn about the rights and responsibilities which citizenship entails? Can the rights and responsibilities be acquired without a loss of the identities immigrants bring with them?

SCHOOLING, IDENTITY, AND DEMOCRACY

In this paper, I shall examine how Canadian schools have attended to the socialization of immigrants for democratic citizenship, and how they have affected cultural maintenance. How does the social system of the classroom affect the way students judge themselves, and how they treat other people. I am asserting that there is a relationship between the conditions of social participation in the classroom, and the identities of the people who participate in the social system, and the way they judge and treat others.

Before going further, it is probably a good idea to explain the process by which identities are formed and developed. Identities are formed and developed from the point at which individuals recognize that they are separate from the environment, and from others in their environment. At that point they become participants in the process of social interaction. Increasing separation from the environment is accompanied by increasing ability to control the environment, and influence others in the environment. Over time, the ability to choose the goals toward which one strives, and the means of achieving those goals, become basic dimensions of a person's identity. As they mature, people come to expect that their behavior can determine the achievement of the goals they seek (Seeman, 1959).

Individuals approach one another to validate assumptions they hold about their own identities. If the responses they receive are consistent over time, their identities will be well integrated.

> To the extent that the society in which one lives is stable and well-organized, the pursuit of a clearly defined career is greatly facilitated. But when participating in societies in which the component norms are not mutually consistent, it becomes progressively more difficult for any (hu)man to integrate his (or her) various images into a single unit. When the differences are too great, a (hu)man may suffer from inner conflicts, and at times the pain may become so acute that he (or she) may suffer dissociation (Shibutani, 1961, p. 246).

People who feel that they are set apart from themselves are considered self-estranged (Fromm, 1955). Such people sometimes feel disembodied in the sense that they feel they are required to present themselves to others in ways that do not accurately reflect the definitions they have of their own identities (Laing, 1965, p. 66–93).

Social interaction is an essential process in identity formation, because people learn who they are from the responses of others to them (Cooley, 1922). When people share common definitions of the situation, and hold mutual expectations for one another's behavior, they can interact successfully, mutually reinforcing one another's identities.

People's identities are subject to enhancement or reduction as a consequence of their perception of the discrepancy between who they are, and what they may become. When people can voluntarily select a standard to apply to themselves, knowledge of discrepancies is likely to motivate them to change their behavior to achieve the standard. When people must involuntarily apply standards to themselves against which they consistently fall short, the results are less positive; they are likely to develop negative self-images. The more they are forced to focus on this evidence of defective identity, the more they are likely to dislike themselves.

There is a close connection between the possession of a positive self-image, and the capacity for treating others as equals. People who have low self concepts, or who are authoritarian, are more likely to hold prejudicial attitudes toward others. People who hold prejudicial attitudes toward the members of one group are likely to hold prejudicial attitudes toward the members of other groups.

Through the process of schooling, people learn about society's definition of a "normal" identity, their own capacities for fulfilling that definition, and the consequences of discrepancies between society's definition and their capacities. People cannot exercise their rights of democratic citizenship equitably, unless the opportunities and constraints on their citizenship are distributed without regard to status attributes such as gender, language, ethnicity, religion, or color. How do Canadian schools affect the development of democratic citizenship? How do they affect the development of the children's identities?

Although it is not the only institution which socializes the young for democratic citizenship, schools are central to the process. They are also potent institutions for influencing the identities which students acquire. The question I want to focus upon is: How do schools affect student's identities as democratic citizens?

The treatment of children when they first come to school, or to a particular classroom, is the first step in the process by which the school influences the acquisition of democratic identities. How are children treated when they first come to school or to a classroom? Are they welcomed as desirable members of the group, because they have background characteristics and experiences that are valued in the classroom? Or are their background characteristics and experiences seen as problematic? In other words, do they bring to the school or class stigmatized identities?

Because individuals approach one another, in part, to validate assumptions they hold about their own identities, the way students are initially treated when they enter the school or classroom has a consequence for the way they see themselves and others like themselves. Prior to entering school, children can manage certain aspects of their identities by participating in, or withdrawing from activities. The boundaries between any given child and other children are in large part under the child's control. But, in school, children are highly visible to one another and to the teacher. Any characteristics—dress, manners, or behavior—which distinguish them from others is immediately available to others to use in their interaction with them. The simple presence of children in the classroom conveys social information over which they exercise very little control; their "information preserve regarding self" (Goffman, 1961) is open to violation, and their identities are open to manipulation and stigmatization. Do teachers express respect for the children in their classes regardless of the variation among them in dress, manners, and behaviors? Or do they demand conformity to familiar—but often unexamined—"Canadian" norms?

Schools represent a new set of relationships for children. Significantly new kinds of learning—apart from the learning prescribed by the school's mandate—will occur as a consequence of their participation in school. Three important dimensions of school life are the way the school defines membership, the way the teachers decide what human qualities need to be changed, and how the teachers go about changing them. Each school and classroom establishes ways in which children may be categorized, so that it is possible to determine whether individuals possess the attributes qualifying them for membership, and what relevant qualities or states need to be changed. These definitions are expectations or demands for the way in which children are to present themselves. Through the process of labeling by others, particularly by others who hold significant power, people learn new self-identifications (Spradley, 1970; Goffman, 1961).

School officials and teachers collect large amounts of information about children at the time of their admission to school, and throughout their school careers. The information is passed from grade-to-grade and from teacher-to-teacher. Record keeping and transmitting—themselves legitimate aspects of the school's work—often produce situations in which the reputations of children precede them. For teachers, student reputations are their identities, at least in so far as the identities are known in the school.

The information made available through the process of identification is easily transformed into empowered social standings, supported by the internal structure of the school. The grade level designation appearing on the binding of textbooks of elementary school children (for example, the number of footprints or squares) is an easily decoded symbol of social standing relevant only within the confines of the institution. When the designations that exist to facilitate categorization of children for instruction are translated into a hierarchy of empowered social standing within the classroom, they become a means by which aspects of the students' identities can be held up before them as evidence of some defect.

When most or all of the members of a particular group share the same or very similar cultural group characteristics, they begin to associate the characteristics with the social standing of the group within the classroom social system. Processes such as classroom grouping at the elementary level, and tracking (or streaming) at the secondary level, have implication for the way children define themselves; for " . . . to move one's body in response to a polite request, let alone a command, is partly to grant the legitimacy of the other's line of action" (Goffman, 1961). In "allowing" themselves to be assigned to a particular class, group, or track, students are granting, in part, the institutional definition of their identities.

It is the process of social interaction between students and teachers that is central in affecting the students' identities as members of distinctive cultural groups, and as democratic citizens. It is through social interaction that meaning and social control are transmitted. Complex cultural rules govern every aspect of classroom interaction, including conversation between teachers and students, the distances between them, and their patterns of movement.

For children whose backgrounds deviate from the school's definition of a normal identity, participation in school is potentially problematic. Through social interaction these children may be called upon to abandon the bases of previous self-identification, in order to earn full membership in, and benefit from the program of instruction.

For some children there is a disjuncture between the way they are expected to behave at home, or in their home communities, and the way they are expected to behave at school. The majority of Canadian teachers expect that children will display what they have learned by speaking publicly before their peers at the teacher's initiation. For children from some ethnocultural backgrounds, this arrangement inhibits their participation. At home these children are expected to observe others, participate with others in a given activity, and, when they are ready, initiate a self-designed test of their abilities. For such children, the public display of what they have learned at the initiation of the teacher is an arrangement quite different from the cultural practice to which they have become accustomed.

The patterns of speech in Canadian classrooms is sometimes quite different from the patterns to which some children have become accustomed through participation in their own cultural milieu. And, in some cases, the classroom patterns are the reverse of those to which the children have been exposed. For example, teachers typically engage children in conversation when they first come to school, as a means of getting to know them. Among the members of some ethnocultural groups this is the opposite of conventional practice. In these situations, people speak to one another only after they have become familiar with one another through careful and prolonged observation.

In Canadian classrooms it is customary that the teacher initiate activity. Some take this arrangement for granted because, from their cultural perspective, the teacher is the most important person and, thus, may legitimately initiate activity designed to elicit behavior from the children that can be observed and judged. In this arrangement, the lower status individuals, the students, perform for the high status individual, the teacher. For students from some backgrounds this practice is peculiar because, from their cultural perspective, high status people perform activities so that low status people can learn them. In fact, in some ethnocultural groups the public display of one's achievements is considered ill-mannered. People from such groups do not draw attention to themselves. Group membership and group cohesion are especially important; self-promotion is seen as a threat to group maintenance. Thus, arrangements such as show-and-tell or practices such as public praise for individual achievement—practices which are conventional in the context of Canadian schools—run counter to the cultural practices of some ethnocultural groups.

Cultural rules also govern other aspects of social interaction. The person who may initiate conversation, the manner in which topics are introduced into discussion, and the amount of time that must transpire before one person has spoken, and the next may speak, are governed by cultural rules. Among the members of some ethnocultural groups, the preferred conversational gambit is to permit the listener to set the topic by asking an open-ended question. In Canadian classrooms, teachers ask direct questions which establish the topic of discussion, waiting no more than one second for a reply. Among the members of some ethnocultural groups, it is customary to pause for a longer period before speaking. Teachers sometimes misperceive that students from such backgrounds are uncommunicative, unable to answer their questions, and, in some cases, retarded in their development. Some students misperceive the teacher as rudely interjecting just as they are about to respond or, because the teacher has interjected, they misperceive that the teacher did not intend or expect a response.

One wonders whether these practices are compatible with socialization for democratic citizenship, and the retention of unique cultural identities. One wonders whether schools are fostering integration or some other adaptive response. Inferential information about the impact of schools—especially schools in British Columbia—on the identities of students, and their socialization for democratic citizenship, is available from a study conducted by the Law Related Education group at the University of British Columbia.

Direct evidence of the level of support for democratic citizenship is available from the results of the British Columbia Charter Survey, although it was not designed for this purpose (Ungerleider, 1989). These data enable an assessment of how much high school students know about their rights, and of their attitudes toward the granting of those rights to others, one index of the degree to which these students have been socialized for democratic citizenship. These data also permit us to gauge whether or not Canadian birth, the speaking of English, or one's subjective ethnicity have an impact upon knowledge of and attitudes toward the rights and freedoms defining democratic citizenship in Canada.

The survey was administered to a stratified, proportional, random sample of 3,161 British Columbia secondary students in grades 8 through 11. It sought to determine how much knowledge the students had about the rights and freedoms contained in the *Canadian Charter of Rights and Freedoms*, and whether they were in agreement with the rights and freedoms.

Table 9.1 provides a detailed view of the respondent's answers. In the table, items from the Charter have been grouped into six clusters of rights

TABLE 9.1
Percentage Correct and Percentage in Agreement
with Provisions of the *Canadian Charter of Rights*
and Freedoms **for British Columbia Secondary**
School Students (organized by clusters of rights).
(N = 3161)

Rights	Correct Responses		Agree Responses	
	Mean %	Rank	Mean %	Rank
Language	74.8	1	73.6	1
Equality	67.5	2	64.5	3
Fundamental Freedoms	66.9	3	60.2	4
Mobility	62.8	4	68.4	2
Legal	57.2	5	57.9	5
Democratic	52.7	6	55.5	6

and freedoms. It would appear that the attention devoted to language rights generally, and the importance placed upon them in the school, have given them a prominence among high school students. However, the students fare less well in their knowledge of their democratic rights of citizenship. Agreement with the provisions of the Charter, organized by clusters of rights for each sample group, is also presented in Table 9.1. The secondary school students gave highest support to language rights, and least support to democratic rights.

The data collected by the British Columbia Charter Survey also shed light on the impact of the respondents' place of birth on their knowledge and attitudes. Some 9.5 percent of the sample was born outside of Canada. As Table 9.2 shows, place of birth did not influence knowledge of the rights and freedoms contained in the Charter, or the students' willingness to agree with its provisions. In both cases, the difference between those born in Canada, and those born outside of Canada, was not statistically significant.

The data also permitted an investigation of the relations of the first language spoken by respondents, to their knowledge or attitudes toward provisions of the Charter. Some 10.8 percent of the students reported that the first languages they spoke were other than English. There was no statistically significant difference in knowledge of the provisions of the Charter between those for whom English was, and for whom English was not the first language spoken. Nor was there a significant difference between these groups in terms of their agreement with according others the rights and freedoms contained in the Charter.

Students were also asked what language or languages they most often

TABLE 9.2

Percentage Correct and Percentage in Agreement with Provisions of the *Canadian Charter of Rights and Freedoms* for British Columbia Secondary School Students by Country of Birth (N = 3129), First Language Spoken (N = 3101), Language Spoken at Home (N = 3099), and Ethno-cultural Group Identification (N = 2909).

	Number	Correct Responses Mean %	Agree Responses Mean %
1. Country of Birth			
Born in Canada	2828	61.8	61.8
Not born in Canada	301	63.0	62.9
Level of significance		N.S.	N.S.
2. First Language Spoken			
English	2731	62.0	61.9
Not English	340	62.1	62.4
Level of significance		N.S.	N.S.
3. Language Spoken at Home			
English	2937	62.0	62.1
Not English	162	61.8	60.3
Level of significance		N.S.	N.S.
4. Ethno-cultural Group			
Canadian	1848	62.0	62.0
Not Canadian	1061	62.6	62.7
Level of significance		N.S.	N.S.

spoke at home. Some 5.1 percent of the students in the survey said that they typically used languages other than English in their homes. Table 9.2 shows that there were no statistically significant differences between those students who typically spoke languages other than English, and those who typically spoke English at home, in terms of either their knowledge of their Charter rights and freedoms, or their agreement with the provisions of the Charter.

These data also permitted an investigation of whether subjective ethnicity was related to the knowledge or attitudes of the respondents. Subjective ethnicity is the subjective identification people have with a particular ethno-cultural group. Students were asked to indicate the groups to which they felt they belonged. Students who identified as Canadian, English-Canadians, English-other, and Canadian-other were grouped together, and compared with those whose identifications gave primacy to other ethno-cultural groups. Table 9.2 shows that there were no statistically significant differences between students who subjectively identified themselves as Canadian, and those who did not.

A self-esteem scale (Rosenberg, 1965, pp. 305–307) was administered

TABLE 9.3
**Self-Esteem of British Columbia Secondary School Students
by Country of Birth (N = 1516), First Language Spoken (N =
1609), Language Spoken at Home (N = 1501), and
Ethnocultural Group Identification (N = 1400).**

	Number	*Self-Esteem Score*
1. Country of Birth		
Born in Canada	1366	4.62
Not born in Canada	150	4.34
Level of significance		p. = .01
2. First Language Spoken		
English	1439	4.61
Not English	170	4.46
Level of significance		N.S.
3. Language Spoken at Home		
English	1429	4.60
Not English	72	4.35
Level of significance		N.S.
4. Ethno-cultural Group		
Canadian	900	4.67
Not Canadian	500	4.49
Level of significance		p. = .02

at random to approximately half of the sample of high school students.
The data gathered with the scale, presented in Table 9.3, enabled an
examination of the relationship between self-esteem, and the same set of
variables employed above. There is a consistent pattern in these data,
indicating more favorable self-esteem among students born in Canada,
students whose first language was English, students who presently speak
English at home, and students whose subjective ethnic identification is
Canadian. The differences between students born in Canada, and those
not born in Canada, and the differences between students who subjectively
identify as Canadian, and those who do not were significant.

CONCLUSION

One might ask what can be inferred from these data about the way that
Canadian schools have responded to challenge of diversity. The support
for rights and freedoms among the high school students is indicative of the
relative impact of schooling on their socialization to a democratic ethos.
These students have apparently been socialized well without regard to their
initial place of birth, the languages they first used, the languages they use
at home, or their subjective ethnic identification.

The evidence also indicates that a significant proportion of students have a subjective identification other than as English-Canadians. Approximately 33 percent of the sample of secondary students identified themselves with ethno-cultural groups other than English-Canadian. This figure exceeds the proportion of students born outside of Canada (9.5%), the proportion of students who indicated that the first language they learned was other than English (10.8%), or the proportion of students who indicated that the language presently spoken in their homes is other than English (5.1%). This indicates that continuation of ethnic identification is important to a sizable proportion of students.

Although the differences in self-esteem are small, the pattern is consistent across all variables. Students from backgrounds different from their native-born, English-speaking, Canadian-identifying counterparts exhibit lower self-esteem. Consistency in interpretation suggests that there is something about the way that these students have been socialized that leads to lower self-esteem. And, given the salience of schooling in the lives of all children, it seems probable that there is a relationship between self-esteem and what takes place in the classroom. However, because the differences are relatively small, it is still safe to say that these students are "integrated" rather than "alienated."

Writers concerned with democratic theory sometimes distinguish between two kinds of citizenship. One is the participatory or civic conception of democratic citizenship; the other is the representative or civil conception. The former, attributed as flowing from Rousseau, sees democratic citizenship as a "way of life" in which equals define and pursue commonly held goals. The latter, attributed to the more individualistic traditions of English legal and constitutional history, sees democratic citizenship as a legal and social status defined in terms of rights and obligations. Where the civic conception emphasizes participation as an end in itself, the civil conception sees participation primarily as a means to other ends. The civic conception places priority on the public or, at least, places the public on an equal footing with the private. In the civil, the private takes precedence over the public.

The development of democracy in Canada has followed the path fashioned by the civil conception of democracy. Given Canada's close ties with English legal and constitutional traditions, this is not surprising. Nor is it surprising that the development of citizenship in Canada has been more instrumental than expressive—a means to an end, rather than an end in itself.

In an analysis of the ascendancy of the ethnic idea in North America, Smith (1981) identifies more than a half dozen forces which are thought to make for nation-building;

> Franchise extension functioned to give citizens the sense that they were
> involved in national decision-making; the creation of national armies height-

ened feelings of participation in great national enterprises; the emergence of
secondary cleavages—those most noticeably following party lines—cut across
primary cleavages of race, ethnicity, and religion thus fostering an orientation
towards the whole; and the meeting by the state of the citizens' need for
such things as decent conditions of work, adequate standards of education,
and an appropriate amount of leisure time gave them concrete and tangible
reason to advance it their support . . . . The creation of symbols transcending
purely local modes of identification stimulated their adoption of a national
frame of reference; the articulation of a set of core values, internalization
of which was made part of the process of becoming a citizen, served the same
end; and clearly spelled out formulations of the nations' character, containing
explicit reference to the role each of its parts had played in the making of
the whole, did much to heighten the sense of those parts that they were
involved in the life of that whole and so made their support for it more readily
forthcoming (pp. 230–231).

Although it can trace its origins to the political thought of the Enlightenment, the concept of Canadian citizenship has been ambiguous, if not
obscure. In fact, until 1947 there were no Canadian citizens. Until that
time, Canadian citizens were simply British subjects residing in Canada.
And, until 1976, a person regarded as a Canadian citizen was also a British
subject owing allegiance to the Crown.

The concept of Canadian citizenship has also been inextricably connected to Canadian immigration policies, the relations between French and
English, and the status of treaty Indians and Eskimos. As Carty and Ward
(1986) have put it, "Canadian citizenship, at least in so far as the immigration and naturalization processes reveal, has been a concept rooted
more in electoral need than in any highly developed principles" (p. 70).
They have asserted that: "If native birth, migration, immigration policy,
and naturalization law have provided the raw materials of the Canadian
political citizenry, the franchise was the tool used in its making" (p. 71).
Cognizant of the variations in the definition of the franchise over time,
Carty and Ward assert that all laws pertaining to the franchise have had
two fundamental consequences. The first is that they have defined the basic
political units in Canada. The second is that they have identified "the
segment of the population which was to be propitiated, solicited, organized
and manipulated by practicing politicians in their competition for office"
(p. 71).

Throughout its history, " . . . [in] the slow evolution of a single national
franchise, the egalitarian political ideals commonly associated with suffrage
reform in a liberal democracy were always qualified in Canada" (Carty,
1986, p. 73). Until the latter part of the 1940s, most Canadians who were
of Chinese, Japanese, and Indian ancestry could not vote (Roy, 1981).
Treaty Indians and Eskimos who were not veterans could not vote before

1960. Only after 1960 could Canada be said to have a universal franchise. It would take still another 22 years before the concept of citizenship represented by the political thinking of the Enlightenment would be entrenched in law in the *Canadian Charter of Rights and Freedoms*.

In reviewing the history of the extension of the franchise in Canada, Carty and Ward assert that "these activities have not been informed by any consistent notion of a Canadian citizenship nor any regular patterns institutionalizing political rights" (p. 76). One consequence of the politically expedient approach to the issue of citizenship is that consensus is lacking about the essential elements of a national political community. This is a signal, according to Carty and Ward, to the electorate that the basis of Canadian citizenship itself remains at issue.

It would probably be a mistake to attribute immigrant acquisition of democratic values to their socialization in the Canadian context. As important as that is, the socialization of immigrants for democratic citizenship could not have been accomplished to its present level in the absence of tight controls over the numbers and types of immigrants entering Canada.

Throughout its history, Canada has maintained tight control over the immigrants that it accepted. In contrast to Britain, where the goal of its immigration policy was to meets its obligation to Commonwealth subjects, Canada's immigration goals were related to its social and economic development. While Britain practiced an "open-door" policy for all British subjects, Canada employed rigorous selection criteria.

Throughout its history, Canadian policy makers have expressed concern about the ability of indigenous Canadians, vast numbers of whom were themselves immigrants, to accept additional immigrants. On Thursday, May 1, 1947, Prime Minister W. L. Mackenzie King stood before his fellow parliamentarians in the House of Commons and gave prominence to the notion of absorptive capacity. The House had been debating a bill to amend the immigration act then in force. His initial remarks seemed to link absorptive capacity to domestic economic conditions: "The government will seek by legislation, regulation, and vigorous administration, to ensure the careful selection and permanent settlement of such numbers of immigrants as can advantageously be absorbed in our national economy" (Manpower & Immigration, 1974, p. 201).

In his remarks, King attempted to counter the specter of immigration negatively affecting the prevailing standard of living by emphasizing careful planning and selection of immigrants. "The essential thing," said King, "is that immigrants be selected with care, and that their number be adjusted to the absorptive capacity of the country" (p. 205). The government's objectives were, in King's words, "to secure what new population we can absorb, but not to exceed that number."

Drawing attention to the connection between the selection of immigrants and discrimination, King asserted that "Canada is perfectly within her rights in selecting persons whom we regard as desirable future citizens" (p. 205). King asserted that:

> There will, I am sure, be general agreement with the view that the people of Canada do not wish, as a result of mass immigration, to make a fundamental alteration in the character of our population. Large-scale immigration from the orient would change the fundamental composition of the Canadian population. Any considerable oriental immigration would, moreover, be certain to give rise to social and economic problems of a character that might lead to serious difficulties in the field of international relations. The government, therefore, has no thought of making any change in immigration regulations which would have consequences of the kind (Manpower & Immigration, 1974, p. 206).

Mackenzie King simply described what had been, and continues to be, Canada's view about immigration.

ACKNOWLEDGMENTS

I am indebted to a number of people for their thoughtful suggestions and criticisms of the original manuscript presented to New Challenges to Socialization for Democratic Citizenship—a conference held at Rutgers, The State University of New Jersey, New Brunswick, New Jersey on October 27–30, 1988. I am especially appreciative of the comments of Bruce Jennings, Associate for Policy Studies, at The Hastings Center, and Jerome Black, Department of Political Science, McGill University. Their detailed suggestions were helpful to me in revising the manuscript. They are nevertheless absolved of any responsibility for the shortcomings of this paper.

REFERENCES

Berry, J. W. (1984). Multicultural policy in Canada: A social psychological analysis. *Canadian Journal of Behavioural Science. 16(4)*, 353–370.

Black, J. (March, 1982). Immigrant political adaptation in Canada: Some tentative findings. *Canadian Journal of Political Science. 15 (1)*, 3–27.

Black, J. (December, 1987). The practice of politics in two settings: Political transferability among recent immigrants to Canada. *Canadian Journal of Political Science. 20(4)*, 731–752.

Carty, R. W., & Ward, W. P. (1986). The making of a Canadian political citizenship. In Carty, R. W., & Ward, W. P. (Eds.), *National politics and community in Canada* (pp. 65–79). Vancouver: University of British Columbia Press.

Cooley, C. H. (1922). *Human nature and the social order*. New York: Scribners.

Employment and Immigration Canada (1987). *Profiles of Canadian immigration*. Ottawa: Minister of Supply and Services Canada.

Fromm, E. (1955). *Escape from freedom*. New York: Holt, Rinehart, & Winston.

Goffman, E. (1961). *Asylums*. New York: Doubleday.

Harney, R. F. (1988). "So Great A Heritage as Ours": Immigration and the survival of the Canadian polity. *Daedalus: Journal of the American Academy of Arts and Sciences. 117(4)*, 51–97.

Laing, R. D. (1965). *The divided self*. Middlesex, England: Penguin Books.

Manpower and Immigration (1974). *Immigration policy perspectives*. Ottawa: Information Canada.

Newman, W. (1975). *American pluralism*. Toronto: Prentice Hall.

Roy, P. E. (1981). Citizens without votes: East Asians in British Columbia, 1872–1947. In Carty, R. W. & Ward, W. P. (Eds.), *National politics and community in Canada* (pp. 151–171). Vancouver: University of British Columbia Press.

Rosenberg, M. (1965). *Society and the adolescent self-image*. Princeton, NJ: Princeton University Press.

Seeman, M. (1959). On the meaning of alienation. *American Sociological Review. 24*, 783–791.

Shibutani, T. (1961). *Society and personality*. Englewood Cliffs, NJ: Prentice-Hall.

Smith, A. (1981). National images and national maintenance: The ascendancy of the ethnic idea in North America. *Canadian Journal of Political Science. 14(2)*, 227–257.

Spradley, J. P. (1970). *You owe yourself a drunk*. Boston: Little, Brown & Company.

Ungerleider, C. S., Echols, F., La Bar, C., & Daniels, L. B. (1989). Constitutional rights and citizenship. In Coombs, J., Pakinson, S., & R. Case (Eds.), *Ends in view: An analysis of the goals of law related education*. Vancouver: Centre for the Study of Curriculum and Instruction.

10 Government as a Source of Assistance for Newly-Arrived Immigrants In Canada: Some Initial Observations

Jerome H. Black

INTRODUCTION

Prior to the crystallization of the principle of multiculturalism in the 1970s, what could be construed as the effort of the Canadian government in the area of ethnocultural pluralism pertained mostly to the integration of the foreign born into Canadian society (Breton, 1986). That effort—especially in the provision of concrete assistance to the newly-arrived immigrants— was far from monumental (Hawkins, 1988, chapters 11, 12). At best, help was uneven and haphazard; at worst, many immigrants had to fend almost entirely for themselves. These problems were rooted both in certain inadequacies in the direct provision of assistance (what would be expected under the aegis of established programs, and delivered through government bureaus and agencies) and, correspondingly, in a heavy reliance upon the "private sector." Sources of assistance in the latter domain meant, for some immigrants, friends and family members—including, of course, those who had served as official sponsors; for other immigrants, "private sector" support consisted of reliance upon more formal entities, such as agencies and organizations of the relevant ethnic group and/or those of the wider voluntary community. Unfortunately, not all immigrants had access to these nongovernmental sources which, in any event, varied tremendously in the amount and quality of assistance that they could provide. Government subsidization of some of the organizations made less of a difference than might otherwise have been the case because funding arrangements were inconsistent and the amounts often inadequate. Compounding the

167

problem was a marked failure on the part of government to coordinate the various sources of assistance, both within and between public and private sectors.

Even today, government inadequacies in the settlement of immigrants are very much in evidence. The insufficiency of funding and the unevenness of access to useful sources of assistance remain significant characteristics of the system. The situation of immigrant women, by itself, is indicative of serious, ongoing inequalities. Many are denied access to government services because of their dependent status vis-a-vis their sponsors and, especially, their husbands (Ng, 1988). Nevertheless, if only as a general statement, the current governmental effort can be said to be more substantial, both in the direct delivery of assistance (at all levels), and in its supply of more generous and realistic aid for the organized voluntary sector (Hawkins, 1988, chapter 15).

Still, it is unclear whether the government's present day role in the process of immigrant adjustment is as considerable as perhaps might be expected, given the significant expenditures and effort involved. Some critics would, no doubt, point out that a large gap exists between effort and impact, and that the discrepancy is largely due to the way in which services are (or are not) delivered.[1] For example, the delivery of services is often insufficiently decentralized, therefore denying access at a level where need for them is greatest (for instance, the neighborhood). As well, services are often insufficiently coordinated to take into account the multifaceted nature of many of the problems that immigrants must confront. But even purposeful attempts at coordination on the part of government are not always successful, leading, in some areas, to wasteful or, what is worse from the immigrant's point of view, confusing duplications of service and, in other areas, to large omissions in coverage. The gap may also be due to, or widened by, the inability of immigrants to take the initiative and to make use of available services. Some immigrants, because of negative experiences they may have had with government in their former countries, may feel apprehensive about approaching a new government for assistance. Other newcomers, accustomed to the practices of more traditional societies, may find the bureaucratic structures complex and difficult to understand, or even intimidating. Frequently, the problems inherent in the organization of these services are exacerbated by the immigrants' inability to use them, resulting in an imbalance between what the government offers and what is actually taken advantage of by the immigrants. Perhaps the most obvious example of this is the bureau or agency that only operates in one language, but which must try to provide services to immigrants who lack proficiency in that language.

---

[1] Some of the problems to be noted are commonly discussed in the literature (see, for example, Social Planning Council of Metropolitan Toronto, 1970 or Bogen, 1987).

That immigrants might actually prefer to rely on other, more "traditional" sources of assistance, such as family and friends, or agencies and organizations of the receiving ethnic community, constitutes another reason for the under-utilization of governmental services. Partly because of the social and/or ethnic ties and a common language, these interactions occur in a context in which a greater sense of trust between immigrants and those helping them can develop. Interaction in this environment is also likely to take place in a context of greater understanding and empathy, engendered by the shared immigration experience. It is thus possible that even in the more contemporary period, some immigrants, even those apparently capable of drawing upon governmental services, still turn to "traditional" sources of assistance.

The highly complex interrelationships among the different needs of the immigrants, their subjective preferences for one source of assistance over another, the availability of alternative sources, and the variations in the effectiveness of these sources make it difficult to develop comprehensive models that might accurately predict how readily immigrants turn to government.[2] The fact that the different sources of assistance, and the way in which their services are consumed, cannot easily be distinguished from each other poses another difficulty. Obviously, social and ethnic connections, as well as other voluntary agencies, cannot completely replace government. While they may be able to substitute for some governmental services, they are just as likely to act as brokers or intermediaries, by assisting the newcomers to make full use of government facilities or, in more urgent situations, by advocating on their behalf. Certainly, with regard to many critical matters involving immigration documentation, citizenship procedures, welfare benefits, interaction with government in some fashion is axiomatic. Distinctions between the governmental and nongovernmental sectors are also blurred by the existence of government grants and subsidies to various ethnic and community service groups, designed to be used expressly for immigrant assistance. Finally, the fact that access to government services varies according to the "category" of immigrant further complicates the matter. For instance, under current guidelines, immigrants entering Canada officially designated as refugees are more likely to be the beneficiaries of government programs than those who are sponsored by family members, who are expected to turn to those members for assistance. (Further complications would result from the consideration, not undertaken here, of immigrants who have entered illegally and/or whose claims for refugee status are in dispute.) These complications, in

---

[2] Multiple jurisdictions present another complication. For example, in the Canadian case many social assistance schemes, from which immigrants might benefit, are the responsibility of provincial governments, meaning that eligibility criteria, and thus accessibility, vary from one jurisdiction to another.

addition to the lack of systematic research on the contemporary role of government in the area of immigrant assistance, at least in the Canadian case, (as well as data limitations to be duly noted) force the present analysis to acknowledge its exploratory and, in parts, speculative character.

Three questions that bear upon the increased governmental profile in the area of assistance to immigrants are to be considered herein. Two of these are quite straightforward, and are driven by the need to gain even the most basic sort of information: how much do recently-arrived immigrants actually use governmental sources of assistance (relative to other sources) and, a natural companion query, which types of immigrants are likely to do so? These questions are explored using data from a 1983 Metropolitan Toronto area survey.[3] The focal point here is the survey's component of adult immigrants—i.e., 18 years of age and older—who at the time of the interview had resided in Canada for no more than five years; in fact, on average, only two and one half years had passed since their arrival. Moreover, these recent arrivals belong to one of four ethnicity categories: British, South European, East European, and British West Indian. Not only does having several such origin categories provide a natural comparative perspective, increased variability in the distribution of individual-level characteristics offers another perspective on the "types of immigrants" who are more likely to use particular sources of assistance. In point of fact, a wide variety of immigrant traits and experiences might be linked to the use of particular sources of assistance. Some, such as higher levels of education and knowledge of the host country's language(s) are suggested on intuitive grounds, or on the basis of research in other areas of immigrant adjustment or, indeed, from some of the "bureaucratic encounter" literature identifying these, or similar sorts of characteristics, as resources that would ease access to, and facilitate successful interaction with, government.[4]

The policy implications that attend these questions are both quite immediate and concrete, thus giving impetus to the expeditious search for

---

[3] A brief description of the survey's methodology is given in Black and Leithner (1987, Appendix A).

[4] There is, of course, a vast, even bewildering, cross-national literature on immigrant (and migrant) uprooting and resettlement, and much of it relates immigrant background characteristics to numerous facets of adjustment or maladjustment. Discussions abound about some of the more routine characteristics that are to be considered here, such as education and language proficiency. See, for example, Richard C. Nann's introductory essay in the volume he edits (1982). However, few, if any, focus directly on how such traits relate to the use of governmental sources of assistance. Moreover, some additional kinds of traits that are considered in this essay, such as the immigrants' previous political experiences, are rarely examined. For an introduction to some of the elements in the bureaucratic encounter literature that might be relevant here, see Katz, Gutek, Kahn, and Barton (1975), Hasenfeld (1985), and Hasenfeld, Rafferty, and Zald (1987).

answers. Certainly, knowing to what extent government assistance is relied upon is basic information policy makers need to know in order to determine the relevance of government for meeting the newcomers' adjustment problems. Perhaps more importantly, such knowledge can help government get a fix on how well current efforts deal with the problems confronted by immigrants. Data about the use of alternative sources of assistance would also, of course, be quite valuable, feeding in to more considered decisions about the allocation of available resources, including how to divide the assistance effort between the private and public sectors. Specific knowledge about which immigrants, with which traits and experiences, turn to alternative sources of assistance adds a valuable dimension to the decision making process, allowing for, among other things, the design of special programs targeted at particularly "needy" subgroups. Still, because of limitations in the data set on hand—including its status as a single-city study—it will be difficult for this study to offer specific suggestions in this regard. What is lacking, in particular, are measures tapping preference for specific sources of assistance, contextual information on the government services used (such as the languages in which they were offered), and the reactions to, and evaluations of, the bureaucratic encounters.

The third question examined here is less subject to the above-mentioned difficulties, because it takes the sources of assistance data as a given (the independent variable), and tries to determine whether or not they bear any relationship to the incorporation of immigrants into Canadian politics. The existence and nature of a politicizing effect, associated with the use of the governmental sector, are of particular interest in this regard. The policy implications attached to this question are of interest to those who may be concerned about some broader aspects of immigrant settlement, because it is premised upon an expanded view of the immigrant as a fuller "citizen," not only as an individual oriented to the "output" side of government in general, and as a consumer of government services in particular but, as well, as someone who has the capacity to demonstrate some political initiative as a participant. Since previous research has indicated that many immigrants begin to involve themselves politically even during the first few years in the new country (Black, 1984, 1987), it is at least plausible that some part of this politicization is engendered during the process of involvement with government officials and their programs.

The novelty of the proposition—no research in the area is known to this author—belies its policy significance. This is especially so in a country such as Canada, where the need for immigrants intending to settle permanently has been, and continues to be, a major factor in the country's development yet, at the same time, where the commitment of immigrants to do so cannot always be taken for granted. Historically, this lack of commitment manifested itself in subsequent outmigration. In the contemporary period, this is no longer as significant a problem, but the large numbers of immigrants who delay or avoid taking out Canadian citizenship remain a source of concern.[5] Insofar as political incorporation is one index of a commitment to be more fully part of the new nation, knowing that a larger governmental role has a politicizing effect would provide a rationale for the encouragement of political incorporation. The view herein expressed is that encouragement should indeed be provided and, in response to possible arguments to the effect that this would add to the problem of "too much participation" and "demand overload," it must be noted that the alternative is potentially far worse. The possibility of newcomers not developing a commitment to the nation and its political structures or, what is worse, expressing feelings of alienation because they feel they have no stake nor interest in them, is far more serious. Moreover, Canadian history is replete with examples of what happens to ethnic minorities that remain, for one reason or another, outside of the political mainstream.

Positive implications of a relationship between sources of assistance and politicization may also extend across the generations, with the promise of benefits for the children of the immigrants. To the extent that participation is engendered among the adults, then they have the possibility of serving as role models of participatory citizenship for their offspring. This would facilitate the efforts of other agents, especially the schools, by allowing them to concentrate on reinforcing the children's "inherited" participatory tendencies and, more importantly, on developing other facets of citizenship that link up with participation, but also go beyond it to include an emphasis on social obligation, tolerance, and respect for the rights and politics of other individuals and groups. The instilling of qualities such as these would be especially welcome in societies that proclaim and celebrate their multicultural character.

The connection between sources of assistance and involvement in Canadian politics is examined last. The next section provides a brief background sketch of each of the four ethnicity groupings considered here, introduces the survey questions that are used to measure sources of assistance, and begins the process of answering the first two questions. The section after that contains the individual-level analysis, which carries on with the process of examining immigrant traits and experiences, and their relationship to alternative sources of assistance. The analysis of assistance and politicization follows, after which comes a conclusion, which reviews the main findings and considers some loose ends.

The Immigrant Groups and Measures of Sources of Assistance

The South European category is very nearly a single ethnicity category. Seventy-eight percent are Portuguese, and this is quite evident in the nature

---

[5] According to the 1981 Canadian census, for example, about one third of all those who were foreign born had yet to take out Canadian citizenship; among those who had immigrated between 1970 and 1977, the figure approaches fifty percent. For a review of the relevant Canadian literature on citizenship, see Frideres, Goldberg, DiSanto, and Horna (1987).

of the category's characteristics. With an average of only 8.2 years of schooling, they are the least educated of the four groups considered here, and many (about 60%) cannot function well in English, while most do not have much urban experience.[6] They have immigrated principally for economic (35%) and family (37%) reasons. Sixty-four percent have entered Canada under sponsorship and, overwhelmingly, their sponsors were close relatives (77%). Generally speaking, the group's profile—low educational level, difficulty with English, and lack of urban experience—suggests that the South Europeans would be less capable of drawing upon government services. (Previous urban experience should facilitate the transition to the cities of Canada and, in addition, past city-living might indicate that the individual is more accustomed to dealing with the formal government apparatus.) At the same time, it is unclear to what extent organizations within the ethnic community would be able to "pick up the slack." While the Portuguese community in Toronto is fairly large, geographically concentrated, and vibrant in many respects, it is still a relatively new community, and its formal structures and institutions lack the strength and cohesiveness found in many other communities.[7] If government and the community organizations, indeed, represent limited options, then the South Europeans may not have much choice but to rely on the family and friends, many of whom they are joining in Canada.

Twenty percent of the East Europeans are Russian in origin, but most of them (62%) are Poles, many of whom apparently left their homeland in the aftermath of the suppression of the Solidarity movement. This is reflected, in part, by the 37 percent who cited political reasons for their decision to immigrate—by far the largest percentage given by any of the four groups. It is also reflected in their entry status; about the same proportion of East Europeans as South Europeans were sponsored, but considerably more (45%) of the former were sponsored by groups and organizations mobilized to help them "escape" from the turmoil and disappointments in their homeland. The contrast between the two European groups is clearly evident in other areas as well. The East Europeans have come from a solidly urban background—89 percent left medium-sized or big cities—where they were likely to have held skilled jobs, many of them at the professional level. This is also reflected in their level of educational attainment; with an average of 15.0 years of schooling, they are the best educated of the four groups, slightly ahead of the British (14.6 years).

Still, at the time of interview, more of the East Europeans were unemployed (26%) and, altogether, only 41 percent had full-time jobs in

---

[6] Only 37 percent had lived in medium-sized or big cities.

[7] Reitz (1980) provides a useful overview of many of the ethnic communities that are referenced in this analysis.

Canada, statistics that likely reflected the difficult time many were having in finding employment comparable to the generally high status positions they had previously held. No doubt, job certification, lack of "Canadian experience," and language—particularly for the 40 percent who cannot function well in English—are the main impediments here. These problems and consequences in terms of unemployment and underemployment may motivate—or perhaps compel is the more appropriate word—encounters with Canadian officials. Still, this might be expected anyway, because of their education levels, and perhaps their prior urban experience, and, indeed, because of former country experiences that create strong expectations of government help. That many entered Canada as refugees is also important, since refugees are given greater material assistance. At the same time, few ethnic communities are as well-organized as those of the East European groups, so there may also be a considerable use of the services offered in these quarters. (It is likely that in some cases ethnic organizations or individuals and groups within them provided the sponsorship in the first place.) While these options would seem to rule out reliance on social groups, there could be a *preference* to use them. As well, many East Europeans were sponsored by close family (45%), and may more readily turn to them for assistance. In short, the East Europeans, as a group, would seem to have a wide range of choices open to them.

The West Indians, among whom Jamaicans form the largest group,[8] can also be characterized in a distinctive way, quite apart from considerations of race. Their mean level of education is 11.9 years, putting them between the South Europeans (8.2) and East Europeans (15.0), but they have even less urban experience and a higher sponsorship rate than the South Europeans. Ninety-five percent of those sponsors were close relatives, but family reunification is not cited by a large percentage as the main reason for immigrating. Those reasons are, in fact, spread out fairly uniformly over the main categories; 26 percent do indicate they were motivated by economic considerations, but about 15 percent in each instance cite political, family, education, and adventure considerations. This mix of characteristics leads to mixed expectations about the kinds of assistance they might turn to; perhaps, with regard to governmental sources, they might fall in between the two European groups. As with the Portuguese community, the various West Indian communities are not long established, and this fact, along with the sponsorship figures, might suggest that social ties play a larger role than the ethnic organizations.

---

[8] Of the 83 (British) West Indians polled, 17 identified themselves as Jamaican in response to an ethnic origin question (which formed the basis for the ethnicity categorization employed). A majority of another 27 who responded "West Indian," however, were Jamaican born; another 15 and 7 respondents claimed ethnicities associated with (British) Guyana and Trinidad and Tobago, respectively.

The British, it is presumed, would draw heavily upon the public sector for help—at least insofar as they confront problems in settlement. In addition to the relative similarities between the two countries, the characteristics of the group—comparatively high levels of education and urban experience—should facilitate the settlement process. At the same time, the importance of economic factors in British immigration might suggest they will rely less on social ties. Fifty-three percent indicated an economic reason for immigrating—the largest percentage, by far, of any of the four groups, and 45 percent actually arrived to take up prearranged employment. Many, it is true, were sponsored (54%), but in a considerable number of cases, the sponsor appeared to be the would-be employer. As for an organizational impact, the British, because they are the dominant group, do not maintain distinctive ethnic community organizations in the same way as the non-charter (immigrant) groups do. Perhaps, if there is any sort of an impact, it would occur in connection with the traditional British churches.

Immigrant problems, and the sources of assistance to which newcomers might turn, were not focal points in the survey, but there are a handful of specific items that should prove useful for present purposes. One involved an open-ended question which queried immigrants about the most important problem they had as immigrants during their first year in Canada.[9] Those who indicated a problem were asked if they had tried to get some help with it and, for those who replied in the affirmative, to whom they had turned for the assistance. Table 10.1 shows that only a handful of newcomers reported having no difficulties with their new life in Canada, and while there were some (mild) group-connected differences—the British and West Indians were somewhat less likely to report difficulties—the significance of such a major change in one's life situation is what really stands out in the data. Some differences do emerge in the kinds of problems mentioned. The three non-British groups were most likely to cite employment-related problems (which brackets, along with joblessness, lack of Canadian experience and certification), and indeed this was true of a majority of the East Europeans. Second in prominence were adjustment problems, and, for the West Indians, climatic concerns as well. By contrast, the British, many of whom arrived with jobs already lined up, were most likely to cite general problems of adjustment, then employment difficulties, followed, in turn, by references to matters immediately related to the immigration process itself.

By no means did all of these individuals seek assistance with these

---

[9] It was anticipated that many among the two continental European groups would respond that language was the most important problem—indeed, 58 percent of them did so—so those who did were asked: "What other important problem did you have?"

TABLE 10.1
Most Important Problem During First Year in Canada

	South European	East European	West Indian	British
A. Had a problem:	94%	96%	84%	85%
(N)	(69)	(96)	(80)	(39)
B. *Type of Problem*				
Immigration related	3%	5%	2%	15%
Language	9	7	2	1
Financial	7	10	0	6
Employment, Job	35	57	38	24
Housing	0	2	3	8
Social/Cultural Adjustment	26	16	25	42
Climate	1	0	23	2
Other	19	3	7	2
(N)	(69)	(90)	(80)	(39)
C. Sought Help for Problem:	55%	59%	41%	34%
(N)	(62)	(90)	(64)	(39)
D. *To Whom Went for Help*				
Gov't Agencies/Officials	6%	53%	31%	29%
Teachers/Counselors	10	7	12	17
Family and Friends				
Family	15 ⎫	7 ⎫	16 ⎫	0 ⎫
Friends	34 ⎬60	13 ⎬20	24 ⎬45	11 ⎬22
Both	11 ⎭	0 ⎭	5 ⎭	11 ⎭
Ethnic Organizations	4	6	0	0
Relig. Organizations	4	0	2	16
Other Organizations	15	10	2	16
Other	1	5	9	0
(N)	(34)	(53)	(26)	(11)

problems, as Table 10.1 also makes clear. Even taking into account the intractability of some problems (such as the Canadian weather), it is still apparent that many immigrants coped, for one reason or another, on their own. East and South Europeans were most likely to seek help (59% and 55%, respectively), followed by the West Indians (41%), and then the British (34%). The last panel in the table speaks directly to the main issue at hand—the sources of assistance named by those who sought help. Only 6% of the South Europeans named governmental agencies and services, while over fifty percent of the East Europeans did so, interestingly, more frequently than their British counterparts (although the small N–size for the latter should be borne in mind). In fact, West Indians were as likely to cite government agencies as the British. Even if the definition of the public sector is broadened to include references to the educational system (teachers and counselors, primarily), the picture does not change very much. The figures for the social group as a source of aid form a near mirror image of these results. Very clearly, South Europeans, as expected, relied quite heavily (fully 60%) upon their family and friends. In contrast, only about twenty percent of East Europeans named similar sorts of individuals. The latter figure is close to the one for the British. That the West Indians also counted heavily upon their family and friends was also anticipated. Finally, there is an indication that the more organized private sector is also relevant to some degree. While few immigrants claimed to have turned to ethnic organizations, 16 percent of the British did turn to religious ones.[10]

Since the amount of assistance that is available (or possible) varies depending upon the problem, it is helpful to consider responses to close-ended questions posed about specific sources of aid. All of the immigrants were asked if, since their arrival in Canada, they had ever made use of assistance of five different types. Three of these involved areas that were specifically governmental domains, and in particular, immigration, citizenship, and employment or training. A fourth item was English language classes (of relevance for the South and East Europeans), and, while they would ordinarily be available under government auspices, the possibility that some attended classes in the private sector, or in schools outside the purview of government cannot be ruled out; correspondingly, it is given only peripheral consideration here. The fifth item pertained to ethnic group organizations "that help immigrants."

The results for the three government items (Table 10.2) indicate that usage is fairly high, more so than the "first year problem" data would suggest. Understandably, services pertaining to immigration matters tend to be cited most often, followed by employment and training. Relatively infrequent use of citizenship services is, no doubt, linked to the recently-arrived status of the immigrants, many of whom are a year or two away from meeting residency requirements.[11] Notable intergroup differences include the frequent use of immigration and employment services on the part of the East Europeans. Indeed, as the second panel indicates, many were multiple users of government services. Altogether, 84 percent used at least one governmental service, a figure that is markedly higher than those for the three other groups. The South Europeans turned to government mostly on immigration matters, as did the British, although not to the same degree. From what has been seen already, and from information

---

[10] Unfortunately, the category "other organizations" includes not only responses pertaining to secular voluntary organizations, but as well to other, quite different kinds of organizations, such as private employment agencies; inferences about this category are therefore problematic.

[11] Altogether, only about 10 percent of the recent arrivals had acquired Canadian citizenship.

TABLE 10.2
Use of Various Services and Organizations

	South European	East European	West Indian	British
A. Used Government Services in Relation to				
Immigration	49%	70%	26%	34%
Citizenship	14%	19%	18%	10%
Employment/Training	12%	57%	33%	19%
(N)	(69)	(93–96)	(74–83)	(39)
B. Number of Government Services Used				
0	44%	16%	43%	43%
1	38	34	38	51
2	18	40	19	6
3	0	10	0	0
$\bar{x}$	.73	1.44	.75	.63
C. Used Immigrant Assistance Services of Ethnic Organ.:	11%	32%	9%	1%
D. Attended English Language Classes:	43%	69%	—	—
E. Social Group Helped to Get Assistance:	28%	19%	40%	13%

to follow, both groups' meager use of employment assistance is easily understood: the South Europeans found work through their social networks, and the British did so on their own (again, many with prearranged jobs), or through private channels. By comparison, West Indians tended to seek help in connection with employment concerns.

To some extent, the data indicating less use of the services provided by ethnic organizations enhance the importance of the public sector. Only eleven percent of the South Europeans indicated reliance on these organizations, a figure that is close to that for the West Indians, while usage is virtually nonexistent among the British. Again, the biggest contrast lies between these groups and the East Europeans, whose receiving communities are known to be more capable of providing assistance; nearly a third of these immigrants turned there for help. Note, however, that the question only referenced ethnic organizations. Individuals who turned to religious organizations within the ethnic community, often the key institution, might have been missed, as indeed was the case with those who turned to the more secular voluntary organizations. In this sense, the current figures provide only a conservative estimate of use of the organized private sector.

TABLE 10.3
Source of Help for Finding Present Job[a]

	South European	East European	West Indian	British
Source				
Government Agencies	5%	6%	8%	0%
School	0	4	0	0
Private Agencies	8	7	5	16
Newspaper Ads, etc.	15	34	29	21
Family and Friends				
Family	9 ⎫	6 ⎫	13 ⎫	9 ⎫
Friends	34 ⎬ 52	37 ⎬ 47	18 ⎬ 33	15 ⎬ 35
Both	9 ⎭	4 ⎭	2 ⎭	11 ⎭
Ethnic/Relig. Organ.	0	0	0	12
Self-Employed, "On my				
Own," "Walked in"	17	2	23	7
Other	4	0	3	10
(N)	(53)	(53)	(57)	(31)

[a] Among those with a full-time or part-time job.

Two final results in Table 10.2 can briefly be commented upon. The English language classes item indicates, bearing in mind the reservations already made, that here, too, East Europeans are the most likely users. The last row of figures is based on questions that explicitly identified individual members of the immigrants' social group, and whether or not such individuals helped the respondent to use organizations or services of the five types.[12] That many were helped is a reminder of how difficult it can be to delimit neatly the various sources of assistance. At the same time, the specific finding that the British and East Europeans more readily drew upon these services without help is not difficult to appreciate.

A question about how immigrants found their present job is the final measure used to assess sources of assistance. It was posed to those who currently held full-time or part-time employment—82 percent of both the British and the South European groups, 69 percent of the West Indians, and 55 percent of the East Europeans. As these numbers indicate, strict comparisons with results already seen are hampered because of variability in the size of the data bases—especially so for the East Europeans. Compared with the data already seen, Table 10.3 indicates a very modest role for governmental agencies. No British immigrant, and only a handful of the others owe their present job to efforts on the part of, or information

---

[12] Unfortunately, only a single (summary) question was asked about help received vis-a-vis these areas. In other words, the figures do not indicate in which particular area assistance was received.

from, government. In fact, more found their jobs through private employment agencies, and even more located jobs simply by responding to newspaper advertisements. It is also quite apparent that the impact of social ties and networks is considerable; large numbers of immigrants relied upon people around them, friends more often than not.

Again, there are group-specific patterns that merit some attention. One result, that of the major importance of the primary group among the South Europeans, is by now a familiar finding—about half found their jobs through their social ties. Interestingly, a near equal proportion (47%) of the East Europeans did so as well, a result that does not quite square with previous results, including the 57 percent who indicated drawing upon the services of government in connection with employment and training. Perhaps the discrepancy may be due to the need for the occupationally downwardly-mobile East Europeans to have dealings with government about the vital matters of qualification and certification while, at the same time, they locate interim employment using their social support groups. Still, part of the answer may simply be that social ties (and connections) are as prevalent for the immigrants as they can be for the population at large. This would seem to be supported by the fairly large proportion (35%) of comparatively advantaged British immigrants who also relied upon social ties. Given the fact that so many West Indians were sponsored by close relatives, one might have expected the percentage (34%) relying on such ties to be higher, perhaps even approaching the figure (52%) for the South Europeans. The discrepancy between the West Indian and South European results could reflect the fact that the Portuguese have control over some (low status) occupational niches, access to which occurs through the associated social networks (Anderson, 1974); the West Indians, on the other hand, control few niches. The 23 percent of the latter who found their present job on their own may also be indicative of this.

While it has been useful to consider these domains of assistance on an individual basis, devising summary indices that measure the overall amount of support received from each of the three sources—government, social groups and organizations—would render subsequent analysis much less cumbersome. In each instance, the total number of mentions of assistance was divided by the number of opportunities the immigrants had to use that source. In essence, the analysis takes into account the fact that not all immigrants had a first year problem (or sought help) or held a job.[13] What should also be mentioned is that a special effort was made to avoid the possibility of double counting for the government index. For example, an

---

[13] As well, small (conservative) adjustments were made to restore some missing data—to allow for comparisons across the sources of assistance on the basis of the same number of cases.

TABLE 10.4
Group Means on Summary Measures of Sources of Assistance

	South European	East European	West Indian	British
Source of Assistance				
Government	.26	.53	.29	.20
Social Group	.49	.31	.34	.29
Ethnic/Relig. Organ.	.07	.17	.05	.11
(N)	(66)	(94)	(76)	(39)

immigrant who received government assistance for a "first year" immigration problem, would not be additionally credited on the close-ended immigration services item.

Table 10.4 provides the summary results, and confirms, as one would expect it to, the more evident inferences already made, including the one that government does play a role in aiding immigrants in general, but more for some ethnic categories than for others. Governmental assistance is most strongly associated with the East Europeans, while the British, against initial expectations, appear to rely upon government the least. (After the fact, this is due to problems, e.g., social adjustment, that are not readily handled by governmental agencies, to prearranged employment and, for some, to a reliance upon their social ties.) The other noteworthy result is the significance of the social group for the South Europeans, although the more general importance of social networks for job finding narrows the gap between them and the three other groups. By comparison, the role of organizations matters less, although, again, the inference here is probably conservative. The next section moves away from an emphasis on intergroup differences to consider the relevance of individual-level background characteristics.

"Correlates" of the Use of Sources of Assistance

Many of these characteristics are intercorrelated with one another, so it is best to employ a multivariate technique (regression analysis), so their impact can be gauged in net terms. First, however, the traits and experiences of the immigrants considered here need to be sketched out. Education, English language facility, and urban residency have already been discussed as facilitators of the use of governmental sources of assistance. The same expectation is held for the involvement of immigrants in the politics of their former country. Presumably, the more politically experienced immigrants would be less daunted by the prospect of interacting with Canadian government agencies. Two quite summary measures of the immigrants' political past are used here. One is the degree of interest the immigrants had in the politics of the former country; the other, the number of different kinds of participation acts engaged in while living there (Black, 1987, pp. 740–741). Previous analysis of these two measures confirms the advisability of keeping them separate. For example, many East Europeans reported very high levels of political interest, but did not participate as much as their interest levels might have led one to expect, probably because of their critical views of the regime. This also hints at the limitations of these measures in the present context; they could be referencing negative experiences with government that might be carried over into the new country. On the other hand, they could be tapping experiences that are simply irrelevant to the domain of settlement.

Organizational membership is another kind of experience in the former country that might be useful to consider. Ordinarily, organizational membership would be associated with—indeed it often engenders—the kinds of interpersonal and communicative skills that bear upon access to, and successful interaction with, government officials. It is also, of course, possible that experience with organizational life might be related to receiving assistance from ethnic community organizations. (This would assume that the needed services are available and, again, that there is a preference to use ethnic sources of assistance.)

Some of these characteristics will, at the same time, be negatively related to the social group as a source of support. Presumably, the better educated, those fluent in English and so on, have the option of "going elsewhere," while those who are less endowed may be limited to seeking assistance from their social networks. Foreclosed options may also describe the situation of some immigrant women who come from more traditional backgrounds, where role definitions have relegated them to a peripheral position vis-a-vis politics. Such women, unaccustomed to interacting with government agencies and officials, may feel constrained to rely upon individuals and groups within their more immediate ethnic environment. The fact that many immigrant women have restricted access to important government benefits and services may also be relevant.

Yet another characteristic may be positively related to the use of nongovernmental sources of assistance: attachment to the ethnic group, measured here by the expressed strength of an ethnic identification (as opposed to an unhyphenated Canadian identification).[14] The supposition is that "primordial" bonds of ethnicity might manifest themselves in a strong reliance upon the "trusted" ethnic community and the (typically) ethnically-based circle of family and friends.

---

[14] The full question is this: "How do you usually think of yourself, as (Group), or a (Group)-Canadian, just a Canadian, a Canadian of (Group) origin, or what?" This variable was scored 3, 2, 0, and 1, respectively.

Finally, there are some typologies of situation-based characteristics, where expectations would seem to differ from "cell to cell." One is the social auspices that surround the immigration experience. Here, four categories are considered—the first three entered as dummy variables in the analysis—based on whether the immigrant (a) was sponsored by an individual (including a close relative), (b) was sponsored by a group or organization, (c) was not at all sponsored, but joined family or friends, or (d) was not sponsored, and did not join anyone in Canada.[15] It was thought that individual sponsorship would be associated with the social group, because of the sponsorship arrangement, and group or organization sponsorship (the category most likely to include refugees) with governmental sources of assistance. A second typology, reasons for immigration, is also partitioned into four categories: immigration for political reasons, for economic ones, for family reunification, or (the reference category) for "other" reasons—principally, for adventure, travel, and education. Political, and possibly economic reasons might be associated with the governmental sector, and family-based considerations with the social group. Finally, the immigrant's employment situation at the time of immigration is included, although without clear-cut expectations. Dummy variables representing two possibilities were employed; the immigrant either had a job offer, or came looking for work, leaving as the reference category primarily those who came as students, or who did not need a job.

Table 10.5 reports standardized regression coefficients (beta weights) measuring the impact of these traits and experiences. Its format reflects the exploratory status of the present inquiry—the need to glean some introductory information—in a key way. The four ethnicity categories have been pooled together, thus ignoring what a more refined analysis would most certainly have delved into: the differential impact of these individual-level characteristics across those ethnic origin categories. (Some compensation is gained by the inclusion of ethnicity dummy variables—with the British as the omitted group—allowing for the intergroup comparisons net of the differences in the individual-level characteristics.)

Commencing with the results for government, it is evident that the resource or experience items do not, as a rule, appear to facilitate use of this source. Only urban residency among these background characteristics seems to make a difference (a statistically significant beta of .18). That language bears no relationship could mean several things, including the possibility, an encouraging one, that services are being used by those who lack proficiency in English. Again, contextual information on the particular agencies or services the immigrants drew upon would have shed light on

---

[15] The latter category is comprised mostly of those who immigrated alone, but joined people they knew, or those who immigrated accompanied by relatives and friends.

TABLE 10.5
Regression Results (Beta Coefficients) for Different Sources
of Assistance[a]

	Government	Social Group	Organizations
Independent Variables			
Education	−.15	.06	.16
English Language Facility	−.04	−.11	−.39***
Prior Urban Residency	.18***	.08	−.10
Gender (male, positive)	−.05	.16**	.24***
Past Political Interest	−.01	−.15	−.02
Past Political Participation	.10	.06	.10
Past Organ. Membership	−.01	−.21***	.05
Sponsored by Individual	−.30***	.06	−.05
Sponsored by Group/ Organization	.01	.02	.17**
Not Sponsored but Joined People	−.03	.02	−.17**
Immigrated for Economic Reasons	.13	.08	.20**
Immigrated for Political Reasons	.13*	.01	.07
Immigrated for Family Reasons	.15*	.07	−.00
Had Job Offer	.13	.05	−.22***
Came Looking for Work	.02	.05	−.11
Ethnic Identification	.00	.32***	−.14*
South European	.24*	.31**	.36***
East European	.54***	.08	.19*
West Indian	.32***	.08	−.12
R²/adj. R²: (N = 220)	.40/.33	.25/.17	.37/.31

[a]The equation also included measures of Canadian citizenship, commitment to stay in Canada, and the number of (up to five) individuals with whom the respondent socialized.

Statistical significance at the .01 level indicated by ***, .05 by **, .10 by *.

this possibility. Also encouraging from an equity point of view, but perhaps surprising in the context of theoretical argumentation, is the negative, although not statistically significant, coefficient for education. The weak results for "past politics" and past organization membership also support the idea that the lack of these kinds of resources and experiences do not constitute barriers to the governmental sector.

The results are somewhat mixed as far as the situational variables are concerned. There is a strong negative coefficient for those sponsored by individuals; taken by itself, this result makes sense, since such individuals are less eligible for government sources of assistance (and presumably their sponsors handle many of the interactions with officials). Still, it is unclear why the logic of the situation does not extend to those sponsored by groups or organizations (where eligibility is much greater), and generate a large positive coefficient. The coefficients representing immigration for political reasons and for family reunification are statistically significant, and the one for the other category nearly so. Presumably, the stakes associated with immigration are higher for these individuals, compared with those who immigrated for other reasons.

It is, in fact, ethnicity that makes the biggest difference in the use of governmental sources of assistance. As can be seen, all three coefficients are statistically significant and two of them, the one for the West Indians (.32), and for the East Europeans (.54), are the largest observed in the column. While this more refined analysis confirms the importance that the East Europeans attach to the public sector, it also reveals a prevalent distinction between the British and non-British. That there is a closer connection with government on the part of the latter may represent a "fair" distribution, given that the British already possess a natural advantage in the process of adjustment. More generally, it appears that culturally-based explanations, which take into account the collectivist and contextual experiences of the immigrants, do have relevance for understanding "who" draws more upon government services. It remains subject to question, however, whether or not they would continue to do so, once other individual-level items, not incorporated here, were worked in. To the extent that they do, then the message would seem to be that what is needed is some sensitivity to the cultural factors that might affect how government services are drawn upon.

The summary statistics indicate that the same set of variables explain less of the variance in the case of the social group. There are, however, several specific relationships of which to take note. A couple of these make sense, if reliance upon the social group is seen as the antithesis of reliance upon the governmental sector; for example, past organizational membership, past political interest, and facility with English all exhibit negative coefficients, although only the first one is statistically significant. Interestingly, the coefficient for gender is also statistically significant, but indicates, against expectations, that men turn more to the social group.

What does occur, as expected, is a (strong) positive result for ethnic identification (beta of .32); a sense of ethnic affinity does translate into the use of the social network (although, it does *not* appear to deter the use of government services). Finally, the heavy dependence upon the social group shown by the South Europeans is not simply a matter of stronger bonds; even with ethnic identification controlled, the coefficient for those Europeans is substantial.

The results for ethnic and religious organizations hold some surprises. The failure of past organization membership to bear any relationship to use of this type of source may be due to the incongruity of purpose between past and present organizations. In light of data previously seen, the larger beta for the South Europeans, relative to their Eastern counterparts, is also unexpected. Ultimately, the result underscores the importance of a multivariate approach; taking into account the edge that the East Europeans have in education, and especially in English, indicates that it is the South Europeans who are inherently more likely to rely on these organizations. A surprise also occurs in connection with ethnic identification. A positive coefficient would be expected on the basis of simple intuition, but, as can be seen, what emerges is a statistically significant negative coefficient. That at the same time language "works" in the expected direction only adds to the conundrum. Such results very much suggest the need for further investigation.[16]

Political Involvement in Canada

By taking as a given the actual levels of usage of the different sources, the third question examined here—the relationship between sources and politicization—is not hampered by the limitations associated with the first two questions. While the possible impact of governmental assistance is the main concern of the analysis, the two other sources of help will also be considered as independent variables. A positive relationship in the former instance is expected, based on the possibility that involvement with government agencies and officials raises the profile of government for the immigrant. Perhaps, because matters entail concrete benefits of nontrivial concern to the new immigrant, lessons are learned about the salience of government in general, and about the advantages of further interaction through regular channels of political involvement.

Quite apart from how high the stakes may be for the newly-arrived, there is also the possibility that exchanges with government officials will be satisfactorily concluded, encouraging positive feelings toward the new polity. This, as a possibility, is not suggested by any specific data available here, but from some of the literature on bureaucratic encounters and, especially, the arguments about the importance of different contexts of eligibility in which encounters occur. At one extreme are service bureauc-

---

[16] The impact of gender should also be given further consideration. The initial thinking was that women would have been more constrained to use groups and organizations found within their immediate environment. This does not appear to be the case.

racies that rely on stigmatizing means tests, where the interaction is characterized generally by "a sense of powerlessness on the part of the applicant, and by a low degree of satisfaction"; at the other extreme are service bureaucracies where beneficiaries automatically qualify, often because of contributions they have paid into programs, and where the "norms governing the encounter stress fairness and equity and do not stigmatize the beneficiaries" and who, as a result, derive more satisfaction from the interaction (Hansenfeld, Rafferty & Zald, 1987, p. 399). It is possible that, as regards immigrants, the latter is the more prevalent type of encounter. (In the wake of much anecdotal data on unpleasant contacts, this is by no means certain.) It is also possible that such interactions do not as much politicize the immigrant, as stave off the development of unfavorable feelings that would otherwise be manifested in a negative government assistance-politicization relationship. At the same time, a negative relationship may fail to materialize, simply because those who would be most intimidated, or put off by such encounters, purposefully avoid contact. The null hypothesis, the absence of a relationship, would thus seem to be the most likely alternative.

There are some ideas in the general literature on the role of ethnic organizations that may form the basis for the establishment of both positive and negative relationships between help received from ethnic organizations and politicization. What may be an older perspective, leading to the anticipation of negative relationships, emphasizes that the ethnic community in general, and its organizations in particular, keep the immigrant locked into the community with little significant contact with mainstream society—including its political life. On the other hand, the opposite perspective considers those organizations as bridging agents. While they replicate aspects of the old country's culture, they also, according to this argument, play an important role in helping the newcomers learn about the new society. Rather than completely cutting off the immigrants from that society, then, the organizations seek to incorporate them as members of both the ethnic community and the society at large, and in the process make the immigrants aware of some important facets of the social and political mainstream. One strong incentive that brings the organizations and their leaders to act as bridging agents is the possibility of mobilizing the appropriately-informed newcomers behind ethnic group goals.

The rationale for a negative relationship in the case of ethnic organizations may also apply to the social group. Indeed, if an ethnically-homogeneous social circle reinforced the envelopment of a "protective" ethnic community, then the negative correlation might even be stronger. The basis for expecting a positive relationship is hinted at in the "uprooting and social auspices" literature (e.g., Tilly & Brown, 1968; Choldin, 1973). The line of reasoning in mind argues that migrants and immigrants who join their kin in the new environment will adjust more easily and quickly to the new setting than those who must adjust on their own. Not only do the latter lack ready-made sources of help, they may face the debilitating effects of loneliness and anomie. The evidence for this view is inconsistent, but in any event it is the sociopsychological dimension that is potentially relevant here; the social group provides a psychologically healthier environment for adjustment, which may spill over into other areas, perhaps including the political arena.

Involvement in Canadian politics is gauged by using a variety of indicators that touch on different facets of political behavior and engagement. Two are psychological and attitudinal in nature; partisanship, at the federal level, and expressed interest in Canadian politics. Two others reference actual participation; working with others to solve a community problem, or "communal activity," and contacting politicians or public officials. The fifth measures knowledge about Canadian politics.[17] This multiple indicator approach recognizes the fact that individuals relate to the polity in different ways, and with varying degrees of intensity. Still, this does not mean that a direct and immediate connection exists between governmental sources of assistance and each of these items. While interest in Canadian politics might be directly stimulated, it is hardly likely that interaction with Canadian officialdom leads directly to the adoption of a particular party identification, at least not in the contemporary period. It is rather more likely the case that the interactions increase the incentives for greater general political awareness, stimulating, in turn, a search for interpretative agencies to help the newcomer comprehend the new political environment. Parties play key roles in this regard.

The benefits of a multivariate analysis are quite apparent for this analysis as well. Incorporating all three sources of assistance into the same equation allows for judgment about the relative impact of each (on the different involvement indicators), and for the possibility of controlling for the effects of other factors that may confound the relationships of primary concern (Black, 1987; Black, Niemi & Powell, 1987).

Table 10.6 presents the (beta) coefficients for the primary independent variables, and shows that use of government sources of assistance does have somewhat of an impact on Canadian political involvement. Two statistically significant coefficients are in evidence, .16 for partisanship and .18 for interest in Canadian politics. While this is a restricted result—

---

[17] See Black (1987, pp. 740–741) for question wording and the operationalization procedures followed. There was an initial concern that the contacting item ("Have you ever personally gone to see, or spoken to, or written to, any politician or public official about some need or problem?") might have tapped interactions with government about settlement assistance, and, thus, have "guaranteed" a positive relationship. As will be seen, however, no association at all emerges between the two.

TABLE 10.6
Regression Results (Beta Coefficients): Impact of Assistance
Sources on Involvement in Canadian Politics[a]

Source of Assistance	Partisanship (Federal)	Polit. Interest	Polit. Knowledge	Communal Activity	Contacting Politicians
Government	.16**	.18***	.08	−.10	.05
Social Group	−.04	−.01	−.01	−.02	.01
Organizations	−.10	−.24***	.21***	.45***	.33***
R²/adj. R² (N = 263)	.36/.30	.39/.32	.53/.49	.33/.26	.31/.25

[a]The full equation also included measures of age, gender, education, English language ability, "past" political interest, "past" participation, "past" organization membership, length of residence in Canada, Canadian citizenship, commitment to stay in Canada, reasons for immigration, and ethnicity.
Statistical significance at the .01 level indicated by ***, .05 by **, .10 by *.

government makes little difference for the other three involvement items—partisanship and political interest are, of course, fundamental orientations, and they frequently stimulate other forms of political involvement—perhaps for these particular immigrants further along in time. As well, the fact that there are many other strong independent variables, against which government sources of assistance must compete, makes this modest result a little less so. Finally, neither of the two other sources of assistance is linked (positively) to partisanship and political interest.

What is interesting is the impact that organizations have as a source of assistance. Leaving aside, for the moment, the statistically significant negative coefficient for political interest, organizational assistance appears to facilitate involvement in the areas of political knowledge, communal activity, and contacting. The beta of .45 for communal activity is especially notable, but given the general result that organizational sources of assistance do matter, it is not surprising that they matter more for this group-based participation item. The fact that neither of the two other sources of assistance makes any difference in these three areas adds to this result. As for the negative result for political interest, it appears to be bound up with the British respondents. A reanalysis based on the three non-British groups produces no relationship, so support for the negative hypothesis is not as great as first appears to be the case.

There is, similarly, no corroboration for the idea that (support from) the social group hinders politicization. Nor does it appear to facilitate political incorporation. It turns out, though, that the social group is relevant for the politicization of immigrants. An analysis carried out specifically on the network of individuals (mainly friends and family) with whom they socialized, shows that political discussions with these people are strong and resilient predictors of involvement in Canadian politics (data not shown). This is equally true of the subset of individuals who assisted the immigrants; here, too, there were strong correlations. Unfortunately, as only a minority of "helpers" were discussion partners, their politicizing effect in the context of assistance is limited.

CONCLUSION

This essay has looked at the relevance of governmental assistance for newly-arrived immigrants in several different ways, and has revealed some interesting findings. Still, these results can only claim tentative status. Certainly, additional study is needed if the policy implications associated with the role of government are to be fully understood. It was not possible to answer the question posed at the outset about the magnitude of the impact of government assistance relative to its expenditures and effort. Such a cost-benefit type of analysis would require massive amounts of information on expenditures, government personnel, and the like, which is in principle attainable, and, as well, data that are not readily available—namely, usage-related information, including outcome and satisfaction measures. The current essay was able to examine some limited aspects of usage, relying on evidence available from a Toronto survey of recently-arrived immigrants. It does seem that government plays a significant role in helping immigrants adjust, and based on what is generally known of past efforts, this represents a major improvement. Previously, the task had fallen almost exclusively to the immigrants' relatives and friends and to organizations of the ethnic and wider voluntary communities. But the situation has not evolved to the point that government monopolizes the settlement process. It is clear that sources in the private sector, often at the behest or support of government, continue to play important roles, and not only by providing assistance themselves, but also by helping the immigrants to gain access to government services.

More precise statements about the relative importance of each source of assistance are difficult to establish. The exercise would require, among other things, greater understanding of the nature of the interrelationships that link the particular problems or needs immigrants have, their preferences for using particular sources, and the availability and effectiveness of alternative sources of assistance. From a more practical point of view, such an understanding would make it easier for policy makers to determine how potential policy changes (e.g., more services in one area) might generate a specific set of results (e.g., more consumption of those services).

Sorting out those interrelationships would also help provide a fuller understanding of the observations made in connection with the relationship between immigrant characteristics and sources of assistance. As it now stands, there are many intriguing possibilities, including that some of the characteristics typically seen as universal facilitators of general adjustment (e.g., education, and host country language familiarity) function differently in the case of government assistance (and, in some instances, in the case of nongovernmental assistance). It is also possible, however, that the results reflect successful efforts on the part of government to facilitate access on a wider basis. More certain information about the correlates of the use of governmental sources of assistance would be of interest to researchers and policy makers alike.

Further research into the relationship between sources of assistance and politicization also promises to yield dividends. There is some evidence that seems to suggest that assistance received from government quarters, in the formative period, does have a politicizing effect. This has important implications that are related to immigrant adjustment in the long run, well after the difficulties of the first few years are over. The eventual full political incorporation of immigrants is considered to be an important phenomenon, in fact, a vital sign that immigrants have developed some sense of obligation and commitment to their new country and its political life. That this more robust sense of citizenship among immigrants might develop as a legacy to be passed on to their children makes additional analysis of the role of governmental sources of assistance even more important. If the present effort is on the right track, then the rationale for governmental intervention will be further demonstrated.

ACKNOWLEDGMENTS

The author gratefully acknowledges the support of the Social Sciences Humanities Research Council of Canada (Grant 410-81-0498 and 410-82-0517) and the helpful comments of conference participants.

REFERENCES

Anderson, G. M. (1974). *Networks of contact: The Portuguese in Toronto*. Waterloo: Wilfrid Laurier University Press.

Black, J. H. (1984). Confronting Canadian politics: Some perspectives on the rate of immigrant political adaptation. A paper presented to the Canadian Political Science Association annual meeting, Guelph, Ontario. June, 1984.

Black, J. H. (1987). The practice of politics in two settings: Political transferability among immigrants to Canada. *Canadian Journal of Political Science, 20*, 731–753.

Black, J. H. & Leithner, C. (1987). Patterns of ethnic media consumption: A comparative examination of ethnic groupings in Toronto. *Canadian Ethnic Studies, 19*, 21–41.

Black, J. H., Niemi, R. G., & Powell, G. B., Jr. (1987). Age, resistance, and political learning in a new environment: The case of Canadian immigrants. *Comparative Politics, 20*, 73–84.

Bogen, E. (1987). *Immigration in New York*. New York: Praeger.

Breton, R. (1986). Multiculturalism and Canadian nation-building. In A. Cairns & C. Williams (Eds.), *The politics of gender, ethnicity, and language in Canada*. Toronto: University of Toronto.

Choldin, H. M. (1973). Kinship networks in the migration process. *The International Migration Review, 7*, 163–175.

Frideres, J. S., Goldenberg, S. DiSanto, J., & Horna, J. (1987). Becoming Canadian: Citizenship acquisition and national identity. *Canadian Review of Studies in Nationalism, 14*, 105–121.

Hansenfeld, Y. (1985). Citizens' encounters with welfare bureaucracies. *Social Science Review, 59*, 622–635.

Hansenfeld, Y., Rafferty, J., & Zald, M. (1987). The welfare state, citizenship, and bureaucratic encounters. *Annual Review of Sociology, 13*, 387–415.

Hawkins, F. (1988). *Canada and immigration* (2nd. ed.). Montreal: McGill-Queen's.

Katz, D., Gutek, B., Kahn, R., & Barton, E. (1975). *Bureaucratic encounters*. Ann Arbor: Institute for Social Research.

Nann, R. C. (1982). *Uprooting and surviving: Adaptation and resettlement of migrant families and children*. Dordrecht, Holland: D. Reidel.

Ng, R. (1988). Immigrant women and institutionalized racism. In S. Burt, Code, L. & Dorney, L. (Eds.). *Changing patterns: Women in Canada*. Toronto: McClelland & Stewart.

Reitz, J. G. (1980). *The survival of ethnic groups*. Toronto: McGraw-Hill Ryerson.

Social Planning Council of Metropolitan Toronto (1970). *A study of needs and resources of immigrants in metropolitan Toronto*. Toronto.

Tilly, C. & Brown, C. H. (1968). On uprooting, kinship, and the auspices of migration. *International Journal of Comparative Sociology, 8*, 139–164.

CONCLUSION

11

Socialization to Citizenship: The Successes, Failures, and Challenges to Government

Marilyn Hoskin

INTRODUCTION

Most of the papers prepared for this volume have addressed one of three concerns. The first is how the various majority and minority groups in multi-ethnic societies assess prevailing norms, and attempt to reconcile their own traditions and behaviors to them. Included in this category are chapters addressing such divergent research topics as group acceptance, racism and its ramifications, and social identity. A second has focused on the role which educational institutions play in fostering integration, by teaching how societal norms and group deviations from them coexist in nations committed to democratic values. Under this broad umbrella fall studies of curriculum, teaching strategies, and school environments. The third concern has directed attention to how governmental programs have attempted to supplement school efforts to bring minorities into the mainstream life of the host society. Taken as a group, this collection provides a rich understanding of the minority experience across a variety of democratic societies.

This focus on social norms, and how educational and governmental institutions deal with them, is entirely appropriate to the overall topic of socialization to citizenship. At base, however, it is government in its many formal and informal functions which defines what citizenship actually means. Government decides who will enjoy the rights of residence and what the host society might expect in return. Government also bears direct responsibility for many aspects of the welfare of minorities (access to education, employment, or welfare aid) and indirect responsibility for others (encouragement of ethnic diversity, and promotion of opportunities). Opposition parties regularly keep issues of immigration and integration on center stage politically, indicating that socialization to citizenship has not been automatic or necessarily applauded within host societies. Indeed, some governments or their political opposition actually discourage citizenship (and presumably, citizenship education) for their minority populations.

The objective of this essay is to assess the range, variation, and relative successes of roles which governments play in socializing their majority and minority populations to democratic citizenship. Our focus, to be sure, is on minorities, and especially new immigrant minorities which constitute the most recent challenge to advanced industrial societies. In that context, however, the orientations of national majorities are critical as well. Majorities in democratic systems mold educational programs and constrain government policies. Our task, therefore, is to set the research presented in this volume into the wider context of research on government and aspiring citizens, to identify recurring themes and results, and specifically to assess the performance of governments as they strive to influence, if not direct, the political education of these groups.

To approach this task, we follow an outline which essentially treats the topic chronologically. Governments, after all, are influenced by their histories, by their present circumstances, and by their future plans. We pursue this straightforward framework partly because it is logical, and partly because it provides a rough test of whether governments are basically creatures of other social and economic forces, largely reacting to those forces, continuing established patterns, and only reluctantly responding to new circumstances. Utilizing this approach, we consider (a) government as a sum of historical patterns; (b) government as policy definer of national citizenship, and its ethnic and immigrant variations; and (c) government as symbolic mediator between insecure, but entrenched minorities on the one hand, and its national mainstream on the other.

GOVERNMENT AND THE CONSTRAINTS OF NATIONAL HISTORY

However, obvious the observation may be, we should note at the outset that the vagaries of national historical experience define broad and lasting parameters within which governments must operate. When governments attempt to modify or reverse patterns established over long periods of time, they more frequently than not fail in the effort. Mark Miller has concluded, for example, that where France, on the average, provides an ideal setting for the assimilation of foreign workers, because of its long history as a political refuge, attempts to implement integrationist policies in West Germany appear particularly ill-fated due to a long negative tradition (Miller, 1981).

There is, in fact, a fairly reliable conventional wisdom about which nations have been historically friendly to immigration and integration, and those which have not. We assume, for example, that Canada will continue to be a relatively receptive host (Hawkins, 1972; Reitz, 1980; Palmer, 1975; Samuda, Berry, & Laferriere, 1984). Similarly, the United States has in the main been a committed host, but faces periodic tensions when nontraditional immigration increases dramatically (Dinnerstein & Reimers, 1975; Handlin, 1959; Taylor, 1971; Higham, 1963; LeMay, 1987; Thernstrom, 1982; Keely, 1982; Portes & Bach, 1985). We also assume that Britain, Australia, and other Commonwealth nations will continue to embrace newcomers reluctantly, resurrecting some of their colonial barriers to full immigration and assimilation of minorities (Rees, 1979; Freeman, 1979; Garrard, 1971; Freeman, 1979; Power, 1979; Wilson, 1973; Finifter & Finifter, 1983; Cheetham, 1972). Finally, most densely populated European nations have reached the point where they believe that absorptive or assimilative capacities have been reached, if not exceeded (Miller, 1981; Rist, 1978; Hoffman-Nowotny & Killias, 1979; Hoskin & Fitzgerald, 1989, 1990).

However consensual such conclusions might be, they need to be examined in terms of both logic and precision. In the first instance, conventional truths may in fact be self-fulfilling prophecies, thus precluding the possibility of change. Certainly democratic governments subscribe to the idea that they are, or can be, the masters of their own history and present, rather than prisoners to those collected years. Secondly, the assumption of a tradition which characterizes nations as friendly or unfriendly to minorities is too simple. The definition of "historical experience" is not self-evident, nor is the categorization of democracies as receptive or hostile to the multiethnic challenge. It is not our intention to engage in major reconstruction of historical determinants. It is instructive, however, to establish rough but comparable criteria which reveal similarities and differences among nations. A review of the phenomena most frequently explored in the historical case study literature suggests that three major factors structure such experiences: time, space, and memorable events or conditions.

Lapsed time as Precedent

The simple proposition that lapsed time legitimizes existing circumstances recurs consistently in the literature. Not surprisingly, this factor's measurement is very crude, differentiating between nations where immigrants came and worked into mainstream society, and nations where immigrants came, but remained unwelcome or isolated. Since the level of precision is this general, scholars tend to categorize fairly easily. The United States and Canada have long immigration histories and melting pot populations, and thus find that they must justify any attempts to close the door (LeMay, 1987). Most Western European nations are new to immigration, and thus find it natural to treat new residents as different or even temporary (Miller, 1981; Hoskin, 1985). Still other nations have become immigration nations fairly recently (Israel, Australia), and find themselves struggling to develop consistent policy in the absence of historical guidelines (Finifter & Finifter, 1983; Gitelman, 1982; Aitkin, 1977). When policy changes are initiated, this body of research would argue, both sides must confront the recent and long-term history as a major factor in determining whether the change will take place.

Demography as National Delimiter

Claiming historical predominance necessarily begs the intrinsic question of why some nations developed friendly or open traditions, and others did not. Clearly historical experience is in part a function of geography. Stated most simply, size (and its accompanying variables of number of mainstream social groups, potential for economic expansion, and vulnerability to neighbors) matters. Geographically large nations can absorb more minorities with less visible impact; typically they have also needed them to establish sustainable population levels in some areas; they have also needed them as manpower for economic expansion programs. Although their borders are extensive, the two major democracies in this category (Canada and the United States) share one border, and enjoy the protection of relative isolation from intrusions from other states.

Conversely, small size is seen as carrying inherent limits on both accepting new minorities and accommodating old ones. West German governments have consistently formulated policy toward foreign workers on the negative assumptions of tradition and the limits of size. The Federal Ministry of the Interior's *Record of Policy and Laws Related to Foreigners in the Federal Republic of Germany* (1985) starts out with the specific notation that Germany is not an immigration nation, then goes on to state that: "The absorptive capacity of the Federal Republic has been exhausted at around 4.4 million foreigners. . . . Especially important is the difficult state of the labor market, the intractable problem of providing living room, and the problems of integration. . . . " (p. 4).

Although it is obvious that ordinary citizens or nationals also require jobs and living room, minorities, and especially newly entering minorities, are targeted as a greater source of pressure when space is limited. As such, minorities are likely to confront greater hostility from those who believe they have a prior claim on national resources.

Memorable Periods or Conditions

There is no question that the histories of individual nations are filled with unique experiences. There are, however, well established themes which many of them have shared, and which underlie similar treatment of minorities. One is colonialism and its variations (slavery, long-term occupation, and dominant alliance relations), in which popular, as well as governmental positions treat outsiders as inferior who need guidance, and are expected to be appropriately servile to the greater power. Such experiences have clearly been linked to American treatment of Blacks, and British attitudes toward former subjects in its colonies of Africa, Asia, and the Caribbean (Campbell, 1971; Ashford, 1981; Power, 1979). Some have interpreted frictions between European heritage and North African Jews in Israel along similar lines (Gitelman, 1982). Still, the relationship between colonial experience and negative treatment is not always consistent, as is clear from the case of France, a former colonial nation with a recognized commitment to protection of political refugees (Miller, 1981).

A second and ultimately related influential experience would be nationalism, and its frequent corollary of isolationism. In this instance, political leadership and mass publics combine to define the nation so exclusively, that interaction with foreigners is seen as undesirable or even offensive. Over time, however, economic needs and even border changes bring some of those categorized as undesirable into the country. Faced with the choice of revising national history to smooth their entry, or treating them with minimal civility, governments typically opt for the latter approach. Such an interpretation is consistent with 19th century German attitudes toward Poles and Eastern Europeans, and currently with the Federal Democratic Republic's attitude toward foreign workers from Southern Europe and Turkey (Esser & Korte, 1985; Reimann & Reimann, 1979; Mehrlaender, et al., 1981). It is also relevant to Britain's treatment of the Irish, Eastern European Jews, and postwar refugees (Rees, 1979). The relationship sometimes varies: the United States has experienced periods of strong nationalism and isolationism in which hostility to foreigners was evident, but did not turn permanently against them. And, the converse relationship does not necessarily occur, since nations which conspicuously lack colonial or nationalistic backgrounds (Switzerland, Australia) are not necessarily models of good relations with minority groups (Hoffman-Nowotny & Killias, 1979; Wilson, 1973).

Although the range of historical experiences outlined here is broad and varied, tangible patterns of the ways by which history conditions the roles governments play in dealing with ethnic minorities do emerge. One is that irrespective of the sequence of relevant national experiences (colonialism, war, and boundary changes), a residue of opinion and interpretation flattering to that nation, and less so to others involved, is likely to persist for decades, if not centuries. Some self-criticism may arise, but it is likely to be overshadowed and outlived by rationalizations of the policies and attitudes of the host population. Perhaps nowhere is this tendency more evident than in a nation's educational system, where instruction and materials criticizing national leaders and policies are routinely outnumbered by those portraying a more noble past.

A second pattern indicates that irrespective of experiences, or the residue of opinion, size and related factors (the proportion of non-nationals, economic diversity and capacity, and population density) consistently act as a brake on immigration and multi-ethnicity. Population saturation is an arbitrary concept, challenged by our enthusiasm for the metropolis. Yet it is employed frequently, typically by those who fear *who* the new population is more than the idea of more people per se. It is almost a universal truth that those with demonstrably less to spare are likely to be less willing to consider sharing to be plausible and appropriate.

Third, political leaders utilize historical examples selectively and in ways consistent with their self interest. Most frequently political leaders, in their attempt to find villains responsible for bad times, or threats to the national good, have focused on foreigners or other ethnic minorities. In this overview the similarities between Bismarck, Enoch Powell, and Franz-Joseph Strauss are more striking than their obvious differences. Simply put, leaders use minorities as negative political capital.

Finally, and related to all three patterns noted above, historical experience is difficult to revise or reverse. Revision requires some rethinking or even repudiation of the past. Moreover, not revising is easier. West Germany, for example, has found it extremely difficult to modify a political culture attuned to population homogeneity as a virtue. Similarly, the United States tinkers with immigration quotas, but does not shed its sense of responsibility for the most recent tired and poor. At least in this policy area, initiating motion is more difficult than accepting inertia.

To return to the point raised at the beginning of this section, all governments inherit some of their predecessors' policies, stands, and commitments. Over time, those commitments and directions accumulate, making dramatic political moves risky, and even modest changes in goals or policies difficult. In assessing the success or failure of governments as they seek to assist in socializing minorities to democratic citizenship, therefore, it is important to weight the historical baggage governments carry in the process. Quite obviously, the long-standing American commitment to immigration and integration makes it easier for the United States to initiate multi-ethnic programs, than it would be for Germany as a nation with a markedly different tradition. This and other examples evident from this brief overview should persuade us to include historical tradition, distinctive periods of international relations, and demographic factors in any assessment of national socialization to citizenship.

GOVERNMENT AS POLICY-DIRECTOR

Governments operate under somewhat conflicting assumptions. On the one hand, they generally expect to act in ways which respect and continue patterns evident in their nation's accumulated history. On the other hand, they also expect (and are expected) to inspire citizens to assess political priorities, to initiate policy changes where they are needed, and to develop those elements of the political culture which are the nation's strengths. In this section we accept the fact that governments cannot realistically be expected to produce ideal combinations of continuity as well as change, and move on to examine the question of how governments use their unique, if circumscribed, role as initiator and implementor of official policy on minority issues. To this end, we consider three critical components of policy: (a) policy assumptions concerning immigrants and other minorities; (b) the extent of legal and political rights of minorities; and (c) social and economic policies relevant to minorities.

Policy Assumptions: Directing and Redirecting Priorities

The debates which surround legislative politics in democratic systems provide insight into national attitudes and expectations about particular issues. At their best, policy assumptions should spell out goals and indicate the value which society accords to their achievement. At worst, assumptions are vague or even inconsistent, or poorly matched with the situations they are designed to address. In each extreme case, as well as the larger number which fall somewhat in between, however, government and its opposition are central players, translating national needs and desired states into formal policy. Our question in this section is twofold; how have political leaders used this opportunity to clarify and define priorities associated with this issue, and do common patterns of policy assumptions exist across nations.

It should be noted at the outset that not all contemporary democracies actually have substantive in-migration policies at this time. Germany effectively cut off new immigration in 1973; Britain and other Commonwealth nations have restricted admission to a narrow spectrum of those related to current residents, or those who possess capital or needed skills; and the United States sets up similarly restrictive categories. Although all democratic nations have committed themselves to accommodating political refugees, they also define that category narrowly. We thus discuss policy primarily in terms of immigrants and other minorities who have established residence, but recognize that that limitation is itself an indicator of the cautiousness of host nations.

The broad research literature on policy stances of governments toward immigrant and other minorities is consistent in concluding that policy makers rarely use the process to guide minorities and educate citizens. Rather, political leaders have used policy on this issue to espouse general principles, while leaving the important decisions of implementation to administrative agencies. To be fair, immigration policy in general, and minority socialization in particular are complex issues. At one level, they are basic social welfare issues, asking what value we attach to facilitating economic and social mobility for the world's less fortunate. At another level, they invoke a higher humanitarian, even moral question of whether we have an obligation to alleviate suffering and hardship of fellow humans. At the same time, their solution is pragmatically dependent on the resources of the host nation. And, not insignificantly, their successful conclusion is dependent on the acceptability of the policy to the host nation's citizenry. Policy assumptions, therefore, should address and evaluate goals realistically, reconciling ideal end states with national resources and government commitment.

In truth, virtually no official policies meet such strict standards. Most nations claim to welcome refugees, but avoid questions of how many could realistically be admitted, or how political and economic persecution might be differentiated meaningfully (Keely, 1979; Conradt, 1982). And, most immigration policies read like human rights documents, until specific requirements present lists of job skills, or types of family connections that qualify an applicant for admission. Policy assumptions, in short, are most typically amorphous and generous, but short on guidance for ultimately achieving integration. What characteristics can be identified as common policy assumptions across nations? Perhaps the most obvious is a tendency to *overstate expectations*. Canadian policy is designed to promote multiculturalism; the British counterpart exists to facilitate free movement of Commonwealth subjects; American policy typically is prefaced by a commitment to democratic aspirations, and to provide economic and political opportunities for immigrants (Hawkins, 1972; Ashford, 1981; LeMay, 1987). That characteristic, however, is compounded by the tendency to include statements which are either *blatantly naive or contradictory*. We noted earlier that even though most of Germany's four million foreign workers have been in the country for more than ten years, official documents still refer to them as temporary and affirm that Germany "is not an immigration nation" (Esser & Korte, 1985). Similarly, British policies rarely mention racial tension, even though that is the primary public concern associated with the country's ethnic minorities (Ashford, 1981; Norton, 1984).

At the same time, another key policy assumption is that immigrant minorities play important economic roles. All policies establish categories of desirable skills. And, during different periods, the United States and Canada have joined Germany and France in actively recruiting foreigners to fill specific gaps in the labor market (Rist, 1978; Hoskin, 1985; LeMay, 1987; Miller, 1981). Implicit in this pattern, however, is the idea that immigrants can be used to meet national labor market needs. A possible corollary, however, is one which Germany has added—that such admission need not oblige the host society to facilitate permanent citizenship. Such thinking reflects a less tangible, but ominous assumption that it is legitimate to treat foreigners and other minorities with less basic respect than nationals—indeed, to treat them more as market commodities than people (Essex & Korte, 1985).

Finally, it should be noted that however vague or incompletely defined immigration policy assumptions may be, those associated with *integration* of resident minorities are worse. Some nations embrace self-reliance and individually defined mobility as the path minorities should follow; others assume that legislating the terms of entry is a sufficient governmental role (Ashford, 1981; Esser & Korte, 1985). To be sure, some states (Israel, and to a lesser extent Canada) are visibly active in socializing immigrants, and include some discussion of that in policy statements. The predominant pattern of assumptions, however, is one of vagueness, lack of recognition of existing conditions, and naivete about how the policy fits with other national priorities.

Tensions associated with multi-ethnic policies are both historically evident and contemporaneously serious. The responsibility of policy makers to set the tone of public debates is thus enormous. In fact, given the constraints which historical experience and precedent place on leadership at any point, articulating policy goals and assumptions in either an overall agenda, or in particular legislation may be the best opportunity to shape a national course. In reality, however, that opportunity is typically characterized by (a) over-generalization, (b) naivete, (c) political opportunism, and (d) unwillingness to face political realities.

Basic Policy: Legal and Political Rights

The question of what rights are extended to immigrants and other minorities would seem to be a simple one. Democratic societies are universally committed to basic political rights and protection for those living within their boundaries, and those nations with significant ethnic minorities typically make such guarantees explicit. Freedom of movement and expression, freedom from legal harassment, and legal access to the wide array of social and economic benefits are for all intent and purposes universal. In nations where that welfare net is extensive, minorities are thereby guaranteed a basic level of security and living standard. As David Conradt notes, that link assures that "they [foreigners] do not constitute a subculture of poverty in the Federal Republic" (1982, p. 70). That statement characterizes Israel and British Commonwealth nations as well (Gitelman, 1982; Wilson, 1973; Martin, 1978; Ashford, 1981).

Where deviations do occur is in policy related to citizenship and the associated right to representation. The worst case is that in which policy impedes the immigrants' ability to become citizens. In Germany and Switzerland, governments maintain only minimal naturalization programs, and do not encourage children to expect citizenship. Such policy produces circular reasoning, evident in the statement of the German Interior Ministry document that: "Naturalization should not be an instrument for the promotion of integration but rather should stand at the end of a successful integration process" (*Record*, 1985).

Esser and Korte (1985) conclude that this stance has: "created a lasting insecurity concerning future life in the Federal Republic of Germany, and this in turn affects the everyday life of immigrant families" (p. 189).

To be sure, few nations assume that long-term residents will *not* seek permanent citizenship status at some point. In fact, virtually all others expect that citizenship is a goal of both immigrants and the state, and make no effort to constrain rights associated with it (Layton-Henry, 1987).

Even where direct legal rights are assumed and protected, however, there is no guarantee that minority interest play real roles in the representational process. Direct political activity has been encouraged by government in only rare instances (when, for example, Israeli parties actively vied for the immigrant membership). Despite their size and permanence, political leaders have been reluctant to champion the immigrant concerns, especially when they seem to threaten majority prerogatives. In fact, parties in industrialized nations are often fundamentally divided on this question. Labor and liberal parties find themselves ideologically sympathetic, but constrained by working class hostility to foreigners; in Britain, Labour even supported a repatriation program in the 1970s. Similarly, conservative parties appreciate the stable work force they provide but feel little real empathy for their needs (Hoskin, 1985; Ashford, 1981; Freeman, 1987). The most frequent consequences are the chances that immigrants will become marginal or alienated increase.

Hoskin and Fitzgerald (1990) noted two corollaries of these assumptions. One is that in the absence of party advocacy, the task of representing foreigners has fallen largely to churches, charitable organizations, unions, and homeland associations—organizations whose lack of political clout is painfully obvious (Miller, 1981; Conradt, 1982). A second is that in the absence of centralized programs, responsibility for official policy is widely dispersed among agencies and levels of government. Such a dispersion virtually eliminates the possibility that one unit will become a powerful champion of their interests (Hoskin & Fitzgerald, 1990).

Several of the chapters in this volume have noted that schools characteristically fall short of teaching and advocating full political participation among minorities. That shortcoming is particularly relevant when, as we have just described, governments fail to act decisively to encourage such minorities to take full advantage of the political opportunities inherent in democratic political structures. Since immigrants are especially likely to have an idealized vision of opportunity in their adopted land, the absence of commitment by either schools or political institutions is all the more troublesome. Socialization to democratic citizenship, in short, is seriously handicapped when democratic governments themselves are daily reminders of the contradictions between rhetoric and reality.

Social Welfare Policies: Bread and Butter Socialization

Defining liberal political agendas and encouraging involvement of minorities are both opportunities for government and opposition parties to make verbal commitments to integration. Formulating and implementing social welfare policies, however, involves tangible resources which all groups covet. Enthusiasm for such policies is thus a good relative indicator of the role government plays in helping immigrants and other minorities move into society's mainstream. In this dimension of governmental activity, variations are both notable and amenable to interpretation.

Although all the systems we consider are politically democratic, they have different conceptions of social welfare. Most comprehensive are those of European and Commonwealth countries, whose social welfare net includes full health insurance, employment protection, and virtually free education. The full array is available to foreigners and other minorities on the same basis as citizens. There are, however, two negative aspects of such commitment. One is that the very comprehensiveness of social welfare in these states means that it cannot indicate special governmental concern for minorities. The other is that by offering minorities benefits identical to those for citizens, governments may have assumed that they would not have to define programs specific to minority needs (Ashford, 1981).

The American approach also assumes equality between citizens and minorities. The approach, however, is based on a less comprehensive conception of governmental responsibility. Although benefits are applied to noncitizens, fewer are available, and there is a certain stigma attached to their use. Consequently, minorities face a real possibility of poverty which has no parallel in social welfare states. Perhaps as important, immigrants in particular are perceived as constituting a drain on basic whatever their fair share might be (Keely, 1982). As in European states, American governments have not developed specifically targeted economic or social programs which would hasten their movement into the national mainstream. In fact, the few instances where specially funded programs were unavoidable (as in the case of the Marielle boatlift immigrants) clearly produced negative public sentiment. It is not surprising that the most comprehensive socio-economic aid to immigrants in the United States, as in West Germany and Britain, has come from church and other private groups.

We should note that some programs dedicated to integration do exist, but few would argue that they are extensive or enthusiastically supported. In Germany companies employing large numbers of foreigners have sponsored programs in language and "cultural adaptation." Even though the permanence of foreigners was evident by the mid-1960s, it was not until 1975 that the federal government began to establish integration programs (including language and vocational training). Despite a continuous stream of recommendations from the European Human Rights commissions, most German states initiated only small-scale educational requirements or alternatives for foreign children and their parents. Cynical observers claim that Germany's enthusiasm for vocational training coincides only with recessions which force foreigners onto welfare and, according to public perception, into the world of crime (Conradt, 1982; Koerner & Mehrlaender, 1986).

A contrasting approach is that of the "Multiculturalism" policy embraced by virtually all Canadian governments. At least officially, the government is committed to support programs which preserve an ethnic identity within the framework of Canadian citizenship. However, Canadian enthusiasm is highest at the level of the abstract and noticeably lower when it affects "their own lives, the socio-cultural institutions in which they participate, or their pocketbooks" (Reitz, 1980, p. 384). Canadian policy has reflected this ambivalence, responding incrementally to demands or crises, to the availability of federal money, or to the assertiveness of particular groups (Anderson & Frideres, 1981; Palmer, 1976). Perhaps as important, ethnic groups themselves are not united on whether they want to use resources for ethnic identity programs, or for programs dedicated to improving economic opportunities for younger members (Reitz, 1980). Still, the Canadian commitment is quite specific relative to that of other nations.

What emerges from this discussion is the discomforting conclusion that official policy, which is after all the province of elected governments, is more a creature of historical and contemporary pressures than a product of leadership and principled planning. Policy is most likely to be responsive to economic or humanitarian crises. Despite its unchallenged leadership in at least proposing policy, government in almost every case has passed up the opportunity to define the ethnic mix characteristic of the optimal social system. Not surprisingly, the attendant opportunity to educate the citizenry on the value of ethnic diversity has been passed by as well. As a result, minorities are likely to be seen as utility players or charity cases, and the result has been seen in friction, shifting goals, and constant concern about the capacity of the state to absorb nonmajorities within its borders.

GOVERNMENT AS SYMBOLIC MANAGER AND MEDIATOR

In the previous section we dealt with the active role of government in defining issues relevant to socialization to citizenship: how it has shaped the political agenda and pursued policies critical to the legal, political, and socio-economic integration of immigrants and other minorities. Without doubt, this role is the most direct way in which government influences the process of socialization. However, government and political leadership also play important symbolic roles which are not always linked to specific policies. Citizens look to political leaders for clues on how to behave and what to value; they also note what government and opposition leaders do *not* do. In this section we identify areas in which a governmental role is not direct, but in which it may well be influential. In fact, the "role" need not even be overt, if it is an opportunity to intervene which it does not use. Two general areas are germane to this discussion: (a) management of public sentiment; and (b) promotion of state and local programs, including education, which are critical to minority citizenship socialization.

Opinion Management

We noted earlier that all governments inherit political traditions which may include tenaciously held biases as well as supportive pubic views. At the same time, governments are elected with an electoral license to propose changes, to suggest needed improvements, and to inspire people to think in new or altered ways. We have already seen, in our review of policy assumptions, that governments tend toward timidity when it comes to using policy assumptions to reshape the specific programmatic agenda on minority issues. Here we ask if political leaders more generally use their authoritative positions to influence or manage public opinion on these issues.

It is, of course, difficult to distinguish what political leaders say generally from what they say in relation to a specific policy choice or debate, but there are some clear differences. First, on issues on which the public has expressed strong preferences, most political leaders speak out—generally echoing public sentiments—while at the same time fully intending to avoid enacting corresponding legislative or executive policies. In most of the nations considered here, this practice is common. West Germany has actually enacted fewer than five federal bills of consequence since the early 1960s; the three British Race Relations Acts, as Ashford notes, have not been accompanied by more specific statutes; and it took the United States Congress twenty years to revise the Immigration Bill. Nonetheless, political leaders of all stripes have kept the issue alive and public opinion virulent even without pushing legislation. And, to the degree that there is a discernible pattern to the way political leaders manage popular sentiment, the pattern is negative. The names most commonly associated with public debate include Enoch Powell and Margaret Thatcher in Britain, Franz-Josef Strauss in Germany, and Phil Gramm in the United States. To be sure, firebrands are always more noticeable. What makes their stances most noteworthy, however, is the absence of clear rebuttals from government or opposition leaders. As we noted earlier, parties and prominent groups have opted for neutral stands or silence on minority issues, and individuals sympathetic to the causes of minorities have been no more daring. Public opinion may be negative by default since there is little guidance from pubic leaders to take positive stands (Studlar, 1978).

The symbolic role of government can thus be one of non-influence. By avoiding clear stands and not countering alarmist anti-immigrant sentiment, political leaders leave the issue to chance, to myth, to events which could be erroneously interpreted. As a result, public opinion has become or remained predominantly negative.

Promotion of Programs Beneficial to Minorities

In a real sense the symbolic role defined by this category should be almost painless. Existing programs have been formulated by others, benefit a wide range of groups, and need only to be promoted and praised. In Canada, for example, governments have entered into cooperative agreements with local voluntary or cultural groups to advance multiculturalism. Leaders in the United States regularly attend ethnic festivals, religious ceremonies, celebrations of minority achievement. Political officials take pains to applaud successful educational schools or programs in ethnically defined areas, or to take special note when a Vietnamese refugee graduates first in his or her class. By and large, such programs are inexpensive to support and appear to pay highly visible political dividends.

Given the ease of such efforts, it is somewhat surprising that political leaders are not more involved in promoting not only these specialized projects, but also educational programs in general. In most nations discussed here, elementary and secondary education is controlled subnationally, and virtually all have minority programs whose successes might be highlighted. And, as we have noted, research in this area is burgeoning. In addition to the large journal literature, a body of research is now being generated by educational institutes dedicated to minority issues in education. The most recent edition of *Neue politische Literatur Beihefte* (1988) is devoted to the topic of "Arbeitsmigration und gesellschaftliche Entwicklung" (Labor Migration and Societal Development), in which over three hundred pieces of research are reviewed. The chapters in this volume reference hundreds of studies devoted to educational issues. Any lack of political attention cannot, therefore, be attributed to a dearth of material from which political stands might be derived.

The involvement of government in attending to educational questions has been sporadic, tentative, and probably toned down to avoid the impression of being too enthused about mainstreaming foreign and minority children. To be sure, it is difficult to quantify an *absence* of symbolic acts. We can however, note that a federal government presence in educational programs is not clearly visible. To be sure, in Germany political support for educational programs for children seem somewhat hypocritical in light of official resistance to permanent residence and citizenship. For most, however, support for educational achievement programs should be low-cost and presumably high in benefits. As noted in the chapters in this volume, however, the involvement of political leaders has not been substantial.

The most notable pattern to emerge from the discussion in this section is the absence of a large-scale or systematic symbolic role for government in immigrant and minority issues. Why this should be the case is not immediately evident except, perhaps, in the case of Germany. Indeed, there the Interior Ministry goes on at some length to stipulate that even the goal of integration should not be overstated: "This [integration] does not mean *assimilation*, but rather the participation of foreigners in our society's life as much as possible without damage to their own cultural ties, and above all the appropriate insertion of foreign youths into the work force" (*Record*, 1985, p. 6). In other states, a logical if not very satisfying explanation of the absence of symbolically supportive behavior might be that any impression of pandering to minority groups might be politically risky, especially to legislators with significant concentrations of minorities in their constituencies.

In short, even symbolic behavior runs some of the risks associated with more direct and more costly actions. An easier path is noninvolvement; and one with potentially great rewards in symbolic negative behavior. As the chapters in this volume have demonstrated, host populations need but little prodding to react critically to those who are different or newcomers. Given this array of choices and accompanying costs, it is less surprising that governments and political leaders have not played out direct or indirect roles very extensively.

CONCLUSIONS

We began this essay with the specific task of identifying governmental roles in the process of socialization to democratic citizenship in multi-ethnic societies. Having reviewed the topic logically, and attempted at least a first cut at reviewing examples from the cases examined in this volume, we should be able to offer some tentative conclusions as to how government and its political affect socialization. The cases studied here suggest several patterns which might be considered in future research.

First, governments are definitely constrained by their pasts: traditions and significant events become part of a collective memory that persists and sometimes grows. Governments characteristically yield to those pasts more often than they attempt to modify their lessons or change their implicit directions. Even without colonialism, colonial stereotypes implying inferiority and danger to the mainstream persist, and few governments stake their reputations on the need to put that aspect of the past to rest. Consequently, stereotypes continue to plague minorities and their ultimate place in the society.

Second, size and attendant demographic factors present vivid national analogies to personal fears about overcrowding, living space, and the supply of economic resources. Small nations, especially those with negative histories, will experience more difficulty in reconciling minority needs with majority fears, than those with greater space and reservoirs of natural resources. An exception to that general rule would appear to be Israel, whose need for loyal citizens has eclipsed what would be typical resistance to newcomers.

Third, despite their monopoly on legitimate political authority, governments have been loathe to utilize it to address immigrant and minority issues squarely. Political debate has rarely been committed to an alteration of existing policy assumptions; policy is almost universally incremental, reactive, and explained in ad hoc terms. Although consistent with our earlier contention that traditions are hard to crack, the preference for continuity appears singularly inappropriate in settings where large numbers of immigrants have been admitted by the same governments, where they face predictably difficult situations, but where policies and expectation are vague or unhelpful. Nonetheless, that preference prevails across virtually all of the nations studied here.

Fourth, a common policy stance is that minorities and immigrants should be officially treated like ordinary citizens wherever possible. Although that has an egalitarian ring initially, examination of this pattern cross-nationally reveals that a corollary is that little or no further attention is seen as necessary. Such a position means that basic social welfare is the same for citizens (who know the system and who presumably are already integrated into some parts of it) as for immigrants (who need help in being integrated). As noted in several chapters, informal groups have assumed major roles in easing the transition of immigrants and other minorities, with little or no guidance from governments.

Fifth, symbolic governmental roles have not been significant in aiding the causes of immigrants and minorities. In fact, the incidence and extent of those roles has been minor. Perhaps because these groups do not yet constitute visible constituencies, political leaders rarely take on their concerns systematically, and there is very little evidence that individual supportive actions are extensive. In fact, much more visible have been the negative crusades of those who would keep foreigners out. The tired and the poor appear not to make good copy or substantial political capital at this time.

Finally, we should note that historically, immigrants have proven to be relatively tough stock. Perhaps because they expect little, the little they get does not discourage them from seeking group acceptance and opportunities to make eventual headway into the mainstream. In fact, the efforts and activities documented by other papers presented here may always have been better facilitators of ultimate integration. That government is not consistently the key player we might wish it to be is disappointing in some respects, but should not lead us to think that minorities will not find alternative paths to democratic citizenship.

REFERENCES

Aitkin, D. (1977). *Stability and change in Australian politics*. Canberra: Australian National University Press.

Anderson, A. B., & Frideres, J. S. (1981). *Ethnicity in Canada*. Toronto: McGraw-Hill.

Arbeitsmigration und gesellschaftliche Entwicklung [Labor migration and social development]. (1988). Special Issue of *Neue Politische Literatur Beihefte*. Bonn: Neue Verlag.

Ashford, D. E. (1981). *Policy and politics in Britain: The limits of consensus*. Philadelphia: Temple University Press.

Campbell, A. (1971). *White attitudes toward black people*. Ann Arbor: Institute for Social Research.

Cheetham, J. (1972). Immigration. In A. H. Halsey (Ed.), *Trends in British society since 1900* (pp. 181–198). London: MacMillan.

Conradt, D. P. (1982). *The German polity*. (2nd Ed.) New York: Longman.

Dinnerstein, L., & Reimers, D. (1975). *Ethnic Americans: A history of immigration and assimilation*. New York: Praeger.

Esser, H., & Korte, H. (1985). Federal Republic of Germany. In T. Hammar (Ed.), *European immigration policy: A comparative study* (pp. 165–205). Cambridge: Cambridge University Press.

Federal Ministry of the Interior. (1985). *Report of Policy and Laws Relating to Foreigners in the Federal Republic of Germany.* Bonn: Government Printing Office.

Finifter, A. W., & Finifter, B. M. (1983). *Political socialization of international migrants: American migrants in Australia.* Paper presented at the annual meeting of the American Political Science Association, Washington, DC.

Freeman, G. P. (1979). *Immigrant labor and racial conflict in industrial societies.* Princeton: Princeton University Press.

Freeman, G. P. (1987). *The state and immigrant minorities.* Paper presented at the Conference on Ethnic and Racial Minorities in Advanced Industrial Democracies, South Bend, IN: University of Notre Dame.

Garrard, J. (1971). *The English and immigration.* London: Oxford University Press.

Gitelman, Z. (1982). *Becoming Israelis: Political resocialization of Soviet and American immigrants.* New York: Praeger.

Handlin, O. (Ed). (1959). *The newcomers.* Cambridge: Harvard University Press.

Hawkins, F. (1972). *Canada and immigration: Public policy and public concern.* Montreal: McGill–Queens University Press.

Higham, J. (1963). *Strangers in the land.* New York: Free Press.

Hoffman-Nowotny, H. J., & Killias, M. (1979). Switzerland. In D. Kubat (Ed.), *The politics of migration policies* (pp. 193–208). New York: Center for Migration Studies.

Hoskin, M. (1985). Public opinion and the foreign worker: Traditional and nontraditional bases in West Germany. *Comparative Politics, 17,* 193–210.

Hoskin, M., & Fitzgerald, R. C. (1990). Public acceptance of racial and ethnic minorities: A comparative analysis. In A. Messina, et al. (Eds.), *Ethnic and racial minorities in advanced industrial democracies.* Westport, Connecticut: Greenwood Press.

Keely, C. (1982). "Immigration and the American Future." In Liebman, L. (Ed.), *Ethnic Relations in America,* pp. 28–65. Englewood Cliffs, NJ: Prentice-Hall.

Keely, C. B. (1979). The United States of America. In D. Kubat (Ed.), *The politics of migration politics* (pp. 51–66). New York: Center for Migration Studies.

Koerner, H., & Mehrlaender, U. (Eds.). (1986). *Die "neue" Auslaenderpolitik in Europa: Erfahrungen in den Aufnahme—und Entsendelaendern* [Foreigner politics in Europe: Experiences in receiving and sending nations]. Bonn: Verlag Neue Gesellschaft.

Layton-Henry, Z. (1987). *The political rights of migrant workers in Western Europe.* Paper presented at the conference on Ethnic and Racial Minorities in Advanced Industrial Societies. South Bend, IN: University of Notre Dame.

LeMay, M. C. (1987). *From open door to Dutch door: U. S. immigration policy.* New York, Praeger.

Martin, J. I. (1978). *The migrant presence.* Sydney: Allen & Unwinn.

Mehrlaender, U., Hotmann, R., Koenig, P., & Krause, H. (1979). *Situation der auslaendischer Arbeitnehmer under ihrer Familiengehoerigen in der Bundesrepublik Deutschland* [Situation of the foreign exchange workers and their families in the Federal German Republic]. Bonn: Freidrich-Ebert Stiftung.

Miller, M. J. (1981). *Foreign workers in Europe: An emerging political force.* New York: Praeger.

Norton, P. W. (1984). *The British polity.* New York: Longman.

Palmer, H. (Ed.). (1975). *Immigration and the rise of multiculturalism.* Vancouver: Copp Clark Publishers.

Palmer, H. (1981). "Canadian Immigration and Ethnic History in the 1970s and 1980s." *International Migration Review,* 15, pp. 471–501.

Portes, A., & Bach, R. L. (1985). *Latin journey.* Berkeley: University of California Press.

Power, J. (1979). *Migrant workers in Western Europe and the United States.* New York: Pergamon Press.

Rees, T. (1979). The United Kingdom. In D. Kubat (Ed.), *The politics of migration policies* (pp. 67–95). New York: Center for Migration Studies.

Reinmann, H., & Reiman, H. (1979). Federal Republic of Germany. In R. Krane (Ed.), *International labor migration in Europe* (pp. 63–87). New York: Praeger.

Reitz, J. G. (1980). *The survival of ethnic groups.* Toronto: McGraw-Hill.

Rist, R. C. (1978). *Guestworkers in Germany.* New York: Praeger.

Samuda, R. J., Berry, J. W., & Laferriere, M. (Eds.). (1984). *Multiculturalism in Canada.* Boston: Allyn & Bacon.

Studlar, D. T. (1978). Policy voting in Britain: The coloured immigration issue in the 1964, 1966, and 1970 elections. *American Political Science Review, 72,* 46–64.

Taylor, P. (1971). *The distant magnet.* London: Allen & Unwinn.

Thernstrom, S. (1982). "Ethnic Groups in American History." In Liebman, L. (Ed.), *Ethnic Relations in America,* pp. 3–27. Englewood Cliffs, NJ: Prentice-Hall.

Wilson, P. R. (1973). *Immigrants and politics.* Canberra: Australian National University Press.

CONTRIBUTORS

Chaim Adler is Professor of Sociology of Education in the Department of Sociology at the Hebrew University in Jerusalem, and also Director of the National Council of Jewish Women Research Institute for Innovation in Education at the Hebrew University School of Education. His main research interests are the education of children at risk, education and social and political change, and the sociology of youth and youth culture. His publications include "Israeli Education Addressing Dilemmas Caused by Pluralism—A Sociological Perspective," in D. Rothermund and J. Simon (eds.), *Education and the Integration of Minorities*, and, with M. Inbar, *Ethnic Integration in Israel—A Comparative Study of Moroccan Brothers Who Settled in France and in Israel.*

Jerome H. Black is Associate Professor of Political Science at McGill University. He has written extensively on a variety of topics in Canadian politics; his current research focuses on immigrants to Canada and their political behavior. Dr. Black's publications on this topic include: "Age, Resistance and Political Learning in a New Environment: The Case of Canadian Immigrants," *Comparative Politics* 20 (1987); and "The Practice of Politics in Two Settings: Political Transferability Among Recent Immigrants to Canada," *Canadian Journal of Political Science* 20 (1987).

Hartmut Esser is Professor of Sociology at the University of Cologne (Köln). He is an expert in the areas of quantitative research techniques and has widely written on these and especially on the philosophy of research. His current work focuses on school and social problems encountered by immigrants and minorities. In his widely published research on the topic he distinguishes among the various minority groups and the educational policies which should be guided by awareness of such differences.

Ilana Felsenthal is an educational psychologist connected with the NCJW Research Institute for Innovation in Education at the Hebrew University in Jerusalem. She is interested in curriculum reform and teacher training.

Clive Harber is Lecturer in Political Education at the University of Birmingham where he is responsible for initial and in-service courses for teachers. Dr. Harber's research interests and publications are in political socialization and political education in Britain and Africa. Among his most recent publications are: *Politics and Education in Africa*; *Political Education in Britain*; and, with C. Brown and J. Strivens (eds.), *Social Education: Principles and Practice*. He is also co-editor of *Alternative Educational Futures* and *Political Education in 1984*.

Hans Hooghoff is the Project Manager for the National Network for Development Education (NNDE) at the National Institute for Curriculum Development in the Netherlands, and is that Institute's senior curriculum advisor to teacher training institutions in the areas of social studies and the humanities. Dr. Hooghoff's recent publications include *A Planning Manual for Social and Political Studies*: *Strategy and Planning of the National Network for Development Project*; and *Curriculum Development in Political Education, Particularly the International Dimension*.

Marilyn Hoskin is dean of Natural and Social Sciences at the State University College at Buffalo. She coauthored *The Political Involvement of Adolescents* with Roberta S. Sigel, and has published extensively on the political acceptance and integration of immigrants in Western democracies.

Israelit Rubinstein is a researcher at the Hebrew University's School of Education NCJW Research Institute for Innovation in Education. Together with Professor Chaim Adler she developed an experimental program to train teachers to cope effectively and sensitively with the demands of multiethnic education.

Roberta S. Sigel is professor emirita at Rutgers University. Her work is in the areas of political socialization and gender studies. Among her books are *Learning About Politics*, the *Political Involvement of Adolescents* (with Marilyn Hoskin), and *Political Learning in Adulthood*.

Charles Ungerleider is an Associate Professor of Education at the University of British Columbia and the Director of teacher placement and research there. He is particularly interested in problems related to multicultural education and to the impact of the mass media, especially television, on education. Among his publications are the book (with E. Krieger) *Television and Education* as well as chapters and numerous articles on this and related educational topics in Canadian journals of education.

Author and Subject Index

Italicized page numbers refer to pages with complete bibliographical information.